TODDLERS
AND PARENTS

ALSO BY T. BERRY BRAZELTON, M.D.

INFANTS AND MOTHERS
Differences in Development

T. BERRY BRAZELTON, M.D.

TODDLERS AND PARENTS

A DECLARATION OF INDEPENDENCE

A Merloyd Lawrence Book

DELACORTE PRESS/SEYMOUR LAWRENCE

PHOTOGRAPHS BY
Edward Tronick
AND
Denise Zwahlen

Copyright © 1974 by T. Berry Brazelton

All rights reserved.
No part of this book may be reproduced in any form
or by any means without the prior written permission
of the Publisher, excepting brief quotes used in connection
with reviews written specifically for inclusion in
a magazine or newspaper.

Manufactured in the United States of America

Fourth Printing—1975

Library of Congress Cataloging in Publication Data

Brazelton, T   Berry, 1918–
    Toddlers and parents: a declaration of independence.

    "A Merloyd Lawrence book."
    Bibliography: p.
    1. Children—Management.   2.   Infant psychology.
I.   Title.
HQ769.B6743   649'.122   74-2342
ISBN 0-440-08750-X

Contents

Introduction

The Importance of These Years

A struggle for independence and self-mastery must be waged by all children between the ages of one and three. The struggle is not theirs alone, but calls for great patience and understanding from all who live with them. To this striving for inner control, each child brings his or her particular strength. The theater in which the struggle is waged will also differ from family to family, with one child testing himself against, and supported by, an ever available mother, another by both parents, by a substitute caretaker, or a variety of siblings. In the family profiles that make up this book, I have tried to show both the universal nature of this struggle, and the many possible ways in which it can be resolved. Though the struggle will not be resolved completely until later in life, if ever, the more autonomy a child can achieve at this age, the better able he or she will be to move on to the next developmental task. In *Childhood and Society*, Erik Erikson describes the critical importance of this stage in the overall life cycle: "From a sense of self-control without loss of self-esteem comes a lasting sense of good will and pride; from a sense of loss of self-control and of foreign overcontrol comes a lasting propensity for doubt and shame."

With the child's first realization of independence, of the ability to "leave," come fears of separation. An overwhelming feeling of dependence balances the drive for autonomy. It is this ambivalence which makes life with a toddler so full of drama, shifting rapidly from intense conflict to warmest intimacy. Unless a child can be given support while he works out this ambivalence, he can never be independent of those around him. He will be at the mercy of cues or triggers from the environment which will remind him of his struggle and set it in action within him. The "temperamental actress" who does not get her way demonstrates this same kind of struggle as she raves and rants around the studio, throwing objects, tearing her clothes, insensitively berating the innocents around her. In an adult, this is seen as a regression to an infantile state. It is painful for others and it is devastating for the person himself. Unless this struggle can be resolved successfully in infancy, it must live on, ready to surface whenever the proper set of circumstances call it up. Each of us as adults remembers this inner conflict, and the painful aspect of it is recalled as we watch another person in its toils. This memory is one of the reasons why parents find it so difficult to tolerate a temper tantrum in the child. Many parents would find it a relief to lie down on the floor in a parallel tantrum.

How much does an environment shape a child? A great deal, but less than we used to think. In the 1950s there was still a pervading belief that the outcome of a child's personality development was entirely the responsibility of his parents. We know now that it is not that simple. Parents do not need to be loaded with helpless guilt, anticipating the errors they will make with their child. By implying that all responsibility is on parents, we are saying that *unless* parents find the one right way, any mistake they make will ruin the child. This creates a heavy burden of anxiety for a parent who cares. My own conviction is that each child is born with particular strengths and marked individuality. These individual differences influence the parents and all people around the child as much as they, in turn, will affect him or her. No parent ever feels the same about two children, for each child calls up a different set of responses. Because of these strengths, and a resilient individuality, a child can absorb a great many mistakes on his parents' part. Hence my best advice would be: when in doubt, follow the child!

At the same time, however, every child deserves an environment responsive to his individual needs, one which can change as he changes. Childhood is long in the human. Nature obviously intended the child to be dependent for a long enough time to set his individual clocks in time with the society around him—his culture, his extended family, and his immediate family as represented by his parents. He has time to try his own wings, to make mistakes, to test himself against people around him who may also make many mistakes—before the appropriate meshing can be found. I see this toddler age which I have chosen to describe, the years from one to three, as a turbulent period of such trials and errors. In these years, each member of the family must make his own adjustment to the wide swings between "yes" and "no," "me" and "you," with which the child is faced. The child is constantly learning from reactions around him how to tune his own behavior. It is a valuable and even crucial time. It may also be a painful one. But if parents can see it as a vital bridge to the next set of achievements, and not just an assault on them by a miserable child—it may be easier for them to participate with pleasure as well as pain.

The big job for the child of this age is that of resolving the struggle between being controlled by outsiders and of learning controls for himself. The sense of autonomy which comes from resolution of this struggle leads to the feeling of competence which is at the root of any child's future progress. It is in this period that a child first becomes subject to his feelings of aggression, begins to be aware of the power which he has over others, of his sexuality, of being different from others, of feeling differently for different people—primarily for mother versus father—of being able to choose parts of each parent and of each sibling to be like and parts to reject. The child also is just beginning to have some control over these feelings. But the awareness of control is barely beginning at this age, and is not yet linked to the feelings. The feelings are likely to be vulnerable, tender, and can quickly be stunted or shoved under for a long wait before they reappear.

A child can be encouraged to express his feelings. He can be taught to understand himself by recognizing them. He can learn to enjoy the pleasure of mastering them to increase his choices in life. This raises the question of how much a parent should or can do to foster self-expression. I think there is danger in parents urging a child to indulge every emotion or let angry feelings get out of control, under the impression that they are freeing the child. Getting out of hand can frighten a child and make it even harder for him to express the very feelings which may need release. My advice is to support and encourage self-expression but also to show the way to its mastery when self-expression seems to get out of control. The parent must be ready with appropriate and understanding controls from the outside. As Erikson said on this same issue, "Firmness must protect him against the potential anarchy of his as yet untrained sense of discrimination, his inability to hold on and to let go with discretion. As his environment encourages him to 'stand on his own feet,' it must protect him against meaningless and arbitrary experiences of shame and of early doubt."

Support given in the form of understanding and tolerance is more beneficial than complete permissiveness. After a real blow-up, a parent in control of his own feelings can say, "That's enough now. It is hard being so angry. But part of growing up is learning not to scream and kick when you feel that way. You are learning that now. You are learning to tell me how you feel, and not just yell and cry. That means you are growing up."

The excitement which children demonstrate when they have learned a sense of inner control is one more testimony to the real drive which is built into children to learn how to do things for themselves. Joe's awareness in Chapter X that he does not have to say "no" all the time is particularly poignant. This excitement is its own reward and drives a child toward maturity. It is also the essence of the pleasure in being mature at any age.

These ages, one to three, are almost the last ones in which parents can expect to play an undiluted role. As school approaches, the effect of peers and of teachers becomes more and more important. So it is an opportunity for influencing their child's development which will never be the same again.

This is a reason for parents' fighting to maintain as close a relationship as they can with the child through this period, in spite of day-care or having to share him with other care-takers. Conflicts which are relatively easy to see at this age span will go underground and be harder to dredge up as time goes on. This is an important age for parents to assess themselves as well as their children. In order to do this one must be aware of the kinds of conflicts the child's behavior calls up. A parent must understand his own reaction to the child as well as the child's behavior. I hope this book will bring to light the "normal," healthy needs and strivings of this age in such a way as to enable the parents to see their own role in helping the child to a happier, fuller future.

Prologue

The first birthday party was over and the apartment testified to its success. There were bits of toys, puzzles, cake and ice cream evenly distributed on floor, walls, and furniture up to the thirty-inch level. Year-old Susan was in her bed at last, exhausted and beatifically asleep.

Her young parents were grimly washing cake frosting off doorknobs and chair rungs and vacuuming crumbs off rugs and sofas. As Mrs. Thompson opened the door to the broom closet, her hand stuck to the doorknob. Her hair was streaming, her face flushed, her clothes spotted with bits of food, saliva, and white frosting. She was speechless and doggedly compulsive as she cleaned up the debris. Mr. Thompson was exhausted. It had been an unusual afternoon for him, following four toddlers around the house, anticipating problems before they happened—pulling one baby away from electric cords and catching another as she began to climb onto the coffee table, separating two year-old infants who were pulling each other's hair. He had found that as he followed them they became more active, leading him to new adventures— behind the television, into the bathroom, dropping ashtrays and cups as if to keep him busy and happy. When he extracted one active little boy from the bathroom and from flushing a diaper down the toilet, he found himself getting angry and crotchety—out of proportion to the child's action. As he spanked the baby's hand, the boy looked up at him with surprise and hurt in his face. Mr. Thompson was suddenly weary and frantic with the feeling that he was letting himself lose control. He wanted to run away to the office, to forget this "festive" occasion, to leave it to his wife and the other mothers who sat calmly in the living room while he worried.

This father's reaction is surely a familiar one for any mother. Her guilty feeling as she allows herself to lose control about something superficial reflects her anxiety about the negative feelings which are called up when she has been stressed too far. Mr. Thompson's relative lack of experience with this active, exploring age, coupled with the provocative reactions of the toddlers when he attempted to contain them, act together to build up into an ever ascending spiral which can be halted only by a definite reaction. Mr. Thompson's overreaction serves an important purpose—both for him and for the infants. Although the punished toddler may appear hurt and surprised, the definiteness and the limit which such an incisive response implies may be a real relief to the baby as well. The wish to fly away is not unique to fathers, and Women's Liberation justly calls for equality in this area. Fortunately for dependents, this flight reaction can be overcome when positive action is taken.

Feeling strangely relieved by his outburst, Mr. Thompson gathered the appealing culprit into his arms to hug him and bounce him into the air. The hurt look changed to one of pure joy. The baby squeaked with delight, crowing "dada, dada."

When each had worked off enough of their tension by cleaning and straightening the disorganized apartment, the couple sat down together. They began to review the past year, and all the changes it had brought to their household. The baby Susan had been welcome, but she had come before they felt they were "ready." In the nine months of pregnancy, each of the parents had struggled with feelings of inadequacy. They had been readier by the time Susan arrived, but they recalled their anxiety which rose as she ran the gamut of newborn behaviors.

Their first feeling—"Will she survive?"—gave way to "Will

we survive?" and changed into utter joy when she began to smile, to vocalize, and to respond to them in the second month. From then on, the rest of the year had been a mixture of anxiety about whether they were measuring up to the perfect roles they'd set out for themselves, and delight with each of Susan's new stages of development.

What an exciting year it had been! Susan had led them to peaks of joy and depths of despair which added up to an experience unlike any other they'd ever been through. They recorded every new step she'd made. Had they been able to assess themselves, they could have seen what bores they'd become—recounting the details of each new step to any willing or unwilling listener. Mrs. Thompson entered into competitive comparisons with other young mothers, as though struggling for some coveted prize. Mr. Thompson found himself unable to resist calling home to see what new miracles Susan had performed. The couple were truly in love.

This first year is an important experience and money in the bank for the future relationship of parents and child. Without this kind of symbiotic attachment in which the parents take a very personal, even narcissistic pride in each new achievement on the infant's part, the next few years might be even rougher. The depth of attachment which these parents have been able to achieve by completely identifying with Susan is a rich, rewarding atmosphere for the flowering of her early personality development. The security she feels in such a household is important for her future. She starts life feeling wanted, feeling worthwhile, feeling an excitement from each new developmental achievement which comes from within her and is reinforced by her doting parents.

But, this also sets the stage for a rather turbulent second year!

TODDLERS
AND PARENTS

CHAPTER I

Declaration of Independence

One Year

"No! no! no!" Loud wails were coming from the closed bedroom. Susan's father rushed to see what had produced such an unusual outburst. When he opened the baby's door, Mr. Thompson found her standing, sagging at the side of her crib, eyes closed, wailing semiconsciously. As he rushed to her, she woke up sleepily and renewed her cries. Mr. Thompson picked her up to comfort her, just as Mrs. Thompson came in. Susan grinned and began to babble. Her parents were so relieved to find her intact that they cuddled and rocked her, further waking her in the process. As they began to tire and tried to quiet Susan to go back to bed, she became wider awake. She struggled to get out of their laps; she howled when they tried to replace her in her crib. She became wilder in her efforts to get away from their tightening grasps. The more determined they became, the more frantic her efforts to free herself. Mr. and Mrs. Thompson began to try maneuvers designed to seduce her into her bed. Dolls, fuzzy animals, her blankets began to make an impressive display. All of her new toys were assembled and added to the pile. A bottle of milk was warmed and allowed to cool on top of the pile. Mr. Thompson swore at Mrs. Thompson, she rebuked him, and Susan staggered merrily around the room.

Susan has had enough sleep to regain some of her resources which had been worn out by the birthday. She is physically revived, but psychologically frayed. Anna Freud has called this "the disintegration of the child's ego" at the end of a long day. As her parents' tension builds, she is sensitive to it, and handles it by more aimless behavior, more provocative demands for limits from them.

There is no question but that this building up of tension between parents and child needs definite resolution for the child's sake. Otherwise, like Susan, the child is forced to wander around, searching for ego boundaries of his own. This is expensive for the child and leaves him anxious and unsure where the inevitable blow must fall. A definite end to this buildup would resolve the tension between them and give Susan the security that someone else was in control of her destiny.

Finally exhausted, Susan lay down beside her father's chair, curled up, and put her thumb in her mouth. He gingerly picked her up and began to put her in her bed. With this, she screamed and began to thrash at him, saying "No, no!" all over again. Nonplussed, he looked helplessly toward Mrs. Thompson. She began to giggle at his boyish appeal for help. They both sat down on the floor, laughing at their complete conquest by a mere infant. Of course, the laughter dispelled their tension and Susan calmed down to watch them. They were able to plop her in her crib to cry for a few seconds, and she fell gratefully to sleep.

It is constantly amazing to me how sensitive infants can be to the levels of tension in the air around them. Even though she was certainly functioning at a less than optimal state of consciousness, Susan sensed immediately the change in the atmosphere and responded to it. This adds further to my thesis that her need for definiteness and limits from her parents springs from a lower level than her brain's cortex. She can "sense" when they mean business, even when she is half asleep and her highest decision-making processes are not functioning. Decision-making at a time like this is really not available to her, and it becomes necessary to function with her at a more primitive level—comparable to Pavlovian conditioning. Leaving her to her own primitive responses must contribute to more disorganization rather than less. A "spoiled" child can be seen as a disorganized one searching for patterns of organization which are not available within him. When parents don't step in at a time like this, they are leaving the disintegrated baby to his own resources which are not functioning well enough for this kind of overload.

Susan woke at her usual hour, reliable to the minute. She stood up in bed, hanging on to the crib rail with one hand and waving the other in the air, as she delivered an extensive repertory of words and inflections. At this time of morning, her efforts to rouse her parents fueled her resourcefulness. She started with the first words she'd learned, "mama," "dada," "baba." "No! no!" was liberally salted between each new effort. She rose to newer words which were more complicated than simple syllables, and cried out "doggie," "baybee," "whazzat."

Approximately 75% of infants are able to make word demands at a year. The first words are the simple vowels attached to an explosive consonant. As the exploration of such speech sounds proceeds, the baby senses that certain ones (mama, dada) produce a more rewarding response from the environment. He quickly learns their value and by nine months of age has fixed them as producible responses. These simpler sounds are intrinsic and need little reinforcement from the environment—although infants in institutions or those whose environments do not respond to early exploratory speech tend to lose these early productions, and a general delay in speech may result. Certainly the importance of "contingent reinforcement," or a response to such attempts at the time of the exploratory efforts, becomes apparent in the quantity and richness of further efforts from the infant.
A caretaker usually will reinforce the infant's utterance by a repetition of it with a new inflection, a new addition. If the addition is within the capacity of the exploring infant, he

may attempt to imitate it and to add it on to his previous accomplishment. This then becomes a kind of "shaping" from the environment.

Deaf children who cannot hear their own exploratory efforts may lose the incentive for further speech development because of lack of intrinsic fueling—called "feedback," a necessary source for internal reinforcement. A baby who does not explore speech sounds for his own pleasure as he lies in his crib in the second half of the first year should be checked for auditory competence. His own internal realization of his capacity must be the first step toward building speech. The combination of internal feedback and rewarding reinforcement from people around him provides the necessary raw material for building a complex speech structure.

There are several other reasons besides deafness for delayed speech in normal children which can be documented:

(1) A physically active child who never stops moving, for whom learning motor skills is more important than exploring his sensory capacities, may learn to speak in a rush at a much later date, in the third year, when he needs it, and when his brain's maturity makes it easy for him to produce speech all at once—without trial and error, without exploration and the frustrations which are necessary when learning to speak in the second year.

(2) In a family which places too much emphasis on speech, parents may be unaware of their pressure on the child to speak. Each utterance of his may be followed by such tense reinforcement or such complicated additions from them that he damps out his efforts in order to escape their tense expectations.

(3) The complexity of a large family with many siblings responding to his speech efforts and with a constantly changing series of stimuli from the environment may overwhelm an infant and he may withdraw into a protective cocoon. Never provided with solitude, he has little chance to explore his own productions and to strengthen them enough for use in his complex surroundings.

(4) The other motivating force for speech may be a need for something, and the toddler's realization that a word cue

may lead those around him to give it to him. In large families with siblings near his own age, spoken language may not be necessary. Other kinds of language are understood by small children, and they respond to the baby by fulfilling his request before he must verbalize it. Parents who respond too eagerly may find that they have not allowed the child to build up the incentive for speech. Delaying their responses until he can verbalize his need, at a time when he is mature enough (by two years), may push him to produce speech.

(5) Bilingual families may create a confusion of phonemes in the child's environment which can postpone speech until the third year. Since this is only a delay until he can sort out his confusion, and most children will be able to speak both languages after the delay in assimilation, I have never worried about this. One set of Chinese twins who heard Chinese at home but English around them were not speaking at two years—except to each other. Then, their intimate speech consisted of words which were unintelligible to anyone but themselves and a trained linguist—for each word was a mixture of part English and part Chinese. The words were definite, reproducible, and meaningful when this rule was understood.

When her linguistic accomplishments failed to draw her parents, Susan began to soar to new heights. She produced a string of syllables, with inflection and emphasis, followed by laughter and a responsive message. She attempted a "hi" and a long telephone conversation, followed by a "bye," as if she were imitating her mother's daily phone conversations. She pointed to objects in the room with attempts at naming them. She shook her crib, banged her head on it, and cried out. She flopped down to sit in her bed and turned momentarily to the large stack of toys left over from the previous night. None of them interested her, and she picked up the half-empty bottle left from the night before. Sitting in bed she explored it, and found she could elevate it and get milk for herself. She heard a sound from her parents' room and quickly dropped the bottle, as if she weren't ready to reveal this kind of self-sufficiency. As they stirred and began to make noises which meant that they were coming to her, her babbling took on a

renewed excitement. She became her most charming self—laughing out loud, running through her newest verbal repertory, watching the door carefully. As they turned the doorknob, her squeals and giggles reached a peak and she held out her arms to be picked up.

Mr. Thompson came to her while Mrs. Thompson prepared her breakfast. Sleepy and disheveled, he grudgingly took her out of her bed to change her. She grabbed for his ears and his nose, explored his mouth with her fingers in the tenderest caressing manner, gurgling and craning to look him in the face. As her seductive powers won him over and he awakened fully, they talked cozily to each other for a few seconds.

He placed her gently on her back on the changing table. She became a whirling dervish. She wriggled, squirmed, turned herself over, extracted herself from his slipping hands, and slithered off the table to crash onto the floor at his feet. She screamed loudly in a long wailing forlorn note, and brought her mother in a rush. Mrs. Thompson looked reproachfully at Mr. Thompson, picked Susan up, and hugged her to her breast. As she soothed the baby, she increased Mr. Thompson's anguish by carrying her away from him.

The number of falls which an infant this age can achieve is staggering. Not only does he see to it that he is constantly exploring a new precarious situation, but the force of his need to explore and to resist any limit on his exploration is so precipitous that no parent can expect to get through this age without such accidents. Hence, it is wise to be prepared with a rug beneath the changing table, a carpet on the stairs or a gate at either end, and cushioning under the crib. The other factor is that there is little fear engendered in the child by falling—and, hence, little is learned from these falls. Fortunately the skull of a year-old toddler who is learning to navigate and to balance is cushioned for falls. Nature must have expected them. The anterior fontanel (soft spot) does not close until eighteen months of age in most children, and allows the skull to give with each whack, acting as a cushion for the brain inside it. A fall which results in unconsciousness or a dazed, unconsolable child must be taken seriously, and medical advice sought. Other bangs on the head are frequent and such a part of this age that they can be taken with a grain of salt.

Mr. Thompson's anguish at having allowed her to wriggle free is a common parental reaction, but it doesn't help.

I am not encouraging parents to allow their infants to fall without attempting to prevent it. There are ways of teaching a baby this age new skills which may cut down on some of the accidents. For instance, one can spank him when he is too active on a dangerously high changing table. He can be taught how to climb and to descend stairs at this age. When he gets the feeling of how to lower a leg to feel the step below him, he will take descent on as a project, to accompany the easier learning of how to ascend the stairs. If he persists in letting go of a sofa or table rim to fall straight back on his head, he can be shown immediately after a fall that he can bend in the middle to sit before he lets go. He may be interested enough to learn this himself as a new achievement. The dangers of overprotecting a baby at this age are two: (1) by rushing to stop his exploration one may interfere with his desire to explore, and (2) if every fall is greeted with anxiety and concern from the environment he may learn a fear of injury which interferes with the courage to explore. It's a fine line one must learn in child rearing.

When Susan had quieted, Mrs. Thompson took over the changing process and Mr. Thompson retired to the bedroom. As soon as Susan was on her back, she began to twist, to whirl, to scream "no! no! no!" as if she were being attacked. Her mother gave her a toy to explore, which she threw on the floor. Mrs. Thompson called for Mr. Thompson, to bring her bottle to quiet her. Susan took the bottle, held it up to look at it, and smashed it onto the floor beside her mother. Standing in milk and broken glass, Mrs. Thompson began to weep. Susan was intrigued and reached up toward her mother's face as if to comfort her. Mr. Thompson stepped in and changed the child's diapers.

There are at least two other ways to change diapers, with the infant standing and walking around, or with him flattened on his belly astride the waiting diaper. With a firm hand pressing down his buttocks, the infant is relatively unable to move any but the upper half of his body. However, learning to place pins or to snap snappers with one hand while the subject is on the move is a real parental accomplishment. Outwitting the

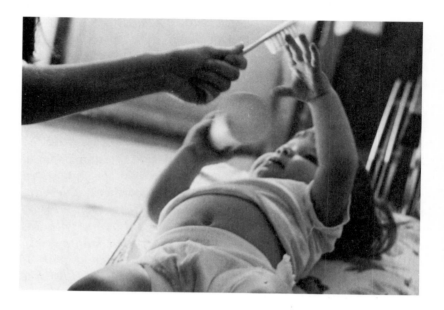

parent is so rewarding for the infant at this age that he rapidly learns ever more exotic ways of prolonging the game. I suspect that this is a major incentive for early toilet training of less passive infants.

At breakfast, Susan became her most delightful self. She babbled cheerfully, waving her spoon and empty cup to emphasize her inflections. As Mr. Thompson tried to read his paper, she leaned over the side of her chair, cocking her head to attract his attention, saying "hi, dada"—a sure interruption. Mrs. Thompson placed a bowl of dry cereal in front of her for her to feed herself. Susan dived into it with both hands, scattering the bits over her table and the floor. As she picked them up and mouthed them, her sticky hands became slathered with cereal bits. Adeptly she licked them off all sides. Finally, after the excitement of maneuvering her hands had begun to wear off, she swept the bowl and remaining bits onto the floor.

Mrs. Thompson could have foreseen this. Had she given Susan two or three cereal bits at a time, keeping just behind her interest, Susan would have kept at finger-feeding longer and more precisely. The competing excitement of a large movement such as the grand sweep of her arm coupled with the clatter of the bowl and consternation of her parents is out of proportion to the fine motor achievement of her pincer grasp (thumb and forefinger). For a moment, the challenge of maneuvering her hands to eat the stuck-on bits held her interest, but not for long. The fine motor manipulation of bits of food is certainly one way to interest a baby this age in self-feeding, but he will tire easily. Hunger in the second year is rarely a motivating force for self-feeding.

Mrs. Thompson patiently swept up the bowl and the bits of food, offering bits of banana and hard scrambled egg next. Susan ate a few bits of each, but was much more interested in distracting her father from his paper. She began to struggle to stand in her high chair, waving both arms as she did.

She might as well be put down on the floor now. Her interest in movement and in teasing her parents has outweighed any interest in her breakfast. Trying to keep her seated and eating would be fighting a tide, and would result in pressure from her parents with perhaps undue emphasis on feeding. This is not a good time to try to push table manners, nor is it at all wise to worry about the quantity of food consumed. A baby this age is so distractible that it is better to follow his whims, providing one meal without surrounding distractions. His needs are so easily met—namely, two ounces of iron-containing protein such as meat or egg, one ounce of orange juice or fruit, a pint of milk or its equivalent, and a multi-vitamin product are entirely adequate for each twenty-four hours.

Mrs. Thompson attempted to reseat Susan and to interest her in her cup. She gave Susan the cup with a bit of milk in it. Susan had been feeding herself out of her own cup for a month. She drank a few sips dutifully. Mrs. Thompson moved away to fix breakfast and Susan upturned the cup on her head, the rest of her milk oozing down over her hair. Mr. Thompson gave up. He began to help with her feeding, attempting to spoon egg into her. She accepted a few bites at first dutifully. As he offered the next bite, she closed her mouth firmly and shook her head back and forth, upending the spoonful of egg into his lap. Patiently he offered her more milk in her cup, holding it for her this time. This brought out a violent thrashing from her arms which splattered the cup and milk across the kitchen. At this point, both parents conceded. Susan was placed on the floor to roam.

Their ordeal was not ended. As they tried to eat, Susan stood at their knees, smearing sticky hands on Mr. Thompson's business suit. She asked for food off their plates. If they offered it to her, she played with it, smashing it into her mouth or smearing it on her hands, and then on them.

This provocative teasing with food is out of hand and it is evident that she is manipulating them with it. A child at this age is caught between his desire for simple attention from his parents and his growing realization that this is not all he wants. Although simple attention served him well in the first year, he is beginning to need to explore himself. The first self-realization comes with "trying himself out" in relation to his environment. Provoking his parents to anger or to more violent interaction proves a kind of exciting potential of which he is just becoming aware. Unless Susan's parents shut it off by a firm, definite reaction, the possibilities for exploration will keep her at it for quite a period.

By the time Mr. Thompson had finished his breakfast, his stomach was tense, his clothes smeared, and he fairly bolted out of the house. Mrs. Thompson reminded him to kiss them goodbye, but his heart was not in it. The combined experiences of the birthday party and the vanquished breakfast made him happy to have a role outside the house.

Mrs. Thompson sighed and settled in for a long day. As her father shut the front door, Susan looked sadly after him, subsiding like a punctured balloon on the floor. She put her thumb in her mouth, called out "baba," which was her word for her "lovey," her blanket. Her mother grasped this opportunity to open the playpen in the kitchen, and to put her in with her "baba." Susan curled up in a ball, with her thumb and her blanket, while Mrs. Thompson cleaned the kitchen, grateful for the respite.

Can playpens still be used to contain toddlers without restricting their exploratory efforts? Certainly this was one use which suited both Susan and her mother. Symbolically it meant subsiding to Susan, and to Mrs. Thompson it offered a period of time in which she knew Susan was safe and at peace in a familiar place. Many active children might be too frustrated and furious with such an obvious confinement, but there are advantages in maintaining limiting safe areas as long as one can. Soon Susan won't put up with this. I have expressed my feeling about the importance of "loveys" (in Infants and Mothers). *Growing up is such a difficult process, is full of such frustration, of such turmoil, and of the ups and downs we have just seen in Susan. In a society which fosters as much early independence as ours does, it seems obvious that we as parents must also respect the importance of balances to this expensive independence. I feel it is an important kind of learning for a child to be able to comfort himself, to subside with a familiar, beloved crutch. Learning for himself how to master the valleys as well as the peaks of experience must increase the possibility of creating a well-rounded person for the future. I do deplore overuse of such crutches. Too many mothers use them as ways of shutting off the peaks in their children. Pacifiers are too often used as plugs. The siphoning off of important energy into the oral sphere at a time when it could be used for exploring and learning in other areas should certainly be weighed against the immediate convenience of "plugging up" a demanding child.*

Susan's quiet period did not last long. She was in a transitional period of giving up one of her two naps. As soon as she got carried away by the urge to walk, she began to be too restless in bed for a nap. Short periods of subsiding like this took the place of a longer nap in the morning, and she was ready for a real nap after lunch. As soon as she was up, rattling the bars of her playpen, Mrs. Thompson took her out of it to explore the house. She toddled from one room to another, arms stretched out at her sides, hands high, balancing as she staggered forth. Her gait was wide and it took her entire resources to master it. She chortled as she walked from room to room, flopping gratefully on a chair in each room. As she gained confidence she picked up a toy in each hand, waving it in the air as she walked. This was the first brave effort to combine any other activity with the all-absorbing job of walking.

An observer can estimate how much experience in walking the toddler has had by: (1) how wide his gait—it narrows as he learns; (2) how facile his balance—if he recovers easily after a threat to his balance, he has had many such opportunities; (3) what other behaviors he can add to walking—a baby who can stop, turn, listen, or lean to pick up a toy has been walking long enough to add many new achievements; (4) how devious his path—a staggeringly direct line is all Susan can master, and any interfering interest would cause her to flop on her seat. She can do only one thing at a time for the present.

Susan's parents had explored the house for traps for her. She was so excited with her new locomotion that she spent most of her waking time going from room to room, endlessly tripping over doorsills and rug ends. Half of the time she caught herself and kept going. The other half, she fell forward on her face or head. Not daunted, she was up and going again. But, as she tired, she began to explore the floors, the baseboards and lamp cords, the cabinets at her level. Then, her resourcefulness in finding detergents, cleaning fluids, or other toxic substances came to the fore.

*The house should be constantly searched for such "traps."
Electric plugs must be covered. Toxic substances must be kept
under lock and key. The experimentation which is uppermost
at this age just cannot be trusted. One mother of twins tells
me that she has spent some time "teaching" her children not
to take pills, and that this helps. If so, it is worth the time
trying to teach a toddler what he can do and can't, but one
must not rely on his rather whimsical memory. In our present
pill culture, poisoning by such commonly used pills as aspirin
and contraceptives is a daily event. Far too many infant
deaths can be attributed to it. Always have an emetic (such
as Ipecac) on hand and a poison booklet to tell you how and
when to use it. Waiting until you need it, is learning too late.
(See the list of poisons at the end of this chapter.)*

The same urge to move and explore sent Susan up the three
stairs which were available to her. She climbed up and tee-
tered at the top. Mr. Thompson rushed to show her how to let
herself down. As soon as she'd learned to dangle a foot until
it touched the lower step, and to let herself down backward,
Susan practiced that with the same fervor.

As long as Susan was the one who was moving from one
room to the other, she was happy. When her mother took the
initiative and left her behind in a room, Susan dissolved. She
screamed, looked helpless, and fell into a puddled mass in the
middle of the room. Although she could easily have followed,
she seemed suddenly unable to bring herself to her feet.

*With the realization of independence and the ability to
"leave" comes an overwhelming feeling of dependence. They
balance each other in the depth of investment. At this time
when Susan is becoming so aware of the choice she can make,
the anxiety about being left behind peaks. A baby cries when
his mother turns her back on him, when she ignores him,
when she talks to someone else. A closed door takes on the
significance of being left. The trusting sense that the mother
is available gives him the necessary capacity to make such a
choice for independence. Ambivalence is at the root of this*

choice, and the experience of it, the mastery of it, are at the base of the child's ability to become a really independent person. A mother who is not there, or one who cannot allow him to struggle with this choice, undermines his future adjustment. This separation may be as difficult for the mother as it is for the child. The satisfaction of the first year's closeness is now threatened. Mrs. Thompson must allow Susan enough time to realize she is left, to protest it, and to find her own way of coping with her feelings. The frustration will drive her to learn how to follow her mother rather than sitting as a helpless lump in the middle of the room.

This same desperation came to the surface whenever a sitter came to the house. As soon as Susan realized she was to be left behind, she dissolved and became a screaming, helpless rag doll. When the Thompsons and Susan went to visit a neighbor, Susan became a demanding, whimpering baby. She climbed up into her mother's lap, sat with her thumb in her mouth, or climbed up and down endlessly. As Mrs. Thompson tried to talk to her neighbor, Susan put her hand over her mother's mouth. If Mrs. Thompson ignored her constant demands, Susan gradually relaxed and became interested in her surroundings. But only on *her* terms. If her mother made an effort to put her down or interest her in a toy, Susan redoubled her clinging demands. Since these embarrassed Mrs. Thompson, she often increased her own efforts to force Susan to separate. A struggle ensued, one which Mrs. Thompson invariably lost. The determination which Susan called up was difficult to match.

This is hardly a helpless age. The strength coupled with fury which surrounds this struggle is basic. It is better to have it surface at this age than in the teens or twenties or thirties. A mother's job is the difficult one of offering her baby the necessary support for both sides of the ambivalent struggle between separation and security. Added to that is the fact that most mothers have not completely resolved this struggle for themselves, and reliving it is tough. An awareness of the necessity for and the importance of the struggle to the baby is a big help.

The morning was a succession of episodes in which Susan and her mother tested each other's limits. Mrs. Thompson was dogged in her determination to finish her chores—cleaning, dishwashing, and bedmaking. Susan could be put off for periods but invariably returned to hound her mother. When Mrs. Thompson could drop what she was doing, sit down on the floor with Susan, and enter into a game with her, Susan seemed quickly satisfied and willing to give her up again. She came to her and pulled on her dress, saying "see" or "whazzat" interminably unless her mother stopped to comment. When she did stop, the baby seemed happy and staggered away to find something else.

Although her main interest is in exploring her newly found walking world, Susan could be interested in a few toys at this age. Pull toys certainly fitted into her new schema. A low climbing area on which she could ascend and descend could interest her for "long" periods (of fifteen to thirty minutes). Toys which had parts to be fitted interested her for relatively short periods. She liked to stop at a chair and place cubed

blocks inside each other, dump them out, and go on to another chair. She liked her cup and spoon in one chair where she could reach them. There, she banged the spoon around in the cup, tested using each, dropped them and went on. A favorite game was that of bringing a toy to her mother, then demanding it back. This game of giving and taking could go on endlessly.

This is a favorite game at this age, and is obviously aimed at testing out the area of ambivalence that is of such concern. "Mine" versus "yours" and "I give" versus "I take" are good areas to sort out and understand.

Hiding a toy, then returning later to find it as if by chance and with feigned surprise, was also a favorite game. She had begun to imitate her parents. She put a tie of her father's around her neck or a scarf of her mother's, and wandered around delightedly. But at the center of each bit of play was her focus on her mother. It seemed clear that each of these served the major purpose of drawing her mother in, if she was available. Her games were heightened with mild play-acting and speech inflections, with giddy feigned laughter, with "hi," "whazzat," proffered toys—all in an effort to draw her mother into her play.

This is not a time for long, involved play alone. She is too aware of her struggle about separating and too afraid of losing touch with her anchors.

By lunchtime Susan was beginning to wear out, having lasted through the morning without a nap. Her mother had begun feeding lunch to Susan early. By eleven, she had begun to whine, to demand more constant attention, and the struggle to put off her feeding until noon had become impossible. Mrs. Thompson sat her in her chair, and fed her bits of soft hamburger and luncheon meat. Susan popped them into her mouth greedily. Without the distractions which had been present at breakfast, she concentrated on the job at hand. She held a spoon in her left hand, waving it around, while she fed herself efficiently with the thumb and just two fingers of her right hand. The cup with little servings of cold milk was managed over and over by her. She consumed an eight-ounce portion of milk in ten minutes, poured into the cup by her mother in small sips at a time.

Cold milk in the cup distinguishes it from the "gestalt" of the warm bottle. The spoon is not easily used by a baby this age and can be used as a "place holder," to occupy the competing hand. This frees the preferred hand to pick up food more efficiently. If both are free, the tendency to pass food back and forth, to find more complicated and interesting ways of manipulating it, competes with the feeding process.

Gratefully, she fell into her bed for the nap period. As she was undressed and diapered, she made a token squirming protest or two, but these lasted briefly, and she seemed as concentrated on their goal as was her mother. Mrs. Thompson looked gratefully at her as she slept. The morning had been an easy one, but she was exhausted.

Mothers are surprised and even ashamed at their own lack of endurance with small children. But they needn't be. There is nothing as exhausting as giving attention constantly to someone else, as trying to concentrate on one line of action while another equally as important is in the offing, as trying to keep a train of thought which is interrupted over and over, and as being aware of the tremendous responsibility that one has for the inquiring, resourceful, nosy little being in the next room.

Mrs. Thompson fell on top of her bed and was asleep immediately. She had planned to get several things done during Susan's nap—and was startled into consciousness an hour later by Susan's cries for "mama." Susan was ready to go again. The old zip on the changing table returned, the struggle over getting dressed was renewed, and the teasing demands were back in action.

A short period of rest acts as an injection of adrenalin for a baby this age. Remarkable resilience in such tiny packages.

Leaving half of her household chores unfinished, Mrs. Thompson dressed Susan for a trip outside. As soon as she realized that they were about to go on an "adventure," Susan's struggles with being dressed ceased. She was ready to go! Bundled into her stroller, she sat absolutely still for fifteen minutes. Mrs. Thompson needed to tidy up and put her own clothes on. This immobilized position in the stroller continued throughout their walk. Although Susan's eyes were in constant motion, her face and body were still and taut for the entire hour's ride. When her mother pointed things out to her, she turned to look at them briefly. If a dog ran by, she followed him with her eyes. When an elderly neighbor came up to tweak her on the cheek, she drew back almost imperceptibly, then sat stonelike for the rest of the well-meaning lady's assaults. After they drew away, her mother heard her let out a long sigh.

Awareness of strangers and sensitivity to intrusions are at a peak at this age. It is not a time for doting grandparents or well-meaning aunts to rush in and pick up a cowering baby. Especially assaulting is eye-to-eye contact. I find I can get by in a medical examination at this age, if I allow the baby to sit in his mother's lap, allowing him a chance to retreat back to her at will, and if I never look him in the eye.

Susan's immobility in the stroller is economy. She is freed of competing activity in order to concentrate on, and take in, every cue. This kind of sensory concentration in the stroller is out of proportion to her capacity to concentrate anywhere else. Perhaps the movement involved in being pushed around can take the place of self-initiated activity for a period.

She especially liked to watch small children. The peak of their excursion was the playground. There, she was content to sit still and watch other children for as much as an hour at a time. Even when her mother put her on the ground, she was stationary. She clung to her mother's knee, watching the activity across the playground. So intent was she, and so involved, that if someone spoke to her or touched her, she jumped and was startled.

This vicarious involvement must signify a kind of learning by identification. One can see this in children who come home from such a period of watching, and are able to play out a whole sequence that they have only observed.

If her mother made a move or talked to a neighbor on the bench, Susan became agitated. She seemed to need her mother's attention as a leaning post while she was so absorbed in the activities around her. After a period, Susan collapsed, demanded to be picked up and cuddled, nestled into her mother's lap with her thumb in her mouth. This was the signal that it was time to go home. But she also hated to go. She protested the moment her mother made a move to turn toward home. Revived by the protest, she watched a while longer before Mrs. Thompson determinedly headed for home.

By the time they reached the apartment Susan was beginning to be ready for the more active fray again. She began to babble, point to things that they passed on their trip, asking her mother to name them as she did. She was able to repeat a few words after her mother—"doggie," "car"—and preferred pointing to the objects she knew as if she were signaling that she wanted a chance to demonstrate her new word acquisitions.

At home, she began to wander aimlessly around the apartment. She climbed up on the forbidden coffee table, circled behind the television set, crawled over to an electric plug, looking back at her mother for disapproval. Mrs. Thompson was distracted and didn't pick up these cues. All of a sudden, Susan lay down on the floor and began to scream. She kicked her feet on the floor, threw her arms about, and twisted her body violently. Her mother was so startled that she rushed over to pick her up. With this, Susan renewed her flailing and crying. So wild was her activity that Mrs. Thompson was sure she'd hurt herself. She couldn't see anything wrong. She noticed no change in intensity of screams as she felt over her body, pressed into her belly, checked her head for bruises. As she became more frantic, so did Susan. She put her into her bed and ran to telephone the doctor. As she did, Susan's noises subsided and she began to sob. Quickly the child was in control again. When Mrs. Thompson went in to see her, her violence returned, but this time it was clear that she was responding to her mother's attention. Mrs. Thompson realized that this was her first full-blown temper tantrum.

The suddenness and apparent lack of reason for these tantrums are always a shock to a mother who has not been through this age before. There was no obvious trigger for this one of Susan's, although there is often a minor one—such as a reproval or temporary frustration. One such as this so obviously springs from an inner need on the part of the baby. Mothers wonder what they have done wrong. There is a myth left over from previous generations that these are a reflection of real disturbance in a child, and are a mark of poor mothering. Also, there are old wives' tales of what one must do to stop them, which is further evidence that they are bad—as if they must be a neurotic symptom, or as if they may hurt the child if they are allowed to go on. This kind of thinking pushes a mother to get into the act. She tries to stop them, or to divert the child to another activity. When her efforts don't work, she gets agitated or angry, tries to punish or contain the infant. She may succeed in pushing them underground and feel successful in her active controlling efforts. Or, more likely, she may reinforce them and prolong them—as we saw Mrs. Thompson do. If she hadn't rushed out to telephone, Susan could have kept up her struggle for quite a while. Both of them could have built up to a peak of tension, in which Mrs. Thompson might have ended with a tantrum as great as Susan's. Learning to understand the reason for tantrums as well as the necessity for them at this age may be the most fruitful thing a mother can do.

Tantrums spring from inner forces in the child over which he is seeking control. Although control from the outside may certainly help him learn it for himself, the ultimate goal will be for him to incorporate his own limit. Hence, the role of a parent becomes that of seeing where he needs controls, and helping the child find them for himself. Had Mrs. Thompson been sensitive to the provoking cues which Susan gave her before this, she probably would have responded with a strong

*"no," which could have settled things. However, the chances
are that Susan might have been so determined to play it out
herself, so pent up with the long afternoon of watching
others, that she'd have eventually come to this kind of active
expression of her inner feelings. One can see a baby this age
who literally creates a struggle for himself in order to end it
with a tantrum. One baby lay down on the floor to scream because she couldn't decide whether to eat a piece of candy or
not—certainly no one cared but she. But she cared intensely!
And her caring was a reflection of the inner turmoil of decision-making that one is faced with when decisions become
one's own, and are no longer made by a parent. In all likelihood the tantrums are necessary and are private expressions
of such turmoil. They are appropriate at this age. I feel that a
parent's role at this time is to comfort and sort out the sides
of the struggle. Certainly, retreating completely for fear of
setting them off, or getting so involved that one ends up having a tantrum, too, is no help to the baby. Picking him up to
love and comfort him afterward, and realizing the fact that
boundaries are necessary whether the baby must respond with
a tantrum or not, may be the best roles a parent can play.*

By the time Mr. Thompson was expected at home, Susan
was building up with one provocative demand after another.
As the usual time for his arrival came, she began to watch for
him. She went to the window, looking out for "dada," and
was waiting at the door when he arrived. As he came in, she
began a frenzied attempt to show off for him. She got down
on her back, kicked, squealed, mimicking in play the tantrum
she had had earlier. Mr. Thompson was tired and hardly
ready for the assault he met. He pulled himself together and
gathered her up in his arms to cuddle and talk to her. She
subsided, looked beatifically up at him, crowing with pleasure
and using all of her new words.

*A father's importance to both mother and infant at the end
of the day can hardly be overrated. Susan had been so ready
for his arrival that a disappointment could have been disas-
trous. No reader who has lived through this long day with*

Mrs. Thompson can doubt what he will mean by way of relief and invigoration to her!

Susan could not be separated from her father. She dragged him to the table to feed her. She ate dutifully for him at first. When she began to tease him with food, he reprimanded her sharply, and she smiled up at him almost gratefully, resuming her careful, obliging eating.

Fathers symbolize control in such a setup. Out of proportion to whatever he may really do, Susan will look to, and expect a controlling response from, Mr. Thompson. Is this built in, or is the need for such a role so great at the end of a long day that he has no chance but to step into it—when the mother's capacity for control is so frayed? I certainly felt myself playing a much stricter role with my own children than I'd anticipated. By way of justification, I blamed it on "their need" and "the need to protect my frazzled wife." I am sure that a child needs very different treatment from his two parents, although they should, and can, agree fundamentally. With two people for the child to play off, to sort out, to imitate, and to identify with, the potential for future development is surely enriched.

After her supper, Susan pulled Mr. Thompson around the apartment, showing him each toy, each stopping place, performing all her newly acquired behaviors. Patacake, peekaboo, give-and-take games all were offered as gifts to this precious new male. When he tried to talk to Mrs. Thompson, Susan dissolved into provocative and tantrum-like behavior. Her jealousy was so obvious and determined that they both had to laugh at it.

Up until now bathtime had been fun. Mr. Thompson would sit and watch while Mrs. Thompson played with Susan in the big tub and washed her off. Now suddenly, Susan began to be afraid of the tub, and today she refused to be put into it— kicking and screaming violently when her mother attempted to slide her down into it. Mrs. Thompson was too tired to struggle and ended by bathing her on the changing table. This was such an ordeal that all she succeeded in doing was a brief swipe here and there—not a bath in any real sense of the word.

This is the beginning of a series of fears—the fear of the bathtub often being the first to surface. Probably this one is a combination of resistance to being handled and manipulated, coupled with an increased awareness of the slipperiness and unsteadiness of a tub at a time when being upright is so new and important. It also comes at a time when outward expression of turmoil is easy and rewarding to the infant—as a way of settling or exploring the facets of the inner turmoil.

Mr. Thompson took over to read to Susan before bed while Mrs. Thompson retreated gratefully to fix their dinner. He read a book which was peppered with words which she could repeat after him. Their period together was a delightful interplay of his asking for, and her delightedly responding with, words and pointing to parts of her body and objects around the room. As she began to get more excited with this game, she asked for her father to throw her up in the air. He became as excited as she and they both began to laugh and giggle. Mrs. Thompson had to step in like a headmistress to remind Mr. Thompson that it was bedtime, and to put Susan firmly to bed, fairly dragging her husband away.

Of course Susan protested vigorously, and was hardly placated by the warm bottle which Mrs. Thompson shoved at her. She threw it over the side of her crib, calling for her father. He went in to retrieve it for her twice before he weakened and took her out of her crib. Intending to rock her to sleep he found she was immediately wriggling to get down. She called for her mother, as if to revive the struggle. Mrs. Thompson was firm as she came in, pushing her husband out a second time, speaking angrily to Susan as she put her in bed. She tied the bottle to the crib side so it couldn't be thrown out again. She closed the door firmly and indicated that it was being closed for the last time. Susan knew that her struggle was over and her wails lasted briefly. Mr. Thompson needed comfort from his wife, for his wish to go back to Susan was difficult to overcome. He felt sad to have stirred her up just before bedtime, and heartless at allowing the separation to come about on an unhappy note. Not so for Mrs. Thompson. She had played out the day to the fullest, and needed and demanded the separation; she wanted her husband to herself.

There are at least two episodes here which hint at the stresses on a marriage which a child can create. The triangle must have firm connections on all sides to withstand the constantly changing attachments, the gamut of reactions introduced by a vital, demanding child. This is a tumultuous time for all three.

POISONS COMMONLY FOUND ABOUT THE HOUSE

Ammonia	Headache remedies	Rat poison
Aspirin	Heart medicines	Reducing pills
Bleach	Insecticides	Room deodorizer
Cement and glue	Iodine	Rubbing alcohol
Contraceptive pills	Kerosene	Rug cleaner
Deodorants	Laxatives	Shampoo
Depilatories	Lighter fluid	Shoe polish
Detergents	Metal polish	Sleeping pills
Diuretics	Paint	Tranquilizers
Drain cleaner	Paint thinner	Turpentine
Fabric softener	Perfume	Varnish
Floor wax	Permanent-wave	Vitamins
Hairspray	solutions	Washing soda

CHAPTER II

Working Parents [1]

Fifteen Months

Breakfast at the Tuckers' was reminiscent of eating in a busy cafeteria. Mr. Tucker drank his orange juice at the sink, shaving cream dripping into it between sips. Mrs. Tucker seemed to be juggling her own clothes and Kara's by hanging them around her neck, holding them under her arms, while she made juice, broke eggs, washed dirty coffee cups left from last night. She called to her husband to get Kara out of her bed. Kara was fifteen months old, and was easy for her parents to work around her in the morning. Although she'd been awake for at least an hour, she had accepted the bottle her mother had stuffed in her mouth to keep her quiet. Now she was standing in bed, bottle hanging out of her mouth, as she rocked the bed noisily to call attention to herself.

When her father came in to get her up, Kara squealed with joy. He was chewing on a piece of toast as he changed her diapers, crumbs from it falling on her wet diapers. Kara, intrigued with his toast, dropped the bottle as she reached for the toast. He dodged her successfully and continued to work on his mouthful. Kara felt spurned and began to twist and turn as he tried to change her. As she became more active, he became more frantic in his attempt to "get it over with." She picked up the excitement and flipped back and forth so rapidly that he was unable to close the pins. He stuck his finger, swore at her, swatted her lightly on her buttocks, and dropped the toast out of his mouth. Finally he stood her up to hold onto his shoulders, and changed her quickly and effectively. Meanwhile, however, he was already five minutes behind in the schedule he'd set for himself—and he'd lost his toast.

Kara had gathered steam from this exciting play with her father, but she sensed his desperation and quieted dutifully to be dressed. There were no clean clothes. Mr. Tucker called out to his wife to bring him a fresh shirt and pants for Kara. Mrs. Tucker was brushing her hair in the bathroom, and finishing her coffee. She called back irritably that she just hadn't had time to wash anything for Kara and that she must go back in yesterday's outfit. Since this was pretty grubby, Mr. Tucker looked sadly at the large pile of ammonia-smelling dirty clothes, extracted the least objectionable set, and slid them on Kara. Kara tried to cheer him up, for by now he looked pretty gloomy. She poked at his eyes, his mouth, his nose until he laughed back at her. With this laugh, her subdued attitude vanished, and she became the active, struggling, teasing mass she'd been before. He felt strangely revived although now he was even more behind.

The sensitivity of a baby to the moods of her caretaker is marvelous. Kara knew when to quiet down and when she could afford to be provocative. This kind of sensitivity to his moods bespeaks an intense and good relationship between them.

He fairly plopped her in her feeding chair. She began to tease him by standing up, but this time she had gauged him wrong. He immediately flopped her back down and firmly belted her into her chair. Although she looked crestfallen, she accepted the definiteness of the strap and his prohibition, and looked around for her breakfast.

I am often asked whether I approve of straps for feeding chairs, and for nighttime, and even whether tethering a child to the porch while he's outside is good for him. Under ideal circumstances I would answer "no" to all of these. I feel that these are implicit infringements on the child's freedom, and are reminiscent of how one treats an unruly animal. I think that children can be taught about the dangers from which these restraints protect them. But this takes time, and it would be a lot to expect a fifteen-month-older to understand. In a household as harried, as rushed as this one, a strap for the feeding chair may well be the lesser of evils. Even though the child may not like it, he is so much safer that his parents can expect *him to put up with it.*

I dislike straps or restraints in bed. Time in bed consumes at least half of most small children's lives. Much of sleep is an active, lively process. By confining a child to one spot and in one position, a strap imposes a large dose of restraint. This may have subtle, subduing effects on his total personality, and on his feeling about his environment. I would not be willing to do this to an active, vital baby without knowing more than we do about its effect on his total personality. If he is climbing out of his crib, and liable to fall, I'd prefer to add crib-side extensions, or to let the crib side down and use the room as the enclosing area. In this way a parent implicitly places restraints on him, but leaves him freedom to move around, to explore, and to live!

As for tethering a child to a porch or fence outside because he can't be watched, I am too appalled even to consider it as a possibility. I have been told by two teenagers that they remember being tied in the yard when they were little. In these memories they see themselves as wild animals being forced by an unwelcoming society to conform to its incompatible demands. The indignity and the horror these kids felt in retrospect were emphasized by the strength of the memories. If a parent cannot be outside to watch a child, he had better keep the child inside. Other than the value of changing scenery and changing pace, there is nothing magical about getting a child "out of the house"—for him!

Mr. Tucker was about to fix Kara a scrambled egg and toast when his wife rushed in. She had finished dressing and realized that she would be late to work unless she took Kara to her sitter's immediately. She knew that Mrs. Stone could feed her breakfast at her house, for this kind of morning was not unusual. She gave Kara a piece of bread to chew on, unstrapped her, zipped her into her snowsuit, grabbed her bottle for the ride, and fairly flew out of the house with Kara under one arm. Her husband looked after them, sadly shaking his head, but rushed to finish his own dressing.

This is a poor start for the day. Not only is it slim pickings for Kara, who has had no real opportunity to touch base with her parents in all this, but the parents will feel cheated and guilty all day. Although life can certainly get out of hand at times when there are many things going on, a routine which provides for leisurely, important interaction between a child and his parents is a must. Otherwise, just as in the case of the Tuckers, there is nothing but emptiness and dodged responsibility to fill up these important periods of family development. Mr. and Mrs. Tucker have missed as much or more than Kara has.

As Mrs. Tucker left Kara at Mrs. Stone's house, she felt a deep sadness and began to wonder why she was always so harried. She suddenly resented having to work, and blamed her job for her frantic life. She had started to work full time when Kara was eight months old, returning to her old job as a medical secretary for a busy surgeon. She had loved her job before the baby came, and they needed the money to supplement her husband's income. She had been determined to get back to work as soon as she felt she'd done her "duty" by Kara. After the baby came, Mrs. Tucker had found it very difficult to give up the closeness to Kara and the pleasure she found in watching her grow and develop. She kept postponing her return to work, until her old boss had given her an ultimatum when Kara was four months old. Hating to give up her job completely, she had compromised for a half-time job and had left Kara with her grandmother for the next few months. She saw this as a weaning period for them both and felt that the idea of giving Kara up to a doting grandmother was easier to bear. She'd wished that she had some idea of the age at which it would hurt Kara's development the least to be divided among two households.

We do need such guidelines. As we develop better caretaking situations, such as day-care centers, it would help concerned mothers and improve the planning at the centers if we knew when infants can best afford separation from a single caretaker. Certainly the first few months are vital to the development of bonds for both infant and parent. This is as important to the parent as it is to the baby. I have noticed that if a mother leaves during or soon after the first grueling weeks, she leaves before she has begun to reap the rewards of a three- or four-month-old baby. This is such a peaceful, rewarding time that it might be seen as the reward for having lived through the big adjustment period of the first two months. If she cared before this, she has only the memory of ambivalent feelings to cement her to her baby in the stress periods which are bound to come.

We also need to know more about which skills and which aspects of personality development are dependent on a single caretaker. In many societies, multiple caretaking is the rule for all babies. But extended families may offer a certain continuity to an infant that disparate caretakers may not. There is some reason to believe that grandmothers and aunts or siblings reproduce the mother's own caretaking to a certain extent. In our society, the disruption may be more severe. If we had some firm data for these aspects of early development, mothers could make more considered choices. As it is, they are at the mercy of pressures around them. Certainly, leaving Kara with her grandmother did make an easier transition for both her and her mother. And it was nice for the grandmother, too!

But after a short stay at grandmother's house Kara had seemed to be getting more and more difficult. At first, the senior Mrs. Tucker had been glad to have Kara and had been sympathetic with the mother's return to work. Half a day hadn't seemed very difficult for the elderly woman when Kara was small and immobile. However, as she began to crawl, the grandmother began to tire. The job of separating hadn't been that easy for young Mrs. Tucker, either. She found herself caught between wanting to tell her mother-in-law what to do for Kara and how, and resenting what she did do.

These feelings are common when a mother shares her baby with someone else. She is feeling competitive with the grandmother, resenting having to give her up, especially to one who has a natural claim on Kara. It may sometimes be harder to give a child up to a grandmother than to a stranger. The feelings of competition and even of wishing to be cared for oneself may be out on the surface under the guise of such resentment about "how" things should be done.

Instead of appreciating the grandmother's help, she found herself criticizing her and wanting to move Kara to a baby sitter. She even felt like spying on her mother-in-law to see whether she did things the same way as they did them at home. Whenever she came to pick Kara up, the two had had a great time and Kara was flourishing. But she felt like an outsider.

It is too bad that we have to make such heavy weather among generations in this country. We are all too conscious of the strains between generations and too ready to let them take over. Kara was certainly profiting from having a caretaker who cared deeply about her. In my cross-cultural experiences, I have been saddened by the awareness that one of the most important losses in our own culture is the strength and the support to all generations of the extended family.

Here is a real example of the price we pay for our separation of the generations into independent households.

Because of the elderly woman's increasing fatigue and her own turmoil, Mrs. Tucker finally decided to find a sitter for Kara. But the sitter's fees were so high for half a day that it seemed sensible to pay a little more for a whole day, and bring home a good deal more pay. At eight months, Kara was taken from her grandmother to stay each day with Mrs. Stone. The Tuckers had looked for several weeks for the best setup for Kara. They had asked friends and neighbors, and had even called the local day-care center to find names. They had figured that one warm, motherly person would be preferable to a more hectic, less personal center. They also wanted someone to whom Mrs. Tucker herself could relate, could speak about Kara, and could complain when she needed to. They wanted a place where there were one or two other babies Kara's age. They felt that she'd learn so much from the other babies, and it wouldn't be as lonely for her as it might be if she was alone.

These are very important and individualized considerations. Most important is the ability of the baby and the mother to feel taken care of by the sitter. Many day-care centers have been too impersonal in the past, and have not paid enough attention to having one caretaker take care of a child—one who likes the child and who can relate to the mother. Fortunately, these attitudes are improving rapidly in most centers, and the new and exciting focus in day-care training is on the mother-child unit rather than just on the child. If the mother feels left out by her child's caretaker (and she is likely to be all too sensitive to such rejection, as we saw in Mrs. Tucker with her mother-in-law), she will suffer, and she is likely to take it out on her child unconsciously. Certainly separation is hard and destructive enough to a mother-infant relationship, and every effort should be made to make it easier. In every case in which the effects of day-care have been studied, the positive gains on the part of the child are directly correlated with the kind and amount of involvement provided for the parents. Carry-over of nurturing into the home is perhaps the most important benefit that a caretaking center can offer a child. Having simple bodily needs and cognitive stimulation offered by a caretaker is not enough unless there is continuity between the nurturing at the center and at home. If the center recognizes the mother's needs and worries, this continuity is more likely.

Mrs. Stone provided all of this, and Mrs. Tucker felt very much at ease about leaving Kara with her. She and Mr. Tucker had both been over to watch Mrs. Stone care for the two babies she already was "sitting" with. They liked the matter-of-fact way she handled the babies' meals and play. They liked her warm cuddliness when one of them was in trouble. What pleased them most was that she seemed perfectly capable of holding all three babies at once, when things were rough. And she wasn't critical of Mrs. Tucker. When she planted an unfed Kara on her, Mrs. Stone seemed equal to preparing another breakfast, and didn't imply in any way that this was tough on the baby. Mrs. Tucker hardly needed to be told that—she was acutely aware of her guilty feelings.

One wonders whether there isn't a certain amount of circularity at work here. Does Mrs. Tucker's unconscious reluctance about leaving Kara every morning interfere with her being more efficient about getting up in time to have a family period before she has to leave her? No rationalization on Mrs. Tucker's part will really explain why this happens so often. As she gets guiltier about it, she also seems more prone to repeat it. Perhaps it would help Mrs. Tucker to be told this, and to be pushed to consider Kara's side.

As she drove on into town to her job, she began to review her reasons for working at all. They certainly could use the money, particularly if they ever wanted to buy a house of their own. Dr. Kahn relied on her, had trained her to suit his ways, and would be lost without her. She had learned to rely on her ability to hold down as complex, as demanding a job as hers. She was proud of it. And when she managed her home well, too, she felt really proud of her ability to manage twice as much as most people in the last generation, and many in her own. She had always been an active, intense person, and as an adolescent she'd hated the boredom of inactivity. When she began to learn about medical techniques as preparation for her job, she'd begun to feel fulfilled for the first time. Not even the close relationship with her husband had challenged this feeling of being important to the many people who came through Dr. Kahn's office. Kara had been the first person to challenge the complete feeling of service that she'd learned in her job. With Kara as a baby she had been engrossed and felt completely needed by her in the same way. But now that Kara was older and more independent of her, she again needed the feeling of being necessary to Dr. Kahn and his patients that she'd come to rely on. But she felt that she was somehow cheating on Kara, and this nagging thought made her uncomfortable and even resentful as she speeded up after a stop light. In fact, she almost ran into a car as she suddenly became aware of how resentful she was to have to feel this way.

This is the biggest danger for women and their children—this unconscious, often unexpressed feeling of "cheating," of guilt about any satisfaction in life besides the "womanly" role of housekeeping and caring for children. Women's Liberation groups are working hard to free women of these incapacitating guilt feelings and I hope they will be successful. So far even they, as a movement, have not been able to face openly woman's "instinctive" need to do a good job as a mother as well as to be free to do other things. I am sure it will be possible to clarify those needs which are basic ones, and those which are mistakenly thought of as conflicting. As long as they are so accepted, they will be conflicting, and our children will suffer.

Just as Mrs. Tucker's unexpressed resentment interferes with her ability to get up in time to give Kara some of herself in the morning, many other possibilities for positive inter-action between a mother and her child can be lost because of unrecognized guilt feelings. Women do have needs other than the caretaking ones which have been assigned to them in the past. In our lonely, nuclear settings it is no wonder that many women go "stir crazy," and many, many more lead discontented, angry, unfulfilled lives. I am not foolish enough to think that a mother who stays at home full of resentment does better by her children than one who leads a more fulfilled, rounded life. Having a fulfilling role besides being a housewife may well give a mother more positive feelings and less negative ones with which to surround her children. The current problem is how to do this best for both parents and children. We cannot afford to continue to ignore the deprivation, the loneliness, the ambivalent depressed atmospheres in which many of our children are being raised. We must look for a variety of solutions, among them ways of freeing working mothers of helplessly complicated guilt feelings so they can do both jobs well. Foremost should be our concern for the welfare of our children. But the psychological welfare of the parents cannot be divorced from this.

Kara was fine. She greeted Mrs. Stone with a wide grin and widespread arms, ready to be hugged. Mrs. Stone sat her in a

feeding table and fed her an ample breakfast. Kara picked up most of it with dainty fingers, but Mrs. Stone found time to feed her a bowl of hot cereal also.

None of the teasing, the scattering of food, the experimental smearing that a child does with his mother seemed to go on here. Not only was Kara not as free to experiment in this environment as she might have been at home, but there was a business-like quality to Mrs. Stone's feeding which Kara picked up and reproduced. The playful quality of a feeding situation which was described in Susan gives way to a different model here. Is there anything lost in the process, or is it just learning to conform to the expectations of another kind of caretaker? Certainly it would be too bad if all experimentation and joyful teasing were lost in this effort—but most children save it for a more appropriate occasion. In other words, they adjust to the demands placed upon them, and save the exploration for situations in which they feel freer.

After breakfast, the other two toddlers arrived. Mrs. Stone had similar hugs for each of them, greeting each of the parents with questions designed to find out how they and the children were—designed to predict how her day with each child might be affected by what was going on at home. This questioning allowed time for the mother or father to make suggestions, to feel included in getting the baby's day off to a start. Each parent lingered at the door after taking off the child's outer garments. As each baby arrived, Kara's excitement mounted. She demanded to be put down on the floor. She wobbled sturdily over to each of the babies, greeting them with "hi" and a poke at the face. Her walking was better than that of the other babies, and she seemed to be demonstrating it as a way of establishing priority. She walked well and steadily, stooping to pick up a toy and recovering her stance without falling. As she walked more, her feet, which had been toeing out at almost right angles, began to point more and more in the direction she was going. Her stance was better now, and her feet were at 45-degree angles instead of 90 degrees. As she stood, her fat bottom stuck out behind, her belly in front, and she seemed to be balancing one against the other. Her back curved inward to compensate for this balance.

All toddlers have prominent bellies and buttocks and a sway-back. They are likely to toe out in an effort to balance side-ways. As they become better at balancing, the feet can assume a more proper direction, and eventually the back muscles begin to improve so that the anterior lordosis can disappear— but not until four or five years of age. Meanwhile, their cherubic postures and figures are not predictions of the fu-ture. I do pay attention to the way children place their feet as they learn to walk. The ones who gradually bring them into a parallel position overcome the duck-like walk that leads to flat feet, knock-knees, and sagging backs in adulthood. Invari-ably a poor stance and outgoing feet lead to poor posture and backstrain later on. It is easy to correct most pronated feet and to improve posture and legs if one starts in the second year. Later than that, it appears increasingly unlikely that corrections will help. Since the way a person will walk is in a formative stage in this second year, and depends largely on how he plants his feet, early correction makes sense if one can predict whether it will be necessary. Improvement like Kara's is a good sign that it will not. Parents should urge their chil-dren's physician to assess this for them in the second year.

The morning passed quietly. Very little of the turmoil that we saw in Susan's day seemed to arise under Mrs. Stone's watchful eye. The three toddlers played alongside each other for the most part. She provided puzzles, toys, a milk bottle to put small objects into, as well as many toys she'd made from cans, bottles, boxes. They were ingenious and as one child tired of a toy, another came over to pick it up. Filling and emptying containers, fitting different shapes into slots made for them, manipulating a spoon and a cup, piling on blocks and knocking them down, pushing rattling cans with a stick were all exciting and absorbing. There was a small jungle gym to crawl up and down on, to hang from, to fall from, and to walk toward. The tears were few: once when the boy walked into a table top (toddlers never look up or even

straight ahead, always down at the ground), another time
when the two girls struggled for the same toy. Mrs. Stone was
expert at diverting impending battles and upsets, but these
two incidents got ahead of her.

*I would worry less if there were more ups and downs. Too
calm and peaceful an atmosphere may not offer as many opportunities for learning about oneself as a child this age*

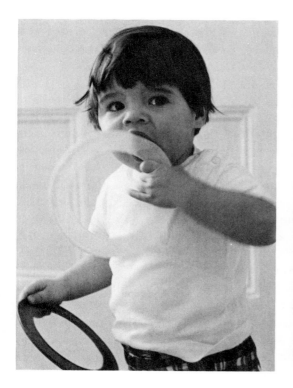

*might have at home. Also, are these children saving their
rebellious feelings for their parents? I wish Mrs. Stone's emphasis on equanimity and "good humor" did not have so
quelling an effect on the children.*

After lunch the children were placed in separate cribs for
long naps. They were geared to sleep for at least two hours or

longer so they would be ready to stay up later with their families in the evening. Each set of parents had requested this, and Mrs. Stone had pushed the children to stay in their cribs longer each day. She had had to put them in separate rooms originally, but soon each child had become used to the arrangement and they were ready to sleep or play quietly near each other.

Naps are certainly subject to environmental pressures. The flexibility which children can demonstrate as they conform to the environment's demands is really impressive. A long late nap means later bedtime, and for children whose parents work, it means more time together in the evening.

The afternoon was more active. Kara climbed up and down, and even on top of, the jungle gym. The other two children tried to imitate her, but she was more adept than they. The boy let go of the jungle gym as he reached the top rung and started to fall, but Mrs. Stone was right there to catch him. She pulled out some dress-up toys, and each child draped a piece of clothing around his neck, and strutted around as if putting on a play. She had a session of words and word imitations. She sat the children around a table, asking them to imitate her as she said "hi," "dad," "mom," and a few other words. All of these were already in their vocabularies, and each child appeared to be delighted with this school-like game. As they repeated a word after her, they all clapped their hands, giggled, and bounced. She began to point to parts of the face and body, asking each child to follow her. This delighted them too. These imitative games lasted for nearly forty minutes before the trio began to tire.

Attention spans of this dimension are hard to come by at this age, and it is a demonstration of Mrs. Stone's ingenuity and power over them. I am sure that the contagious aspect of working in a group helps also.

After this session, they played "ball," rolling it from one to another on the table. As it dropped over the edge and out of sight, each child leaned over to find it. Kara followed it behind a box where it had disappeared, pushing the box aside.

This is quite perceptive for her age. Piaget has developed a series of tests of "displacements" to evaluate a child's awareness of space and of the permanence of objects. The ability to follow a ball as it drops out of sight, following its arc to the ground, is commonly achieved at this age. (All three children did it.) To follow a ball which disappears around a barrier and to push aside the barrier in order to retrieve represents more advanced perception. It demonstrates awareness of the ball as an object which does not disappear just because it is out of sight, as well as a concept of objects going around and under other things—which can then be displaced in order to reestablish the presence of the original object. Persistence as well as well-developed perceptual learning is involved in this task. Piaget would call this a "Stage V" achievement, and Kara did well for her age.

This kind of test of a child's capacity to combine several perceptual systems is much more useful in understanding how he or she works than is a simple, rather meaningless I.Q. All of these children can perform adequately for their stage of maturity—for example, saying two words, making a tower of two blocks, pointing to their shoes or clothes on command, scribbling with a pencil, placing a peg in a hole, putting small objects in a bottle and then pouring them out, walking sideways and backwards on command and after a demonstration. But the process involved in learning each thing is in no way demonstrated by such a stereotyped performance. It is more useful to have a series of scales which uncover the thought processes and the ability of the child to combine ideas to reach a goal.

To this end, Sybille Escalona is combining some of Piaget's ideas into a scale of development. We can combine such a scale of motor and perceptual development with others which document the child's ability to relate to other people, to imitate, to initiate activity in order to draw in another child or an adult. Another set of scales might test such intangibles as motivation and flexibility in adjusting to frustration (coping mechanisms). By assessing the child in all these different areas, we could better predict performance and stability for later years, as well as pick out the infants who were at risk for the more complex demands of our society. The latter could be offered environmental stimulation which was appropriate to their needs, and which might provide them with better experiences to build upon. Unless this experience is offered as early as possible, the chances of salvaging most such children are passed by the ages of four or five years. We learned this sore lesson from Head Start programs which reached many children too late to change their stereotyped ways of coping and learning.

As the afternoon progressed, the children became more and more active and noisy. They began to watch the front door, and went to the windows as if they were watching for their parents. They began to be aware of clothing as if anticipating being dressed, and performed the only acts of which they were capable—removing shoes and socks. As fast as Mrs. Stone could put on one child's shoes and socks, another had removed them, chortling with glee at upsetting Mrs. Stone. By the time Kara's mother came for her, she had removed her shoes, pulled down her pants, and put her snowsuit around her

shoulders. She stood in the midst of the floor, naked from the waist down, well covered from the waist up, waiting in regal splendor for her mother to pick her up.

Mrs. Tucker was delighted with this picture, and giggled with Kara as she dressed her. On the way to the car, she hugged her and both looked forward to the next few hours together. Unfortunately they weren't to be easy ones. All of Kara's stored-up negativism came surging forth as soon as she was home. She lay down on the floor to kick and scream when Mrs. Tucker tried to take off her snowsuit. Screams and resistance increased in vigor and intensity as long as Mrs. Tucker tried to calm her down. When she finally gave up and stormed out of the room, Kara began to sob "mama, mama." This brought her mother back to her and she clung pitifully to her, emitting loud racking sobs.

This is a typical response in this age group, due to the combination of fatigue, the pent-up excitement of getting home to her mother, the steam which she'd stored up all day, plus the opportunity and safety her own surroundings provided to let herself go. I would worry more about a child who never let himself go to this extent than I would about one like Kara who saves it for home and safety. But such behavior is not easy for a parent to understand and appreciate.

Mrs. Tucker was turned off by Kara's sobbing and felt like a failure all over again. She, too, was tired and Kara's tantrum reminded her of her own exhaustion. Her enthusiasm was dampened, but she pulled out some games to play with Kara. She took out "their book" and sat down to read to her. Kara curled up cozily next to her mother. When Mrs. Tucker came to the end of a familiar sentence, she left the last word for Kara to say. They finished almost the whole book this way.

The telephone rang just as they were building up to the climax which Kara loved. Mrs. Tucker jumped to answer it, leaving Kara alone. Kara began to wail inconsolably, tried to climb off the couch to follow her mother, and fell just as her mother returned from the phone. When her head hit the floor, Kara let out one more cry, stopped breathing, gradually

turned pale blue, and stiffened out in her mother's arms with eyes rolled back. Almost immediately, she began to scream and thrash in one of her usual tantrums, and Mrs. Tucker felt thoroughly chided for having left Kara to go to the phone. By this time, Mrs. Tucker was shaken and frayed. She resorted to an old trump card. She put Kara into the bathtub to play. Kara had always loved her bath, and it came as a real shock to Mrs. Tucker for Kara to resist being put into the tub. She cried, fought, curled up her legs, arched her back, clung to her mother—all by way of resisting her bath. Since this was new and she was afraid of another "spell," Mrs. Tucker gave up and dressed her again, attributing her upset to the fall she had just taken.

Not necessarily so, although it may have been a factor. Most children this age go through this distaste for the bathtub (see Chapter I). There are various dodges to help children get through such a period (for they do get over it eventually) —bathing them on the bath table, taking them in gradually while the parent is in the tub, using a wading or swimming pool to help get over the fear. It's not serious. If parents take it as if it were, that only reinforces it as a struggle.

She plopped Kara in front of the television set to wait until the father came home. She was too exhausted to face a feeding now.

Mothers need television as a baby sitter more than babies do. I deplore the overuse of TV in this country for children of all ages, but there are times like this when it is invaluable. I certainly think Kara should not be left too long. She's already pretty jazzed up (see Chapter VIII).

As the front door squeaked, Kara heard it above the blare of cartoons on the television, and made a rapid beeline for her father. She cried "dada" over and over, laying her head on his shoulder when he picked her up, and glaring back at her mother as if she were safe at last. One could almost imagine that she would like to tell her father about all the horrors she and her mother had been through, now that he was home and she was safe. Mrs. Tucker thought of this and found herself feeling a little reproached and irritated by Kara's behavior. For what, she wasn't quite sure.

Here beginneth the oedipal triangle. There is surely no reason for Kara and her mother to compete for Daddy, but this is what is happening. Mrs. Tucker's feelings are too raw and she gets down on Kara's level too easily for her own good—or for Kara's.

Mr. Tucker consented to feed Kara her supper, and perhaps it was fortunate. For Kara refused to feed herself at all. Whereas she had been using a spoon at times, had learned to take a full spoon from her parent's hand and feed it to herself, handled a cup well by herself, tonight she refused to do anything but be fed. She swept the finger food and cup off onto the floor in one adept gesture. She sat there stonily until Mr. Tucker started feeding her. Her mother was so angry and tense by now that she would have spanked her at this point.

They are certainly paying the price for Kara's "good" behavior all day. The need to work out the issues of independence, of ambivalence, of negativism (see Chapter I) is so great that though they can be postponed all day long, they will come out eventually, in a child with strong will and a strong ego. This regression in the feeding situation is to be expected, too. It is also a good sign rather than a bad one, if one considers Kara's need for balancing her behavior during the day with being a baby when she can.

After supper, her father played "horsie" with her, swung her around, bounced her on his swinging foot in "This is the way the farmer rides." As she fell off his foot, she chortled with laughter. All three Tuckers curled up in an armchair, and the parents read prayers and bedtime stories to her. She was beautifully tucked in, and looked beatific as they tiptoed out.

No sooner had they sat down to supper than her wails began in the bedroom. Mrs. Tucker gave her husband a desperate look. She seemed so frazzled and distraught that Mr. Tucker went in to try to quiet Kara. Soon he returned with her in his arms—"to get a glass of water." When he tried to take her back to bed, piercing wails started again. Her mother took her and tried to comfort her. As soon as she scrambled to the floor, she was as gay as a lark. Mrs. Tucker felt her anger rising, and yet she was not equal to the struggle it would mean to put her back. Neither parent could venture to take control, put Kara back, and shut the door in the face of her wailing protest. For an hour and a half of tense, angry interplay, they waited for her to tire so they could put her to bed easily. As she got more tired, she disintegrated even more. Her hysterical play was intermingled with garbled words and sobs before the Tuckers finally got up to put her in her bed. Even then, she cried out and they turned to go back to her, but fortunately for them all, fatigue won the battle.

To the observer, this is patently absurd. The child has had to disintegrate before the adults could make a decision which so obviously should be theirs to make. This kind of parental indecision is less common now than it was in the permissive era, thank goodness. It certainly wasn't easy for the children involved. Although parents would give all sorts of excuses— such as "We can't stand to let her scream," "It's too hard on the neighbors," "She must need something we haven't given her"—there is no adequate excuse. These are all rationalizations for underlying reasons. Why should she want to give up at the end of the day if there is this much ambivalence to play on?

In the case of the Tuckers, it may be partly based on experiences of their own in which separation from parents was hard, or on unresolved fears, or on any number of other personal reasons. I do see this commonly when both parents work, and leave the baby during the day. No amount of reassurance can relieve the Tuckers of an underlying fear that the child has been neglected or mistreated during the day—and that they are at fault. They probably also feel unsatisfied about their all too brief contact with Kara at the end of the day and, without knowing it, feel they should keep her near them to make up for it. But these guilty feelings do not help Kara. In fact, they incapacitate the parents to play an important role for her—that of helping her learn limits and learn how to separate without disintegrating in the process. Somehow it seems to me that being allowed to continue with this behavior will do Kara more harm than any effects of being separated from her parents during the day. She will soon realize that they feel inadequate as parents. If they really want to make up to her for their "other lives," they must help her develop the capacity to understand "no" as well as "yes." To help Kara with her side of this bedtime problem, they could use such gradual weaning procedures as going to her to put her down firmly, giving her a "lovey" or a substitute for them, but at the same time letting her know that she must give up. Night lights, open doors, rocking, bottles in bed are all crutches of the same sort. But no crutch will really replace the parents or help a child unless all are ready to accept the necessary separation of bedtime. Sleep problems are usually parents' problems.

CHAPTER III

Sibling Rivalry

Fifteen Months

Anguished screams roused Mrs. Clancy as she bent over the sink, scrubbing the last bit of egg out of the breakfast frying pan. She realized she was still only half awake, and had been blessedly unaware of the turmoil in the bedroom. As the wails built up she came alive, rushed in to see what was responsible for the baby's crying. Tom, who was fifteen months old, and a slender, rather fragile-appearing little boy, lay on his back on the floor kicking his feet halfheartedly. His crying was the most vital part of him, and as he saw his mother, his cries took on new energy, and he pointed toward his older brother. Three-year-old Michael was a sturdy curly-headed, brown-haired boy who was squarely built like his truck-driving father. Michael now cowered in a corner trying to look as small as possible. To no avail.

Mrs. Clancy sized up the situation in one sweeping glance, bore down on Michael, clouted him hard on one ear. Michael began to scream, clutching dramatically at his ear, rolling over on the floor, deserted. Mrs. Clancy, face reddened, rushed to pick up her baby, screaming back at Michael that more was forthcoming. By the time Mrs. Clancy sat down with Tom in her arms to rock him, Michael was recovering but sat curled up in the same corner as if he were waiting for some signal of reinstatement from his mother. None came, and she rocked harder, crooning comforting sounds to Tom. Michael watched this picture, thumb in mouth, face drawn, and he gradually began to rock rhythmically on his haunches—as if he were imitating his mother, or as if he were somehow trying to get into the charmed circle.

It is easy to identify with Michael and feel the sense of deprivation with which he is left. If he is not to feel deserted indeed, he must recoup his sense of identity by being angry. Since he won't be able to get as angry at his mother as he might want, he will undoubtedly begin to blame Tom—appropriately or not. In this way, Mrs. Clancy has reinforced any negative feeling Michael may have for Tom. By rushing in, making a quick judgment, choosing sides, she has pushed Michael out on his own. In a way she has polarized them even more. Whether her snap judgment was right or not becomes of secondary importance. Her reaction to the acute crisis is understandable and automatic, but her next steps needn't be.

If she could include Michael in her comfort, she would dilute his hatred of the intruding new sibling, and make him feel less excluded, guilty, and angry. In all likelihood, Tom needs less from her than Michael does at a time like this. If Michael did indeed hurt Tom, he is probably more deeply upset, for the guilty feelings engendered in an older child by an assault on the younger are more disturbing than they appear to be on the surface. The older child is truly frightened by the combination of his feelings of aggression toward his weaker sibling and the realization that he hasn't controlled them. Any good, objective nursery-school teacher rushes to comfort the aggressor as well as the victim. But Mrs. Clancy has not got the training or the objectivity of a teacher and her reaction is direct, straightforward—to protect the most vulnerable of her brood.

As she rocked Tom, the likeness between them was striking. Both were pale, blond, and wispy. Tom's hair was thin and shot out in all directions—Mrs. Clancy's hair oozed from a small knot. Tom's long, pale face was drawn into a frowning appeal for help. Mrs. Clancy's looked drawn and tired, although it was early in the morning. As their bodies curled closer to each other in the rocking chair, color began to return to each of their faces, and energy seemed to well up for each of them. When Michael whimpered from across the room, Mrs. Clancy and Tom jumped as if they were unaware of their surroundings. The return to reality and to Michael was not entirely welcomed. Mrs. Clancy sighed and gently put Tom down on the floor, and pulled herself up to return to her chores. Tom let out one brief cry of protest and sat next to his mother's chair as if he were waiting for something else to happen, watching Michael warily. Michael, watching his mother leave the room without acknowledging him, looked first sad, then determined. When he heard her begin to scrub her dishes, he pulled himself together, glanced at Tom, crawled over to the toy nearest to Tom, put it in his mouth, and crawled away to his corner with it. As he had anticipated, Tom screamed again for his mother.

The torture in this act goes more than skin-deep. Michael chose a method of locomotion and a way of conveying the toy away both of which were in Tom's repertory and designed to tease Tom the most. Had he walked over, picked it up in his hand, and walked away with it, Tom might have felt somewhat teased, but the imitation of Tom's own behavior is ingenious. Immediately it threw Tom into a helpless role, cheated of his own ways for retrieval. And the marvelous thing is that they both recognized all of the facets of such an act. This is a negative use of "shaping" which we all use to teach a child a new way of doing things. We choose behavior of which we know he is capable, demonstrate it in the context of a new undertaking, and in that way show the child how to put together a sequence of familiar actions into a new achievement. Michael has done this to heighten the significance of his predatory act. It is no wonder that the maneuver was so successful.

Mrs. Clancy stopped her noisy scrubbing briefly, screamed out at Michael to lay off Tom, and went back to her work. Tom began to crawl toward Michael when he saw that his screams produced no results. Michael picked up the toy with his mouth and crawled to another corner. Each time he moved ahead of him, Tom screamed again. Each time he screamed, their mother called out at Michael. As the crawling, teasing game built up, Tom began to be more and more frustrated. He tried to stagger on his feet to follow Michael. Michael stood up too and whirled past Tom without touching him. This was just enough to unsettle Tom and he fell backwards, hitting his head, and screaming even more loudly.

I am sure that a child Tom's age can make himself fall in a way that will hurt him. Instead of bending in the middle as he falls, and he certainly has learned this by now, his protest over Michael's indignities leads him to "want to hurt himself" in order to put some sort of end to the torture, and to have a reason for getting his mother into the act again.

These wails brought Mrs. Clancy back into the room. Again, she saw Tom lying helplessly on his back, having hit his head. She saw Michael retreating into the distance. Her weariness of the repetition of this situation reinforced her instinctive reactions, and she picked Tom up to cuddle him, hurled a verbal blast at Michael, and sat down to play with Tom to divert him. Having had an older sister to tease her constantly, she knew well how hard it was for Tom. She felt like protecting him from the misery of always being the underdog, always the inadequate one. She felt exhausted by this kind of constant struggle, and found herself disliking Michael most of the time.

The feelings which are revived in Mrs. Clancy are the reason for her exhaustion. They are also the reason why she can't be more detached and objective. If she could, she'd be more effective in handling this situation. As it is, her constant interference is perpetuating the bickering rivalry between her boys. Her feelings are based on past experience with her own sister and her own mother. She remembers her own frustration and feelings of inadequacy at being teased. If she could also remember how her own mother rushed in to protect her, to take her side, to "baby" her, she might see that this kind of reaction from a mother serves to emphasize in the child the very feelings of helpless dependence which she wants him to overcome. By coming when he calls, she places herself in the coping role and strips him of the motivation and the need for learning to cope with his brother by himself. By taking his side regularly, she takes the balance out of such a situation, and she reinforces Tom's one-sided point of view. Then, by identifying with him as completely as she does, she gives him the same feeling of being put upon that she has grown up with. She makes him feel a sense of inadequacy which is self-reinforcing, for he will not learn to cope, or feel equal to the coping, and will believe that he is "bound" to be stepped upon by an older sibling. Such a self-image will not help Tom for the future.

One cannot blame Mrs. Clancy for reacting this way—after all, it is the kind of experience she had had in her own life. But one would certainly like to keep her from handing on such an inadequate means of coping with others in a competitive situation. It is a difficult role for a mother to learn—the instinct to defend the weaker one is strong in everyone, and it is hard to see the value of leaving such a rivalrous situation up to the unequal competitors. I am convinced that sibling rivalry can be a positive learning experience for the involved siblings. It is the triangle (child–interfering parent–child) that keeps it alive as a negative experience. When the mother reinforces the rivalry, not seeing their struggle as a way of involving her and calling her from other duties, the two children will continue the pattern. When she doesn't come, the importance of perpetuating the struggle is soon lost in favor of more constructive play. A positive relationship between the children can never take place when the mother steps in to interfere. Had Mrs. Clancy been able to let the boys themselves work out this interplay with the toy, there is much more likelihood that they would have ended in constructive play together. If I were there to point this out to her, she'd have seen it but she would justify her actions by saying, "But I must protect Tom from Michael. There is just as much chance that they'd build up to a fight in which Tom *would get hurt." I would have to agree with her, but I could also point out to her that she had set up this kind of expectancy in them—that if they ended in a fight, they'd get her into it, and they'd each have their own kind of reward. It's hard to see how Michael could think of his treatment as a reward, but I'm sure he does see it as more exciting than being left to play with a whining, whimpering Tom.*

If she could begin to leave more up to the boys, to weigh and equalize their needs after a crisis, as well as in the buildup period, to press them back on their relationship directly to each other rather than "through" her, I think she might have an easier time herself, and I'm sure she'd further an ultimately healthy and positive relationship between them. They are already dependent on each other, as is evidenced by the intensity of their struggle.

The adult Clancys had reviewed their roles in the boys' rivalry at supper just the night before, wondering what they'd done wrong that made Michael so jealous. Although Mr. Clancy wasn't as involved or upset with their fighting, he found that he too was getting angry with Michael a lot of the time now. When Tom crawled or staggered over to his father to be picked up, Michael was likely to do something very openly destructive. He could shove Tom down, or pull on his leg, or abuse a favorite toy. All of this seemed out of character to Mr. Clancy, who had had such an easy relationship with the older boy, and who had found him open, cheerful, and easy before this. The parents thought he must be going through a bad time and were afraid he was getting "out of hand." In their neighborhood there were delinquents whose parents had not taught them self-discipline or respect for others, and they feared this as an outcome for Michael. These kids all ended up on the streets or in reform schools, and it was nothing to look forward to for parents who cared deeply about their children. Hence Michael's recent, rather sudden change was of major concern to them both.

As they reviewed his reaction to Tom, they remembered how easy he'd been when Mrs. Clancy brought the baby home. They'd talked to him about it beforehand, had prepared him as best they could. They'd read that the older child was more worried about losing his mother's attention than about the new baby himself. So they'd seen to it that Mrs. Clancy spent a lot of time with Michael after she came home with the new baby. In fact, she'd spent so much time with him in the first few weeks that she began to feel that she didn't even know her baby. She even found herself feeling cheated of Tom's babyhood.

This is often an unconscious feeling on the part of a mother with a new baby. In the end, she will feel resentful toward the older child for having interfered with her important relationship with her new infant, and she must balance this against the older child's needs.

As she tried to spend more time with the baby, Michael had shown his resentment in various ingenious ways. He put his shoes down the toilet and was flushing it when she arrived. He emptied all of the soap powder over the kitchen floor. He emptied her drawers, put her underwear around his head and neck, started the vacuum cleaner, turned wastebaskets upside down, called to her for help while she was feeding Tom —maneuvers openly designed to draw her away. As long as she was able to retain her sense of humor about these, Michael was easy and open about his feelings. After four or five months, Mrs. Clancy felt that she'd had enough and that Michael should learn how to cope with these feelings of wanting "more than she could give." She began to punish him for such pranks, and he looked hurt and surprised but he stopped. Now when she was tending the baby, he was more likely to sit down in a lonely corner to suck his thumb or to look forlorn. When his father was at home, Michael could retreat to him and get him to play.

This is the nicest thing for fathers about such a time. Older siblings will fall back on them for comfort. It is an opportunity for Mr. Clancy to solidify his relationship with Michael. It may also be a time when rivalry between the parents may surface. In other words, parents go through such periods of anguish in their children as if they themselves were experiencing the incidents, reliving their own past.

For a while after this, Michael's rivalry seemed to go underground, and he stopped saying "Get rid of that baby" to replace it with "I like Tom." Mrs. Clancy thought that she'd really hit on a good method for helping Michael with his feelings, and whenever any negative ones came to the surface, she found herself trying to shut them up in him. He became a quieter, more thoughtful little boy, but he began to wet his pants again, although he'd trained himself at twenty months just before the baby came. Mrs. Clancy tried several things with this new symptom—she shamed Michael, she spanked him, she put him back in diapers, and finally she even tried to understand it as his reaction to Tom. But it irritated her and she found herself showing her feelings to Michael whenever he made a mistake.

Her irritation not only may be due to the obvious nuisance of having a child regress who has been trained, but it may also be indicative of her own guilty feelings for having deserted him and for not being available now to understand him.

The more her neighbors and her reading about it made her realize how common it was as a response to a new baby, the more irritated she became. She found herself justifying the time she spent with Tom. She made real efforts to free herself to play with Michael, but she was angry at "having" to do it. She had given him a lot of herself and of her time when he was a baby, and she expected him to live up to this new adjustment. Whatever time she freed for him never seemed to be enough, and when she stopped reading to him, he whimpered for more. This enraged her, and she tried to find ways to tease him out of it.

Mrs. Clancy is down on Michael's level. She is acting like a child about a natural kind of protest from him. No child ever gets enough, ever wants to quit something he's liking. To expect him to give up easily is missing the point. Hence one wonders whether Mrs. Clancy isn't already ambivalent and angry about the demands of two children. She is expressing a common feeling that most mothers of two have at some time —that it is asking too much of them to have to split their own "ego" or mothering capacity in two ways. It is a big adjustment period, and one that will pass, as the mother learns that she really can take care of more than one. The tragedy will be if Mrs. Clancy continues to see it as Michael's fault for demanding too much of her and continues to blame him for normal needs of her own. The anxiety this will produce in Michael will reinforce his demandingness.

For a period after Tom started to sit and to crawl, Michael had been happier with Tom. He seemed to play with him, giving him things to entertain him, "teaching" him how to play with simple toys, talking to him. Mixed with this were periods

when he blew up, hitting out at Tom or screaming at him to frighten him. But, in general, he was good with the baby, and everyone was delighted with him. In fact, as the Clancys thought back to this period, they realized that a lot of Michael's good behavior was indeed to gain their approval. Often it had a showing-off quality to it, but Mrs. Clancy needed the respite from her own feelings and she welcomed any sign of good feeling between the boys. Tom lapped it up. He responded with glee whenever his brother came up to him, chortling with laughter whenever Michael performed for him. He tried desperately to perform all of the tasks which his brother set out for him. When Michael tried to teach him to repeat a sound, Tom put much more energy into his attempts than he did for his parents.

This is a common observation that parents make. The motivation to learn from a sibling who is spending his time teaching is out of proportion to motivation at other times. Perhaps it is less complicated coming from a child near one's own age, perhaps the wish to identify with him is different, perhaps it is recognized somewhere as a way of keeping one's idol involved. But it is true that small children will sit for long

periods being taught by someone slightly older, and they will work very hard to please by learning. The model which one child offers to another a little younger must be particularly appropriate to the capacity to learn.

As Tom became more mobile at a year and began to get around, he began to become more of a threat to Michael. Not only was he appealing to everyone as he toddled across the room, but as he toddled, he became much more adept at getting into Michael's play. When the older boy was building blocks, Tom found it exciting to fall into the tower. When Michael was trying to swing, Tom came up to the swing, and was rescued by a frightened parent who stopped any further swinging. Not only were Michael's activities openly curtailed to protect Tom, but Tom's every act was admired openly. When Tom found Michael's prize toy dog and pulled out its eyes, his parents laughed at Tom's ingenuity. Michael found himself cut down at every turn by Tom's new mobility. As his jealousy and anger came to the surface, both parents pushed him away even further, and he felt isolated.

Michael need not be consciously aware of the reasons why he resents his brother at such a time. It is absurd to think that a child as normally sensitive as Michael is to his environment wouldn't sense the nuances and implications of the changes around him. If he had to find a scapegoat to blame for such changes, it is obvious that he would turn to his vulnerable brother. It wouldn't help to blame his parents, and he is too outgoing and vital to turn the blame inward any longer. Hence the sibling becomes the focus for all the pent-up frustration.

Michael soon found that it was effective to tease Tom into frenzies, to use subtle methods such as stealing nearby toys rather than attacking him directly. The structure for retaliation was already too complicated for either Michael or his parents to sort out any longer.

Mr. Clancy had suggested that Michael was too confined with his mother and baby, and that he needed more playmates. He had urged Mrs. Clancy to get the boys out more often as a solution to some of the warfare. After the third rending episode within the hour, she decided it was time to try out his suggestion. She telephoned her mother who lived nearby to suggest that she bring the boys over to play at their grandmother's house. Her mother sounded weary but responsive, and Mrs. Clancy began to dress them for the venture. The children caught the excitement and anticipation in their mother's voice, and they submitted to being dressed in "good clothes" and snowsuits with a minimum of protest. Michael brought Tom's clothes and his own to his mother and even helped her put Tom's socks on him.

This is the other side of a coin. Here he can be very helpful and positive when he's given an appropriate opportunity and appropriate praise. This balanced relationship is hard for a mother to keep going all the time, but perhaps it's no harder than listening to the screams and fights of boredom.

When they arrived at Grandmother's, Mrs. Clancy could see why her mother was weary. She had taken her other daughter's children for a few days and they were all over the apartment. The other family consisted of four active, insistent children—from six years to one year in age. The six-year-old boy was in school, but four-year-old Nancy and three-year-old John were constantly teasing, running after each other, climbing furniture, falling over the year-old baby, and wrecking their grandmother's compulsively neat apartment. She was frantic, and was relieved to see her daughter. Tom and Michael were delighted with the excitement and the activity which their cousins offered. For the next two hours, peace reigned—in the form of active struggling but cheerful play on the part of the three older ones, and quieter play for the two babies. Mrs. Clancy was amazed at the effectiveness of this solution for every age group. She and her mother had the time and peace for cups of tea while the babies played quietly at their feet. Although they touched base from time to time with the adult in charge by standing at her lap, each infant watched the other, laughed, gurgled, vocalized, and imitated the tempo and type of play of the other. This play lasted for nearly two hours.

Two infants of this age communicate at many subtle levels. The tempo, the style, the actual behavior of one baby seems to be picked up out of the corner of the other's eye. Although they rarely seem to be watching each other, they are certainly in tune. As one bangs a toy, the other answers with banging. As one cuddles a doll, the other becomes appropriately motherly to his play object. In other words, it is not only direct imitative learning that one can see, but whole chunks of behavior and its underlying affect that one baby picks up from another at such a time. I have seen a boy cuddling and vocalizing to a doll in a way that he had never done at home before—all in imitation of a similar-aged girl's play nearby. We do not give children of this age enough credit for such closeness and ability to identify with each other. Imitation of age-appropriate actions is a powerful force in learning. Twins can learn large chunks of behavior in one piece of imitation from each other without the usual testing and step-by-step learning.

The older children found just as much pleasure in playing with each other. Nancy and John teased Michael and he teased them back. They ganged up on him but he loved their torture. He and John landed on Nancy when she lay down on the floor, and scrambled around on top of her. Loud screams and noises came out of the trio, but no one cared. The active release of energy and the joy that went with it was fun for both adults to hear as they turned the living room over to the whirling dervishes. Mrs. Clancy wondered why she and her sister didn't get their children together more often. She remembered their last visit together as a nightmare. And now she remembered why. Both she and her sister had spent the entire time tensely interfering with the children's squabbles, their play, their roughhousing, their noise. The two sisters had sat stiffly upright in straight chairs across from each other, jumping at every sound, rushing in to interfere every time there was a protest from the other room, conversing artificially while they listened with half their minds to the children. They had never been relaxed, as were Mrs. Clancy and her mother. They'd been like ruffled gamecocks waiting for cries of anguish from their children. As a result, the visit had been a nightmare of fights, bites, and torn clothes. Each had secretly vowed never to do it again. The children had been apart since then—for over a year.

When mothers interfere in small children's play by hovering over them, they not only take away the spontaneous ups and downs which children achieve for themselves if left alone, but they inject their own adult tensions into the play. When a child strikes out at another in the presence of an interfering or protective adult, the act quickly becomes loaded with all sorts of meaning: "Hit him back!" "Don't hit him!" "Bad boy!" "Children should love each other." All of these put a heightened value on an act which was originally for the child a simple letting off of steam, or a rather primitive, simple form of expressing his feeling. By the time it is reworked by the adult, it has become distorted with the adult's interpretations of what aggression will mean to him in the future, and how one must learn to handle his aggression. These reactions end up loading an act with meanings which take a lifetime to sort out. As a result, and in very subtle ways, the adults convey tension to their children, indeed heightening the importance of aggressive play—and the prophecy of hurting each other becomes fulfilled. In Mrs. Clancy's and her sister's case, we can easily see how their children were trapped into repeating the rivalry of the adult sisters. When adults do not interfere, more positive learning takes place. I have seen one child bite another; when no adult loomed to protect the bitten child, he stopped crying to bite the first one back. Neither child ever bit another child again. Had an adult reinforced it with expressions of horror, this lesson about biting and being bitten back would not have been learned so simply.

By noon, Mrs. Clancy and her mother felt refueled, and she gathered her two boys for lunch at home. Tom glowed with color and peaceful good humor. Mrs. Clancy felt a pang when she realized how infrequently he looked as contented as this. Michael was bursting with energy and bravado. He strutted in front of his mother and the baby, shouting at children down the street, calling back to a barking dog. He fairly swaggered with his newfound equanimity. The morning had been a real outlet for them all.

Peer relationships are important to all ages. Especially in our lonely, nuclear society, it is important to remember that children need outlets besides their parents as much as parents do from their children. It is sad that these must be as contrived and artificial as they often are.

At lunch, the boys began to fall apart. Michael was silly, showing off for Tom. He showed him how to drop bits of food over the side of the table onto the floor. Tom picked this game up promptly and began to tease his mother with it. As she brushed up the food, he watched and waited, then dropped more over. Michael shouted with delight and spurred Tom on. Mrs. Clancy felt her anger rise as she realized that they were "ganging up" on her. But she was so glad to have them working together that she decided to play along with them. She too made it a game, mockingly overreacting to Tom's teasing.

She had worried about his poor eating habits, and it made her very tense when he didn't eat all she put in front of him. She still fed him baby food from jars when he would let her. She had found that he ate better after Michael had finished, so she sent Michael into another room and tried to feed Tom the rest of his dinner by spoon. He took a few mouthfuls, then began to twist his head from side to side in refusal. She sang songs to him, tried her usual games of "Open wide for Mommy," of "One more bite then we're done," of "Michael does it this way." None of them worked today, and she finally gave up to put him to bed.

This concern of mothers about being sure their children get enough to eat is certainly a universal one. It becomes heightened in periods such as this where not only is the child's need for food overshadowed by other interests (in this case, all of

Tom's energy has been played out), but the whole push for independence becomes involved with food habits. The child wants to feed himself and to be fed—often both at the same, impossibly conflicting times. He wants to eat but he wants more to be independent, and if his mother cares and shows it (as does Mrs. Clancy), the latter drive supersedes, and he'd rather go hungry than be submissive. Hence, it is especially important at this time to turn the feeding over to an independent child. It is far too easy for a well-meaning mother to fall into the trap of "being subtle" but indeed exerting pressure to eat on a child. As Tom does, a child recognizes these "games" and subtleties for what they are to him—pressure and a threat to his autonomy. Three meals are not that important and are certainly not necessary. In fact, one good meal a day in the second year is about par for the course. If it contains a minimum of the necessary ingredients—protein, iron, milk, and vitamins (see Chapter I)—the parent is lucky, and the child is adequately fed!

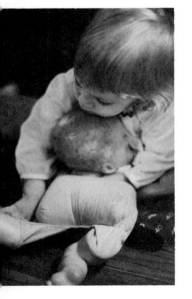

Both children were ready for their naps. They gratefully reached out as Mrs. Clancy placed them in their beds. Each clung to his "lovey." Michael had a bedraggled teddy bear and his thumb. Tom took his bottle to bed with him and fell quickly asleep sucking on it. He continued to suck in brief bursts long after he'd been put to bed. Michael cuddled his teddy to his chest to sleep. As he became sleepier he pushed it down between his legs and under his stomach to rock on it. Mrs. Clancy had been horrified by this use of his teddy bear, and had discussed it at length with her husband. He, too, had been upset when he watched Michael and realized that it was a form of masturbation. They had tried to stop him—by taking away the teddy bear after he was asleep, but he immediately woke up and demanded it back. He seemed so lost, so sad without his "lovey" that they couldn't take it away again. The bear had been a part of his night ritual since he was a small baby. Since Tom had come, it had become more important to him than ever, and the rocking had become part of his sleep ritual. The Clancys had given up on trying to change it for the time, but they worried about it.

All three-year-old children masturbate at times. The word carries such ugly implications for many people that perhaps a new one should be coined. Repetitive, rocking, stimulating activity is a normal and even healthy way for children to learn how to change from a state of excitement to a quiet, relaxed state of sleep. In REM (dreaming) sleep this activity often returns, and it seems to be a common pattern among small children in our society for maintaining a quiescent sleep. In simpler, more "primitive" societies I have seen similar rocking behavior in the REM sleep of three- and four-year-olds, but not as much emphasis on genital activity. These societies do not place the taboos on genital handling in small children that we do, and perhaps the explanation is as simple as that. I'm sure there are many other culturally determined pressures which figure into it also. At any rate, I am certain that genital stimulation is common and not harmful in any way, unless parents are so upset by it that they feel they must interfere. Since their interference must be vigorous to be effective, it seems obvious that it will do one of two things: either reinforce it as a habit in the child, who will carry it on in secrecy and with guilty feelings; or suppress it as a behavior, but force the same tension and need for an outlet into another channel of behavior. The latter may not be a simple overt pattern; instead the tension may show up in the form of free-floating anxiety which is difficult for the child to handle. The parental tension which goes into interfering with it must then be added to the child's own. In other words, maybe it is better for the child to use this common way of handling tension, for he will "grow out of it" if he is left alone by those around him. As the Clancys so sensitively felt, Michael does need outlets at this time. He is trying hard to master many conflicts of his own.

Tom was more restless in his sleep than Michael. Although he was quieter during the day than his brother had been at that age, he moved around the bed in sleep, tossed, turned, and even cried out. "No Mi" came out on frequent occasions. "Mi" was his syllable for Michael, and the dreams of resistance to him were obvious to the Clancys. Long before Tom might have awakened on his own, Michael was awake in his bed, and making noises to try to wake up his brother. He sang to Tom, called out softly to him, finally he slipped over to tickle him. Mrs. Clancy first heard Tom giggling in his bed, crowing with delight at Michael's efforts.

When she went in to get them up, Michael was putting Tom through his paces. "Show me your mouth, Tom." Tom pointed to his mouth. "Show me your eyes!" Tom jabbed a finger in one eye, which teared, but he went doggedly on—pointing to all parts of his body at his brother's command. When Tom couldn't carry a command through, having momentarily forgotten, Michael patiently showed him how to point to his toes or his fingers. Tom squealed at the game.

Here is another example of how much teaching goes on between siblings. The pressure from an older child on a small one to learn can be great. It might be too much pressure if it came from sources other than an older sibling. In such a case there are built-in compensatory mechanisms. Michael is pushing Tom in a warm, fostering way. Disapproval is at a minimum, by "showing" him in a gamelike way. Each success is quickly reinforced by Michael's tacit approval, not by an overreaction of approval which may overemphasize the importance of success. Tom's desire to keep up with and please

Michael is out of proportion to any other kind of motivation I know. Perhaps we should always furnish children with equivalents of siblings and fostering environments, and their cognitive development will flourish as part of their desire to live up to those around them.

In the afternoon, their play was of a different order. Mrs. Clancy wondered why she'd been so upset in the morning. She was able to finish all her dishes, to wash and iron clothes, even to clean a room before her boys began to disintegrate. They played together through the afternoon—Michael directing Tom into activities which he chose. He told him to be a horse while he, Michael, rode him. He showed him how to tear an entire magazine apart. He showed him how to be a bear and growl fiercely. Whenever Tom started off on a venture of his own, Michael firmly but effectively manipulated him back into their play situation. Tom complied, but with growing resistance. At the end of the afternoon, he climaxed this resistance by crawling to his mother and climbing up to hang on her legs. Michael gave up and returned to his own toys.

This long period of directed play is both rewarding for Tom and difficult for him. The rewards are obvious in that he learns so much, has such exciting company as his older brother, and gets a chance at this constant, stimulating interaction. The overwhelming aspect must not be ignored. It must be expensive for a child of this age to keep being directed and redirected, to absorb and handle this much stimulation. In Chapter I we talked of the need for autonomy and sorting out both sides of one's ambivalence in order to establish independence at this age. What happens to this need in a child like Tom who is being constantly overpowered by an attractive but directing older brother? He must learn to deal with frustration, with his own autonomous needs, in very different ways from an only child. Submission must be an early learned pattern. Is it coupled with a burning need to burst forth later, or can it be handled more economically, by such mechanisms as learning to comply and conform in such an effective way that the approval of the older child continues? Perhaps it comes out as a drive for independence later on, for being an individual who is very different from the teacher, the older child. Certainly first and second children are most often very different. The individuation may be fueled by such pressures as these, as well as by the difference in treatment the children receive from their parents.

Surely no one could watch this kind of session and worry that Tom lacked stimulation. The mother is needed to serve a very different role for the second child than for the first. It is no wonder that she might instinctively overprotect the baby after such a period of stimulation. What does her overprotection mean to Tom after he has worked so hard to live up to his brother? It is surely a necessary refuge, but it might also be a reinforcement for his inadequate feelings. Perhaps there are ways of offering refuge and comfort without babying him and making him feel inadequate. He certainly isn't.

Father's homecoming was awaited with a buildup of tension by everyone. Mrs. Clancy began to show her own tension by more activity. She scurried about, leaving Tom clinging to one moving object after another. Tom began to whimper to keep up with her. She shut him up with a short reprimand. This surprised him and he renewed his efforts to follow her. She began to be more biting toward him, saying "no" whenever he tried to reach her. Michael picked up the excitement and began to tease Tom. As Tom began to whimper, both Michael and his mother landed on him with reprimands and "no's." He looked beaten.

What does "no" come to mean to a child when everyone uses it against him? It must take on an added significance—of feeling that nothing one can do is right, that all of the world is against one.

As Mr. Clancy came in the front door, everyone ran to greet him. Michael reached him first and was tossed in the air. Mrs. Clancy rushed up to be kissed and Tom came scurrying in on all fours. As he pulled up on Mr. Clancy's pants leg, everyone else was forgotten. Daddy melted into the greeting he gave to Tom. He picked him up, hugged him, kissed him repeatedly, tickled him to make him laugh, and seemed to forget the rest of his family as he flopped into his big chair with Tom. Michael's eyebrows came together with a dark frown and he retreated into a corner of the sofa to watch. Mrs. Clancy watched him and sat beside him to pat him on the leg. With this attention from her, he began to liven up, and he began to show off for his father. His lively attempts to attract his father's attention seemed to no avail, as Mr. Clancy redoubled his play with Tom.

Fathers come home with needs of their own. After a tiring, demanding day it is hard to step into a demanding, exciting homecoming. Mr. Clancy is probably turning to the baby for his quiet, relaxing responses until he can face the more complicated needs of Michael and his wife. After a period of recharging, maybe he can progress up the chain of command. Unfortunately this comes across to Michael as a kind of rejection. However, part of learning to live with other people is learning about proper timing of communications. If Mr. Clancy can make it up to Michael afterward, the boy will have learned that someone can love him—but at that person's speed, not his own. It is hard growing up and having to learn such complicated things about people.

After Mr. Clancy had revived, and had bounced both boys on his knees for a play period, they all sat down to supper. Eating with father was very different from eating lunch with mother. With him, everything was spit and polish. Michael used his fork, not his fingers. He was expected to say "please" and "thank you" and he did. Even Tom was fed in a much more regimented fashion. Mrs. Clancy didn't attempt to feed him finger foods as she had at lunch. Her husband found it very difficult to tolerate food on the floor or smeared into the table, and she respected this. So she fed Tom entirely by spoon. He ate very little, sitting stolidly with mouth closed for long periods after each bite. But there was none of the teasing protest he'd shown at noon about being fed. He used a more solid passive resistance, except when his father barked at him to take a bite. After complying, he managed to keep such a bite in his mouth for an even longer period. Finally, Mrs. Clancy gave him a piece of Zwieback to hold, in desperation. With this in hand, he began to be freer, waving it, sucking on it, smearing it in his hair. He also began to accept his mother's proffered spoon. But Mr. Clancy couldn't stand the smeared hair and abruptly took away the stick of toast. Tom started to cry, but shut up quickly when he saw the scowl on his father's face.

This is an example of the kind of learning about the differences in their parents to which even small children are equal. The emphasis on manners and order is more important to this father, and both the children know it. They may not like it but they conform. To their mother, quantity of food ingested supersedes such formal aspects of a meal, but she tries to satisfy both her husband and her children's needs. She avoids as much tension as she can. Tom demonstrates his respect for his father by cutting short his protest. How early this learning about each parent sets its mark! It is surely one of the assets of having two adults to conform to. But it may not be easy!

After the boys' supper was over, Michael and Tom began to play together while their parents finished their supper and talked together over their coffee. As their play built up to teasing by Michael and loud protesting by Tom, Mrs. Clancy shrank back in her chair. Mr. Clancy's immediate response was to rush into the room to separate them and to spank Michael. As he picked him up to punish him, the boy began to dissolve and he clung to his father. Mr. Clancy sensed Michael's desperation, hugged him to him, and said, "Dammit, Michael. You can't tease Tom all of the time! It drives me and your mother goofy! I hate to spank you, but I'm sick of it. Can't you learn to get along with him? After all, he's your brother." Michael looked up at his father, listening. "But he breaks up my tower." "Maybe if you showed him how to build up a tower of his own, he wouldn't need to break yours up. You are so good at showing Tom how to do things, and he really likes to do them with you." Michael asked to be put down, went over to Tom, and gently began to show him how to pile blocks on top of each other. As Tom put on a fourth unsteady block and the tower fell, both boys laughed in pleasure at the loud tumble. Mr. Clancy felt revived by this success, and he took over the bedtimes of his boys from his grateful

wife. After Tom was in bed and asleep, he read to Michael—about castles and giants and little boys who conquered them by using their heads, rather than their brawn.

How nice to have a new, fresh look from Father enter the rivalrous situation and give Michael an entirely new way of handling his feelings. By recognizing their importance, Mr. Clancy gives him a more positive way of seeing himself and his brother, and their relationship. Certainly their rivalry is an expression of the strength of their relationship. Both sides of their relationship—the caring and the resentment—are important. Understanding that one can feel both ways about someone is important in learning about one's self and one's relationship to others. This is the essence of what Mr. Clancy provided for Michael in this short explanation.

CHAPTER IV

Parent Alone

Fifteen Months

Single Mother

Mrs. Belew, an only parent, had first brought her Tony to me when he was four months old. He was being breast-fed and was flourishing. She had delivered him by natural childbirth and had found breast-feeding a glorious experience for them both. When she was advised to put him on solid food supplements, she had balked. As her doctor pushed her to feed her baby and shamed her by making her feel that she was depriving him of an important source of nutrients, she came to me. We talked about the relative merits of solid food and whether they were really necessary in the first few months (until extra iron in addition to his mother's milk was needed by the growing infant by five months) and whether indeed solids would interfere with her ability to nurse him. As we talked, it became obvious to us both that she was very protective of the closeness that surrounded the breast-feeding situation. She not only dreaded the threat to this that any other food might mean, but she was desperately afraid that others might intrude on and break into this magical, rewarding unity and destroy it. She was also guilty about how much this meant to her, and somewhere she saw it as wicked that she cared so much for Tony and felt so much pleasure in his response to her.

*This was the first bit of evidence that she saw her lovely rela-
tionship as fragile and undeserved. Although she was giving
as much as she was receiving, the depth of pleasure in such a
mother-infant relationship can be overwhelming and frightening—particularly if a mother sees herself as standing up
against the world to protect it. The guilt which simmers along
counter-balances the really great and rewarding communication between mother and child. For Tony at this age, this
close relationship was pure gold—unless it becomes so hedged
in with protective defensive devices that it cannot grow.*

As we talked about the real issue (which was not a matter
of when to introduce solid food) of raising, of loving, and
giving to a baby, and then being able to give him up gradually,
she began to weep. She saw herself as losing him completely
as soon as there was any sort of a wedge between them.

*Although this is rarely expressed, I am sure there are many
mothers who go through this kind of tortured all-or-none feeling about separating from their baby. It makes it difficult for
them to see the baby's need to be a separate individual.*

With this understanding between us, I was able to offer to
help her see such issues as they came up from Tony's side as
well as her own. At the time when Tony wanted to start feeding himself with his fingers, she found it hard to let him, and
she needed to be pushed. She had hated giving him a relief
bottle of milk and managed to breast-feed him successfully
until he was eleven months old and ready for a cup. By that
time he handled it well by himself. She carried him around in
the daytime and needed to be urged to put him on his belly so
that he could learn to crawl. When he started to walk, she
got him a walker "to protect him from falling," and I had to
press her to let him try his own wings—to fall and bang his
head if necessary. There were several periods when Tony
began to wake at night and cry out for her, and she ran to
him all too readily. When she told me that she found it
"easier" to take him into bed with her at night to nurse and

comfort him, she was able to understand me when I urged her to avoid this pitfall.

The remarkable flexibility which Mrs. Belew shows is coupled with a real desire for understanding Tony's side of it. Instead of doggedly plowing ahead, getting him fixed in a pattern, and then crying for help—too little and too late—Mrs. Belew was always ready to weigh her own wishes and needs against what it might mean to him.

An only parent also risks overwhelming a baby by such closeness. Along with the sleep problems which she might be reinforcing for Tony by responding so readily and so rewardingly to his every night cry, Mrs. Belew was creating a kind of closeness which would be hard for him and her to dilute.

In our culture, sleeping in bed with a parent is too threatening. I have been interested in other cultures (such as in parts of India) where this is not taboo, where the children climb in and out of bed with mother all night long. I wondered where the limits on this came from as the child grew older and incestuous wishes began to come to the surface. As I understand it from hearsay, by four or five years the children no longer come to the mother's bed, and if they do, everyone (including the father) calls them babyish to shame them away. So the limits are there and come up at a time that we might expect them to if we agree with Erik Erikson's stages of psychosexual development. With our customs of privacy and of sexual taboos, a child picks up shaming messages from his environment long before four or five—from peers, from people around him, and from his guilty parent. I am sure that no parent in our culture can allow (or encourage) a child to sleep in his or her bed without feeling guilty and ambivalent about it. If it serves a real purpose, such as it did for Mrs. Belew—of filling a loneliness for her—the guilt is even stronger. It might have made her even more defensive and unwilling to discuss it with me, but it didn't—and this is why I admired her.

By the time Tony reached his first birthday, we had been through many minor crises together. He was a beautiful, strong boy who was not easily frightened or worried, who seemed sturdily masculine with his swaggering gait, his aggressive inquisitiveness, and his sober way of watching and understanding as one showed him how to do things. And he had a sense of humor—he and his mother laughed together, and it was a pleasure to see them play with each other.

When he returned for a checkup at about fifteen months, there were new signs of tension between them. When Tony

began to explore the office, to walk from one piece of furniture to another, Mrs. Belew jumped to stop him. She told him at each turn what he should or shouldn't be doing. She had a new, strained look on her face and Tony seemed sadder. When she removed him from my telephone for the fifth time, he lay down on the floor, screaming in a mild tantrum, and she too began to weep. She told me then that he had started having mild tantrums and saying "no" to her and that she felt herself falling apart as a mother. "What have I done wrong? Is it time to start punishing him? I feel myself getting angry with Tony and I never have before! I really do feel lost and hopeless."

The negativism and tantrums from Tony hit her so hard because they are expressions of another level of separation. As he needs to go through these periods of negative and violent responses to her, he is establishing his own ego boundaries for himself as separate from her. This is truly the beginning of the end of their intensely intimate relationship, and it is even harder for a lone parent. To Mrs. Belew it represents a kind of rejection, perhaps an end to the loveliest period of her life, and an end to a relationship which she never felt she deserved —so it's even harder. The fact that she can let him go without suppressing all of his negativism and stubborn determination is really remarkable. She could make it so difficult for him to express himself that his expression would go underground— and we'd see Tony as a Little Lord Fauntleroy, complying in a saccharine (and ominous) way to her wishes.

We discussed these aspects of separation—how hard they were for her but how important for him. Then we were able to talk about how to "handle" his tantrums, when punishment and limits were important. Until we had established the reasons for her own anguish, she never could have been objective enough about Tony's side of it to see where she needed to act and where she didn't.

The constant overprotection which went into her directions to him at every turn could now be seen as a way of controlling him, of keeping him from getting out of hand, or into trouble which she couldn't handle. In the process of pressing him, she was really provoking him to tease her, to try out dangerous tests, to close his ears when she said "no," and to press for more than this constant, bickering control. He certainly

needed the firm limits she had to offer him—but in smaller, definite doses, leaving room for exploration, testing, and then an awareness of how important the limits were in order to learn them for himself.

Without definite, firm, effective limit-setting from a parent, a child is pushed to find limits for himself. That's hard and often scary, for children seem to know instinctively when they are going too far. To me, a spoiled child demonstrates this kind of anxiety, constantly testing the system for limits which he knows are there somewhere, wanting them to come from the outside rather than having to find them for himself. It's no wonder that his response to being stopped is that of relief.

We spoke of the occasional necessity for spanking him or confining him to his room as punishments when nothing else worked. But to make controls effective, she had to save them for important things, then be definite and incisive.

It must be harder for a lone parent to be sure of what's important and what needs a tough approach. Almost anything can be rationalized, and worked around—and it's often easier to do that than to face the ordeal of punishing a child if one is not quite sure of oneself.

With a lone parent, the area of limits and punishment may be even more important. Since there is no male figure in the Belew household to represent authority, it becomes Mrs. Belew's role. Often it may seem artificial, and she may have to be tougher than she would want to be for the pure value of making a point of authority. It is important that Tony and she both recognize the symbolic value of her authority.

Mrs. Belew began to talk about other areas which were difficult for her. Eating had never been a problem in the first year. Tony had loved food and had never refused a bite. All of a sudden in the past few months he had been refusing whole meals at a time, refusing to eat one food after another, for no reason that she could see. It made her especially angry, for she took great pains to cook him tasty dishes—ones that she was sure he'd like if he would just try them, and she also had done all I'd suggested about letting him feed himself. She wanted to start feeding him all over again, so she could at least see that he tried different new things. She felt rejected when he turned down her cooking, and often she blew up at him. More often she tried to finish a meal he'd refused entirely by spoon-feeding him baby food. She knew he wouldn't starve, but she couldn't stand to see him lose his sturdy masculine build.

We have seen how common it is for refusals of whole meals, for testing of foods, to dominate the feeding situation. This particular situation is harder because she takes it more personally, sees it as a part of Tony's turning away from her, and then rationalizes this by worrying about his losing weight or "his build." Of course these are only part of it, and this kind of manipulating of food and meals is a necessary part of Tony's second year, just as it is of Susan's and Tom's.

Bedtime had become a problem again. She found it very hard to decide when he should go to bed. It was so much more fun to have him around in the evening that she realized she would keep him up all evening if she could. But she knew that wasn't good for him. She had kept him up in the mornings to push him to one nap, then had put the nap as late as possible and had left him in bed as long as he'd stay—so that he would be able to stay up later in the evening with her. When she kept him up later than eight, however, he always went down fighting, and he had begun to wake up at night all over again. Her inclination was to go to him, rock him or read to him, or just love him. She knew now that she mustn't bring him to bed with her, but she needed me to tell it to her all over again. He had begun to wake twice at night, and she thought that maybe she was playing into it.

I think so too. She is likely to be reinforcing it by going to him too soon, by keeping him up longer than is best. She is honest in admitting that her own loneliness motivates her.

But she doesn't quite realize how he's crying for help. His gradually increasing pattern of waking suggests to me that she must soon take a firm stand. All children (and adults) have cycles of deep and light sleep through a night. These seem to be about four-hour cycles in most people, and every four hours a child comes up into light REM sleep. This often takes the form of dreaming, of talking or crying out, of sleep-walking. As children come up to semiconsciousness to dream or call out, they need to learn internal mechanisms for getting themselves down into deep sleep again. Otherwise they must wake up, find comfort or ways to quiet themselves which depend on outside help, and only then return to another cycle of deep sleep. When Mrs. Belew pushes herself in as an outside aid to Tony's returning to sleep, she is really depriving him of the opportunity and the need for learning how to do it for himself. This is another instance of how hard it is for her to allow him real, important independence from her.

The last area was his jealousy. Whenever she was trying to talk on the phone, he managed to get himself into a pickle from which she had to extract him. When she had a friend over, he climbed in and out of her lap, and often he even put his hand over her mouth when she tried to talk. Her friends

thought she spoiled him by letting him torture her this way. When she had a male friend over, Tony went wild. He showed off painfully, was coy with the man, teased his mother mercilessly, and when she attempted to leave him behind with a sitter, he had an endless tantrum which almost stopped her from going out. Then he woke up whimpering during the night. She almost never had dates anyway, but after this, she resolved not to try it again.

She does allow him to overreact, and I agree with her friends. There is too much permissiveness here. What if he is jealous? It's normal for him to hate to share her, but it's pretty important to both of them that he learn how. She must want him to interfere with her other associations or she would let him know somehow that this won't do. It will be better for them both if she can make some meaningful friendships to dilute the intensity of theirs.

At a friend's insistence, she brought Tony to a play group. Tony seemed overwhelmed by the new situation and clung to Mrs. Belew's skirts. As she tried to ignore him and talk to her friends, Tony became more insistent and demanding. He climbed into her lap, put his hands over her eyes, his face in

front of her face to try to divert her. Both intrigued by his clinging and embarrassed in front of the other mothers, she tried halfheartedly to push Tony away. Of course, this didn't help and he redoubled his attempts to intrude into her new relationships. She became more embarrassed and wished she hadn't come in the first place. She pushed Tony off onto the floor to play. He started a tantrum which ended quickly as she picked him up. She looked around to the other mothers for help. They urged her to put him down and ignore him for a while. One of them told her that she'd had exactly this kind of experience when she came to the play group and she had learned that it was necessary to push her child off. Mrs. Belew listened, pushed Tony down again, and turned her back on his protests to talk to the other women. Within a few minutes, he was playing with the other toddlers.

Mrs. Belew's greatest asset is her ability to listen to people who want to help her. In part this springs from a need for support from other adults, and from a realization that some separation is important for both of them. She was also very reassured by the fact that other mothers had had to go through the same experience. One of the problems of being isolated is that it fosters the feeling of being unique, with "different" problems from everyone else. In Mrs. Belew's case, she then reinforces every slight misstep in Tony's behavior as evidence that she is a bad mother and he a damaged child. Seeing other mothers with the same problems will be a real bulwark against this feeling—common to all mothers.

Tony played hard. He watched the other children and began to participate in their games. He tried to dominate the play, pushing one child to the floor. Mrs. Belew started in her chair, as if to intervene to protect the other child. The mother of the assaulted child held her back, saying, "We've learned to let them deal with their own problems. You watch." The child got up from the floor, gave Tony a hard push, then started playing again. Tony registered surprise, seemed to take it in, and settled down to play again.

Tony's speech was more advanced than that of the other

children in the group. He began to try to order them around, half showing off that he could speak. They were playing with crayons and a large piece of paper. He said, "Here, let me do it!" And he attempted to gather all of the crayons for himself. For a few minutes it seemed to work, as each child gave in to his commands.

His ability to command and to use speech in a more facile way certainly came from the more encapsulated relationship he and his mother shared. She had spoken more to him directly than do most mothers, who have other responsibilities. It is interesting that Tony uses this to try to dominate a play situation which is still new and frightening to him. The other children's acquiescence is interesting. They seem to accept his dominance in this area.

Soon, however, each of the children had turned away to play with other things, and Tony found himself alone. He lost interest quickly in his drawings, and sidled over to the group who were climbing on a sofa, imitating each other's antics. He tried once more to enter the group, pushing into their play. This time a boy his size gave him a hard shove, saying "no." Tony landed on his bottom. He sat stunned for a few minutes, looked to his mother to see whether he should cry in protest. She was lost in conversation and hadn't seen this interchange. Tony picked himself up, watched the others, and entered more carefully into their play.

It amazes me how quickly children can learn from each other if they are left to cope with their peers. The other children had sensed that Tony was bad news when he came barging in. They showed him they weren't going to tolerate his behavior. And when he found he had to, he learned from the experience. This alone is worth all of the effort of getting a group together. For Tony it is a timely, valuable lesson.

When it was time for juice and crackers, the children all sat around a table. The mothers ranged themselves at a distance, but watched this event. Mrs. Belew was horrified to see

Tony grabbing for all of the crackers, and jumped to intervene. Again, another mother stopped her and said, "Leave it to them." The boy seated next to Tony pulled Tony's juice cup away, leaving Tony with his hoard of crackers but no juice. When Tony protested and started to reach for his cup, the boy said "no" loudly. Tony seemed to interpret this correctly, shoved the crackers out toward the middle of the table, extracted his juice, and the party continued.

This is an example of the richness of communication which can go on with very little speech. Each of the boys knew what the other was "saying" without any more explicit verbalization than the most useful word at this age—"no." It might seem as if we cut down on other modes of expression when we rely entirely on speech. The reality is that the behavior which accompanies speech is as important to a communication as are the words themselves. One needs only to watch a film of a conversation without the sound to see how much of a communication is expressed in behavior. The understanding of this behavior which children have already built up is as important to learning to communicate as is the learning of words themselves.

At the end of the morning, Mrs. Belew and her son felt weary but refreshed. Tony had had such a good time that he looked back hungrily as they left the group. Mrs. Belew felt she had been given a new lease on life. She had had a chance to communicate with and to share thoughts with other adults —and adults who were going through the same things she and Tony were. It was a real shot in the arm!

Being an only parent for one's children is lonely work. Days can stretch on interminably, relentlessly, and nights are hard to fill up. A job may help to break the powerful monotony as well as providing necessary income, but the ups and downs of a family are all up to the one parent to manage, and it's a demanding responsibility. There's no one else to pick up the pieces at the end of the day, no one to start baths or turn them off, no one to answer the telephone while the baby is being changed, and, most important of all, no one but children to talk to. Children's talk can be fun when it's mixed with other kinds of conversations in a day. But there's a stagnating aspect to it, too. Adults need their peers for many reasons— support, stimulation, and an opportunity to see themselves through others' eyes. The responsibility which an adult feels when he is trying to listen to a child—to understand what the child means, what he is trying to say, to support and encourage him, and then to lead him on into more complex thinking —is strenuous and demanding. In the previous chapters, the mother and father have fed off each other as they met the challenges of the day with their child, and so has the child. One of the most difficult aspects of being a lone parent is that there is a sparseness in it for the child, too. A parent who wants a rich atmosphere for his child feels this extra responsibility. I admire a parent who tackles it head-on and who wants to see the pitfalls and the problems which get magnified in such a situation.

I have rarely felt as useful as a pediatrician as I have in supporting such parents, and providing an ear for their concerns. I have seen that the second year is a particularly hard year for them and their children. The first year is rewarding; each of the infant's new achievements is like a new petal opening up, and the problems are those that lend themselves to a one-to-one relationship. The boredom and monotony may be there, but it's more easily overlooked for a while. And, if the mother or father is working, it's easier to find a good caretaker for a baby. Not so for a toddler. As babies become more independent, more active, more demanding—and more negative—they are suddenly cats, not kittens, and it takes a parent to love them much of the time.

This year can represent a crisis in many ways for a parent alone. Mrs. Belew will weather hers now, with her new-found sources of support. She has the inner resourcefulness to manage anyway, but the richness she and Tony will gather from the play group and their respective peers will help them separate and grow as more fulfilled individuals.

Working Single Mother

An only parent who must work has a somewhat different set of problems. The intense problems of separation of parent and child are already diluted by the nature of their lives. Presumably, the working mother has set up a caretaking situation for her child which is the warmest, most nurturing she can provide. It may be a single sitter (as in Kara's case) or it may be a day-care center. The necessity for working has made it easier to leave and to share the child with another person or persons, but as some of the inevitable turmoil of the second year presents itself, a working single mother (or father) is pressed to reevaluate herself and the relationship.

Mrs. Little had a girl of two and a new baby when her husband "ducked out." She had been prepared for it in some ways, for she knew things weren't going well between them and she'd had the new baby, Ann, in a last-ditch effort to pull the family together. Suddenly she found herself solely responsible for two babies. Her husband had disappeared completely, and there was no support available so she had to think of returning to her work as a schoolteacher as soon as possible. Fortunately, her aunt lived in the town, and she was able to arrange for her aunt to come in to sit with the two girls until she could arrange for a better caretaking situation for them. After a year she found a center where she could take Laura for day school and where Ann could be a part of an infant unit. There was one adult for every three infants, and Mrs. Little felt grateful for this. Her aunt had been exhausted and was glad to be free, though she had been very important and supportive to them all through the crisis.

As Ann came into her second year, everything seemed all set for clearer sailing. Mrs. Little's job was steady. She taught second-graders and came home tired, but she was able to be home for a little bit of the afternoon and for supper and breakfast with the two girls. Although their care in the center practically devoured her salary, she had sized up her option for accepting Aid to Dependent Children, which would have given her an income and allowed her to stay at home, and had decided that she herself needed the outlet a job offered, to help fight the depression with which her husband's desertion had left her. So she accepted the marginal financial situation and proceeded to make the best of it. She worried about her girls and hoped she could make up to them for such a stressed life.

This is the most important ingredient—having a parent who cares, who can overcome his own, sometimes overwhelming problems to want to look beyond to those of the children. Mrs. Little had assessed her strengths and found that she had more for her children if she worked than if she stayed home with them in a state of depression. Although I would certainly always prefer an intact mother-child unit, there are many times and many situations where the children may be better off in a shared environment.

Laura was a subdued, pale, quiet child who looked perpetually worried. She made Mrs. Little feel guilty. But Ann was a bouncy girl of fifteen months who seemed open, cheerful, and able to take everything in her stride. Mrs. Little gathered great comfort from her times with Ann and felt the child was something of a miracle—to have come out of all the misery surrounding her early months with such gaiety and bounce. Three-year-old Laura would sit and watch the interplay between Ann and their mother with longing eyes, as if she wanted to be as open and easy. When Mrs. Little would try to tease her out of her quiet moodiness, Laura would try awkwardly to imitate Ann's antics. She always ended by playing a rather pathetic baby role, which turned Mrs. Little back to Ann.

A child's inborn characteristics seem to play such an important role in shaping the responses of the environment to the child. Laura is quiet and observant and reminds Mrs. Little too much of her own problems for her to respond positively. Ann's characteristics are easier, more cheering, and offer a new outlook to this difficult situation. No wonder her mother responds with such a marked preference. Even at three, Laura is acutely aware of her own contribution to this failing situation. Mrs. Little is almost dividing her own personality among the two—the gay side to Ann, the depressed side to Laura.

When Mrs. Little went to her aunt for help in sorting this out, the aunt was able to point out that Laura was able to take the competition, as long as Mrs. Little made an effort to treat her as a positive individual. To do this, maybe she'd have to take her off alone for periods, to get to know her by herself, and to let her know how much she had to offer which was not in competition with Ann.

This is a very important way of handling a situation like this. It is probably difficult for Mrs. Little to see Laura and Ann as separate individuals unless she makes an artificial separation like this. And because she sees only her own version of Laura's troubles when both girls are together, it would help to get Laura away to see her underlying strengths as well as her superficial behavior. Also, it becomes an opportunity for real cementing—to spend a time alone together just for the purpose of getting to know each other better. I can't recommend this enough to overstressed parents who are losing touch with a particular child.

Ann's makeup had also made it easier for her to make friends with the caretakers at the center. She was coy when they approached her, gay when they played with her, and assertive when they weren't paying attention to her. She seemed economical in all of her responses. She seemed to know what she wanted and how to get it. Mrs. Little enjoyed watching her in action and, of course, she loved the reports from the center, which were always glowing. She worried a little about the ease with which Ann turned people on and off, and she worried about the depth of the relationships she did make. She realized that she and Laura probably cared too deeply, and that what bothered her about Ann was that she was too much like her father.

It is very hard not to place children in "slots"—to associate them with an adult whom they resemble. The biggest problem is that one treats them as if they had the traits of the adult in question, and it becomes a self-fulfilling prophecy. It would be too bad to make invidious comparisons between Ann and her father. A child with an absent parent has a hard enough time with her fantasies of him. She needs an image of him and she constructs one out of this need. If it can be a positive image, it is easier to fill up the emptiness his absence leaves. It is one of the hardest jobs of a parent alone—to try to stress the positive side about the absent parent without emphasizing the negative aspects. Mrs. Little will have to try hard not to devalue Ann's good traits, because she has been hurt by someone whom Ann resembles. A child with one parent has a built-in doubt about "What's wrong with me?" that comes from not having what society thinks of as a complete family. If a parent falls into the trap of reinforcing this by blaming the other parent, by devaluating the other's characteristics, it is natural for the child to take this criticism personally, as if it were putting the finger on "what's wrong" with the child also.

Although Mrs. Little felt she had too little left over for her girls at the end of the day, she could see that Ann was flourishing. The child was vital, excited by life, and delighted to see her mother arrive at the center. By the time she got home, she was negative and full of tantrums. She screamed for what she wanted until she got it. When she was corrected, she lay down on the floor to roll and kick. This open fury was easy for her mother, and she could comfort Ann after it was over, and almost enjoy it at the time. She felt released herself after one of these screaming fits.

This is one reason the antics of a baby in his second year hit us so hard. We can and do identify with his struggle and with his feelings. Mrs. Little needed a chance to scream and kick about her life, too, and therefore could get some vicarious pleasure from Ann's tantrums. I think they are another evidence of Ann's normal development. The fact that she is reaching negativism and its expression at the age which is appropriate for it does suggest that she has already developed a strong ego and one that is following an expected course.

Single Father

Mr. Gray was left alone with his small boy when the latter was fifteen months. His wife had suffered an acute mental breakdown after she had pneumonia when Bobby was a year of age. She had finally been hospitalized three months later, after a stormy, disturbing period for them all. When she left, Bobby and his father were still reeling from the times they'd been through. Mr. Gray was depressed and felt as if he had somehow contributed to his wife's breakdown. He had sought and received therapy for himself which helped him separate his own and Bobby's problems from the entangled situation. When they were finally alone, and the household began to settle down, he realized that Bobby had suffered a great deal. He was a pale, frightened little boy who was very tenuous in his relationships with people, frightened to do anything but please them. He jumped at any loud noise, paled perceptibly when anyone spoke harshly in the room, and never dared incur anyone's disapproval. When his father broke down and wept on rare occasions, or sat sadly in a corner chair by himself, Bobby crept over as if to comfort him, looking up into his face and smiling gently, clinging to his knees.

Precocity of this kind—in which the child seems to take the role of a parent—is not uncommon as a response to a stressed household. It is not an ideal pattern to perpetuate, and I would urge Mr. Gray to see it as a sign of Bobby's distress. As soon as the father can pull himself together enough to help Bobby, he must again assume the role of adult, and Bobby can let go of this pattern. At present, it is obviously a defense against seeing his necessary parent so withdrawn, and he uses a known role of comforter to reach him and to keep in contact with him. It is a sign of Bobby's strength that he can cope with this distress in such a positive way.

As Mr. Gray began to recover, he saw how slowed down Bobby was. He was still crawling, although he certainly knew how to walk. It was apparent that he just hadn't the courage to let go or the incentive to try anything new. He babbled very little and said no clear words except "mama" and "dada" and "please." He seemed to spend his day watching the faces of the adults around him for signs of pleasure or displeasure. Whenever he sensed tension, he tended to huddle in a corner, rocking back and forth from his waist, sucking on his thumb and looking dully ahead. At the end of the day, when put to bed, he lay awake for long periods, rolling his head, sucking his thumb, and staring dreamily at the ceiling.

These are ominous signs of an overwhelmed child—the slowed-down motor effort in not walking, the frightened withdrawal from tension, the eagerness to please at a time when he should be rebelling, the resignation behind the rocking and head-rolling patterns coupled with the dull acceptance of isolation.

Bobby's father spent as much time with him in the next three months as he could spare from his work. He searched for a sympathetic, warm woman to come to their house to sit with Bobby while he was at work. He told her of his fears and concerns about the effect of all of this on Bobby's development. He urged her to work with Bobby gently and slowly. He came home from the office as soon as he could each day, to spend the rest of the evening with Bobby. He read about children of this age, and talked to many friends about how to reach his son. Over the next three months, with this kind of patient concern, the child began to gather steam. He walked again soon after he was walked around by his father. He began to have color in his cheeks, and to eat better when someone was in the room with him, talking to him and laughing with him. The joy he began to express in the act of walking was exciting to see. He no longer withdrew by himself but brought toys to his father or his sitter, asking them to play with him. He began to be less frightened by any disapproval, and even giggled at his father on one occasion when Mr. Gray said, "No, Bobby, leave the television alone." As he became stronger and more vital, the patterns of rocking, head-rolling, and thumb-sucking began to decrease. He slept for longer periods at night, and lay awake less.

Mr. Gray cherished Bobby's rebellion when it began to appear. Having seen the kind of passivity which was the alternative, he was gratified by any kind of vigor. When Bobby started saying "no" gingerly, Mr. Gray played a game of saying "no" back to him playfully. They built up in a crescendo of "no's."

This sensitivity to the gingerly quality of Bobby's first "feelers," and the permission to try out his negativism, is certainly saving Bobby. Had he been left to go on in the same fright-ened, withdrawn pattern, he could have ended with problems as serious as his mother's. This early attention to changing his defense mechanisms, to freeing his aggression and his capacity to establish his own wishes and needs, will salvage Bobby's future.

When Bobby banged a toy, his father imitated and encour-aged him. He began to play give-and-take games with him—rolling a ball to him and asking Bobby to roll it back. They played at pointing to parts of Bobby's body. "Where's your nose? Where are your eyes?" Mr. Gray then pointed to his own and said, "See? They're like Daddy's nose and Daddy's eyes."

By establishing Bobby's awareness of himself, Mr. Gray is also strengthening the boy's feeling of being a person. Then carrying it on into a comparison with him further strength-ens the boy and gives him permission to identify with and be like his father.

By eighteen months, Bobby was a changed person. He was stronger in appearance, and he had vitality and was developing a mind of his own. He began to tease Mrs. Crotty, his sitter. She reported to Mr. Gray that he was becoming very "bad" and wouldn't do what she told him. He refused to put away his clothes, he swept food off his table, he began to protest with mild tantrums when she told him to do something. His father interpreted this as a good sign and saw that Bobby was going through a normal, negative period. He urged Mrs. Crotty to put up with it, and tried to explain to her how important it was for Bobby to be allowed to test her. She grumbled about "sparing the rod and spoiling the child" and began to be less enthusiastic about her times with Bobby. Mr. Gray saw that she had liked Bobby as long as he was a frightened rabbit needing her overwhelming kind of mothering, but probably wasn't equal to allowing him the freedom of rebelliousness and negativism he needed now.

This is a common problem with part-time sitters. They are great for one stage of development which fits in with their own needs and their own image of what children should be —but at another stage they just can't make the necessary bridge to the child. Had she been with Bobby all along, or had she been more deeply involved with him as a total person, maybe she could see what Mr. Gray is trying to show her. It is sad but true that the intensity of the relationship between Bobby and his father may be excluding her and may have not allowed her to identify more completely with Bobby's new developmental stages. At this point, it is necessary for Mr. Gray to decide what is important to his son, and of course, the answer is obvious. He needs the freedom to develop his own strengths.

Mr. Gray felt weary when he thought of replacing Mrs. Crotty. He could see that she was becoming less and less effective with Bobby, and was being turned off, as a result. But he also realized that there was value in maintaining stability for Bobby at this time, just as he was beginning to dare to venture outside himself. Also, he felt overwhelmed at the idea of either spending any more time at home, or having to look for another person to fill the bill.

Mr. Gray had given so much of himself during the stress period that he may be having a bit of a reaction to that, and be starting to resent having to give up so much of himself to Bobby. It is certainly an understandable reaction.

He had just begun to feel freer to have a social life of his own. He had been playing tennis twice a week, and had gone out to dinner for the first time since his wife's illness. He found these outlets reviving and exciting. As soon as he showed a willingness to go out, invitations began to pour in. He felt deluged with opportunities to get away. For the first time, he began to feel torn by wishes other than his concern about Bobby.

A father alone has problems. He may feel deserted with his children, angry at the desertion, and may even take this anger out on them. It must be hard not to. The demands on his time are already great—those of earning a living become coupled with a desire for social life which is often more available to single men than to single women. He can justify his social life with the fact that he may be "looking" for a mate to mother his children. Men rarely can find the same resources to face a lonely life that women can. And society sets them up for the kill. No one is more vulnerable to the demands of everyone around him than is a single man. So he must struggle fiercely to save any part of himself for his children. If he cares about having any special role in their development, he must have some time with them. Fortunately, the amount of time is not as crucial as the quality of the time he spends with them. I remember the anguish which fathers voiced who returned from the Korean War to children who had grown out of their babyhood. They claimed that they felt cheated of very fundamental knowledge of their children when they hadn't been around to see them develop from the start. I think a father who is away most of the time must depend on a mate to transmit knowledge of his children to him when he does return to touch base. When there's no one there but a sitter who doesn't care about cementing this bond, the feeling of deprivation and of missing something must be doubled.

The successful fathers I know who are in lone charge of their small children must make a very special, even an artificial effort to have time with each child. They sense what I feel—that it's not how much time but the richness of the time with them that makes for a deep, understanding relationship. In such times, the child can get to know the good and bad sides of daddy, just as he can learn to show daddy the good and bad sides of himself. A small child's tendency with a father who is home only rarely is to put on his best face. It is especially reassuring when he can show his other side to his father as well.

Mr. Gray began to take Bobby with him when he went to visit other families. He even sought out families with children who were Bobby's age. At first, these new situations were overwhelming for the boy, and he clung to his father. After a few gentle introductions, he began to be able to play with other small children, and it was arranged for him to join a small play group several times a week. Mrs. Crotty was relieved to have him away at such times, and this seemed to

dilute the tension for them. As Bobby began to be more involved with other children in the play group, he began to be
more at ease with his negativism. He could turn it on or off
almost at will. He could sense that it was too much for Mrs.
Crotty, so he began to play a role with her—of being the good,
compliant little boy she liked. And he saved his outbursts for
his father.

*This kind of parceling of his behavior is a good sign. It dem-
onstrates a kind of control, as well as an awareness of priori-
ties with people around him. Whereas he had been compliant
and "too good" with everyone before he began to improve—
out of anxiety—now I feel it is a discriminating response to
what he senses people around him can tolerate. And that's
good. It means he will get what he needs from each one, and
still be able to work out his own needs. But even more important, it means he has gathered enough ego strength to be able
to "give" to other people—even if it is a rather self-centered
kind of giving—that of seeing that they are pleased and not
angered. He has made a great deal of progress.*

When Mr. Gray came home at night, it was almost a regular thing for Bobby to work himself up to a tantrum. At first,
it amused his father to see the little boy searching for something to fuss about. He saw both sides of it—Bobby's fatigue
at the end of a long day of holding himself in, and the boy's
awareness that at last here was someone who could take
whatever he doled out. But after a while, Mr. Gray found
himself getting angry at Bobby for using him so regularly as
an outlet. He justified his anger by saying to himself that he
was tired too, and he felt pretty much like having a tantrum
himself. He spanked Bobby one night after such a display. He
felt so guilty that he immediately picked the boy up to love
him and to apologize. Bobby looked hurt, surprised, then
rather delighted by his father's outburst.

*The relief many children show when they are finally stopped
by a parent is always a surprise. But it points to their need for
limits from the outside, and Bobby is ready for them. This is*

another step in his own ego development and in the dimensions of their relationship.

Tantrums and negativism may be harder for a father than a mother. There may be less ability on the part of a father to tolerate bad behavior as well as good in a child. Perhaps the kind of violence and aggression that surfaces in tantrums means a different thing to a man—more threat about the meaning of loss of control. Men may have more difficulty learning to control and use aggression than do women. At any rate, fathers are likely to find this stage very hard to tolerate without reacting at the child's level. Mr. Gray has been amazing heretofore in his capacity to understand Bobby, and now the need for controlling his reactions may be over.

The biggest crisis occurred when Mr. Gray brought a woman friend home for supper. He had hoped that a female's presence (aside from Mrs. Crotty) might relieve the intensity of Bobby's relationship with him, and he also felt the need for a more normal homelife. But Bobby withdrew into a corner, crumpled up, and began to rock, to suck his fingers, to look off dreamily into the distance. This was so much more frightening to Mr. Gray than had been Bobby's outbursts of temper that he resolved not to try it again soon.

Sharing relationships with a lone father may be a problem for children. Although they are geared to having a sitter or a caretaker during the routine day while daddy needs to work, the expectancy for an intimate unshared time when he is at home may get built up to enormous proportions. I am sure that in a way it is evidence of the economy of relationships that a child like Bobby can muster. He can relate effectively to the daily caretaker but will save all of his real caring for the end of the day. This has its problems. When it is infringed upon, the child can become a raging tiger. One young man told me of an episode in which he took a young woman home "to see whether she would pass muster with the kids" before he asked her to marry him. The three-year-old daughter was openly hostile. She raced into her room, weeping angrily and hid under her bed. When her father cajoled and finally coerced her into coming out to meet Miss Johnson, she allowed herself to be held stiffly on the woman's lap, but proceeded to wet herself and the horrified young woman. His eighteen-month-old boy had one tantrum after another, spit out food as it was offered to him, poured his milk all over the kitchen, and refused to play with either the father or his friend.

I would advise a father who wanted to introduce a new competing figure to his children to do several things in preparation and during the visit: (1) Warn them that she's coming, and see to it that they view her as someone who's coming to see them and make an exciting time for them. (2) Be sure she brings them a present. (3) Spend little time attending to her and much time in the regular routines with them—wooing them to like her will surely work the wrong way. (4) Warn her that they will be negative and jealous and not to be thrown by it. (5) Expect it yourself and understand their jealous antics for what they are—attempts to protect something of vital importance to them.

The tension in the household built up despite Mr. Gray's awareness of his own and Bobby's problems. He decided to leave Bobby at home for a weekend while he went to visit friends. When he returned, Bobby had regressed to such an extent that both he and Mrs. Crotty were frightened by his behavior. Mrs. Crotty began to see the challenge which the child still presented, and Mr. Gray saw how fragile were the developmental steps which Bobby had made. After this, he resolved to stay closer to Bobby until the child had become more solid in his ability to deal with the strained family situation.

Raising a child alone is not an easy task for either the parent or the child. Separation of any duration which is not daily routine is almost bound to throw Bobby harder than other children. The loss of one parent, even if it happened before the child can have any memory of it, places extra value on the remaining parent. And it also magnifies the possibility in the child's mind that this one may leave, too. There is no fear as great and as deeply instinctive in a small child as that of being left alone. Separations must be prepared for, honestly and clearly defined, and there must be the assurance that daddy is coming back. To slip away because it's easier than facing a child's tears, to leave him alone in a strange place like a hospital or even a grandmother's house without adequate preparation and warning, is asking for a severe reaction in a child with one parent. Though it might be better not to separate from him under such circumstances, it certainly might not be feasible. And it probably isn't even necessary— as long as there is a preparation period to which the child can refer during the separation. I always remember a tiny boy who was hospitalized, lonely, crying, but saying over and over, "My mommy said it would be this way." He was clinging to his mother's words of preparation as if she were still there herself. Perhaps a picture of the father, or a shoe or his hat, will serve as an important substitute when he must go away. One little boy whose father was overseas wore his old hat all day long and slept with it at night to keep his memory of his father tangible.

CHAPTER V

No! No! No!

Eighteen Months

Greg was a cherubic-looking eighteen-month-old boy. His face was round, his features regular, and his head ringed with blond curls. He had a sturdy, athletic build, and as he stalked along he resembled a determined athlete—zeroing in on his opponent. He was indeed masculine in build and appearance. His stolid expression was coupled with a way of looking seriously at his surroundings, sizing them up before he acted upon them. With new people, his slow assessment amounted to intimidation. As he stared at a stranger with knitted brows, their cheery, rather empty greetings ("Aren't you a big boy now?") turned to acid in their mouths, as they felt themselves evaluated and pigeonholed for the inanity of their comments.

Why does a serious child make an adult feel like such a fool? It is surely a commentary on the superficiality of the effort which most people make in greeting small children. Certainly, the high-pitched voice we use in speaking to them already puts us at a disadvantage. One expert points out that we pitch our voices to a new register when we speak to a child by way of signaling to him that we are now speaking directly to him. I have tried this and found it true; changing to a higher voice does attract a child's attention. But we must feel a bit foolish for it. And then we do use such inanities as "What's your name?" and "My, how you've grown!" If we are serious in wanting to reach out to a child, there are many ways of doing it which are more acceptable to him—such as sitting down to play with something alongside him, or offering to show him something in which he might be interested, a book or a toy which is appropriate for his age.

His parents had found Greg to be an easy baby. He had learned each new developmental step with patience and practice, and when he mastered it he was very sure of himself. Their efforts to teach him or to push him to learn faster were met with a stubborn resistance which let them know just where they stood. Mrs. Lang had responded to this dogged determination with real pleasure. Greg had never made her feel helpless or as if she weren't contributing her share of mothering to their relationship.

There are few guidelines for young mothers to reassure them about how well they are mothering. The old supports of an extended family—grandparents, aunts and uncles, who could show young parents how they did it and on whom they could rely for support and answers to their questions—have not been replaced by neighbors or pediatricians or child-rearing literature. The parent whose child is so definite in his responses that he does not leave any question as to the appropriateness of their direction together is truly fortunate. I have tried to urge young parents to settle their own insecurity about trying new things out by watching for cues from the child to guide them. This is not as easy as it sounds with many babies. When one can find out from the infant's reaction whether he can accept teaching or more pressure to learn a new step, it certainly makes child-rearing an easier job. Greg is such a baby.

Mr. Lang had reveled in Greg's solidity and strength. He had roughhoused with him, had played hard with him, confident that Greg would whimper when he'd had enough. When the father came home at night, Greg became a gay, alert baby who watched his father's every move and then attempted to imitate him. This kind of communication had been at the base of their relationship from early infancy. Mr. Lang relied on Greg's cues in their relationship, too.

Sex differences are built in early. There is some experimental evidence that male and female newborns show different reactions at birth. In early infancy there are apparent differences in muscle tone and use of muscular movement in males, and a more prolonged attention to visual and auditory stimulation in girls. But the parents' expectations for each sex determine their treatment of the baby so early that it is difficult to call genetic the differences which have become solidified in the early months of life. By this time, both of Greg's parents have created and found a set of "masculine" expectations for him that are implicit in every interaction. Even "feminine" responses (whatever they are) would be interpreted and changed over by this set of expectations. By now, Greg's own image of himself must be set in such a way that he will choose a "male" reaction in preference to a "female" one. Thus the whole issue of whether maleness and femaleness are built in at birth or are learned is a difficult one to determine unless we can establish differences at birth or eliminate the unconscious and conscious differences in early environmental reactions.

When Greg began to be negative in the second year, his parents felt as if they had been hit with a sledge hammer. His good nature seemed submerged under a load of negatives. When his parents asked anything of him, his mouth took on a grim set, his eyes narrowed, and, facing them squarely with his penetrating look, he replied simply "no!" When offered ice cream, which he loved, he preceded his acceptance with a "no." While he rushed to get his snowsuit to go outside, he said "no" to going out.

The initial "no" is no more than a fragile barrier behind which a child this age can hide. If he is taken too literally, he will be surprised and disappointed. Rather than indicating

that a decision has been made, it is a marker for the beginning of decision-making. It is more an effort to establish in the child's own mind (as well as in those around him) that he now has a choice available. Establishing this out loud, he can begin to make a decision—most often the same one he would have made anyway. The "no" seems to affirm his new power to master his own decision-making. This is parallel to the negativism in adolescents behind which they must hide in order to establish their own identities.

His parents' habit of watching Greg for cues now began to turn sour. He seemed to be fighting with them all of the time. When he was asked to perform a familiar chore, his response was, "I can't." When his mother tried to stop him from emptying his clothes drawer, his response was, "I have to." He pushed hard on every familiar imposed limit, and never seemed satisfied until his parent collapsed in defeat. He would turn on the television set when his mother left the room. When she returned, she turned it off, scolded Greg mildly, and left again. He turned it on. She came rushing back to reason with him, to ask him why he'd disobeyed her. He replied, "I have to." The intensity of her insistence that he leave it alone increased. He looked stolidly back at her. She returned to the kitchen. He turned it on. She was waiting behind the door, swirled in to slap his hands firmly. He sighed deeply and said, "I have to." She sat down beside him, begging him to listen to her to avoid real punishment. Again he presented a dour mask with knitted brows to her, listening but not listening. She rose wearily, walked out again. Just as wearily, he walked over to the machine to turn it on. As she came right back, tears in her eyes, to spank him, she said, "Greg, why do you want me to spank you? I hate it!" To which he replied, "I have to." As she crumpled in her chair, weeping softly with him across her lap, Greg reached up to touch her wet face.

The intensity of this conflict and Greg's determination to carry it to a conclusion reflect his intense need to establish his own identity. It must be difficult for a mother to see why a child needs to be punished or rejected to establish himself as a separate person, but perhaps it is as simple as that—when he is intensely loved, it is even more difficult to separate. When his behavior creates even a temporary ambivalence in his parent, then he can more easily feel his separateness.

After this clash, Mrs. Lang was exhausted. Greg sensed this and began to try to be helpful. He ran to the kitchen to fetch her mop and her dustpan, which he dragged in to her as she sat in her chair. This reversal made her smile and she gathered him up in a hug.

Greg caught her change in mood and danced off gaily to a corner, where he slid behind a chair, saying "hi and see." As he pushed the chair out, he tipped over a lamp which went crashing to the floor. His mother's reaction was a loud "No, Greg!" He curled up on the floor, his hands over his ears, eyes tightly closed, as if he were trying to shut out all the havoc he had wrought.

When he began to recover, his thumb went into his mouth and he went into his room to get his blanket. He retreated behind his pattern of sucking on his thumb and fingering his crib blanket lovingly. So often did he need this kind of retreat that he had sucked a huge blister on his thumb. It had become infected at one point, but before Mrs. Lang could get him to the doctor, he had succeeded in sucking out the infection himself—the blister drained, the infection subsided, and his

thumb was ready for another blister. When she reached Greg's doctor, her query had been, "Should I take his blanket away? Will he never stop sucking his thumb? Why should he still be sucking, when I made a tremendous effort to see that he had plenty of sucking as an infant? I always thought that breast-feeding him was the surest way to prevent thumb-sucking."

These are common concerns in mothers of children who continue to suck their fingers at this age—and most children do. In fact, when one stops to realize that it is one of the few autonomous resources a small child has at his disposal for retreating, for handling tension, for comfort, it must be obvious that the things which happen in the second year make it the peak year for the need for finger- and thumb-sucking. I am relieved when a child demonstrates this kind of resourcefulness. I would not expect any correlation but a negative one between how intensely he sucked his fingers at this age and a "habit" pattern in later childhood. In the last generation, parents were more up-tight about habits such as finger-sucking. Their attempts to prohibit only reinforced the pattern, by focusing more attention on it than it deserved, and by increasing tension at a time when the child's sucking indicated his need to retreat from tension.

In a study of the sucking patterns of "normal" children whose mothers did not try to prohibit their finger-sucking, we found that there was an upsurge in the amount of finger-sucking and retreat to "loveys" in the second year, which began to subside naturally by two and a half years. In the children who used this pattern at bedtime and under stress for the next few years, and there were a considerable number, there was none of the "permanent" problems—such as distorted mouths, and habits which persist as a problem into school years—which are used as reasons why a child should be stopped. Unless parents disapprove, a child is not bothered by disapproval of grandparents, peers, or even schoolteachers, and it need not become a permanent problem. If the "lovey" is a blanket which gets dirty and soggy, it can be cut in half —one of which can be washed while another is in use—too small to be obtrusive to disapproving neighbors at the super-market. If it is a special toy, be sure it is one which will sur-vive the intense onslaught of this year (as is shown by the sucking blisters on Greg's thumb). If it begins to fall apart and cannot be mended or refilled, find another, more durable toy. Tie or sew the old "lovey" to the new one until all the old smells, sensations, and feelings have been transferred to the new one. Then, and only then, the old one can be discarded. As you can see, I feel strongly about an eighteen-month-old baby's need for all the supports he can get. It is a rough time for parents and babies!

Mrs. Lang returned to her household chores, and Greg to his. He began to play with his trucks, lining them up in orderly fashion, running them noisily across the floor, and imitating their noises. As he played, be began to talk to them. He pitched his voice higher as he handled a tiny truck, as if he were talking to a small child. With the biggest truck, he began to use a lower, gruff voice. Each truck seemed to be designated by its size to an appropriate pitch of his voice. His voice had a tender quality to it as he chattered to his toys. Words were indistinguishable, but the phrasing, the inflec-tions, the accuracy of imitated speech were all there. The flood of garbled speech was marked with a variety of inflections and phrases. It continued as long as he was not conscious of being observed. When his mother entered the room, the free flow stopped, and self-consciously he began to try to say dis-tinct words. For her, he said "truck," "see," and "my." But the lilting gobbledygook had vanished as soon as he was aware of her.

Earlier, the gobbledygook is used as a form of communication with adults. By eighteen months, the child is well aware that a parent expects distinguishable words. The freedom of pre-speech is saved for isolated free play. It often crops up in the middle of the night when the child is only semiconscious; but not easily any longer. A second or third child is allowed his gobbledygook only briefly, if at all. The older children teach him, correct him, and push him into formal words and con-

structs before he can learn the pleasures of such free speech. By their very ability to "understand" and interpret a baby's prespeech, which seems amazing to adults, they quickly shape a baby into more structure. A first child has the opportunity to explore verbalization in all of its imitative facets.

Gregory had already begun to pick up the last word of a sentence to imitate. When his mother or father made a statement, he emphasized it by attempting to repeat the last important word—always a verb or a noun. The words were usually isolated, although occasionally he began to add a personal pronoun, such as *"my* book" or *"my* dog." More often, it was simple repetition. The consonants and vowels were mixed in predictable, repeated ways. For example, "basket" was "basik." "Doctor" became "docket." Or consonants were often left off the ends of words—"book" was usually "buh," "ride" was "ry." His parents automatically repeated the word, adding the consonant. When he made a one-word utterance, they instinctively added another to it. "Car" was corrected by them to "Greg's car." "Ry" was enlarged to "We'll all *ride* in the car."

In this way, parents add on an expectation for the next step in speech. This is an automatic response on the part of an adult, and needn't be curtailed. However, if there is too much or too constant pressure on the child to enlarge his speech production, he may feel hopelessly frustrated. What could be an opportunity for imitation becomes an insurmountable obstacle for him. When a child stops speaking or is late in producing words, it might be well to evaluate the environment for too much pressure toward speech. A child's inner desire to communicate and to imitate is a powerful force toward learning language. The maturation of his vocal equipment is necessary before he can master the production of speech which he has understood for months beforehand. And, despite sophisticated attempts to teach children to speak earlier, word production comes about on a fairly rigid timetable in the second year—single words in the first half, and phrases, adjectives, and adverbs in the second half. All of a sudden, at two or two and a half, the rush of new productions indicates that he has been storing ideas for a long time.

At this point, Greg left his trucks and began to search around the room. As if he had found what he was looking for, he picked up a prohibited glass ashtray and carried it over to his mother. She accepted the bait and tried to snatch it away

from him. He recoiled and lay down on the floor screaming, clutching the ashtray to him. This was such an obvious play to embroil her in his teasing that she recovered quickly. She said, "Greg, may I have the ashtray?" As if the wind had suddenly been taken out of his sails, he handed it over to her submissively. She realized that she usually plowed head-on into his forbidden behavior, and that when she didn't, it left her with more authority.

Lunchtime seemed as if it might be an oasis for them.

Gregory had always loved food. He seemed to look forward to meals, was gay when he was waiting for them to be prepared, and devoured everything appreciatively. He was deft with a spoon and fork, and had even begun to attempt to use a knife when he saw his father cutting his own meat. He had been using a glass for many months, but clung to his nighttime bottle as part of a bedtime routine. Mrs. Lang had been conditioned to expect a pleasant communicative time between them. He often gurgled appreciatively to her about something she gave him. Occasionally at lunchtime when they were alone, he demonstrated how much he liked something by feeding bits of it to her and then laughing at the way she smacked in approval.

Not today! As soon as he was put into his high chair, he began to whine. She was so surprised that she stopped preparation of his food, and took him to change him. This did not settle the issue, and when she brought him to his chair again, he began to squirm and twist. She let him down to play until his lunch was ready. He lay on the floor, alternately whining and screeching. So unusual was this that she felt his diapers for pins which might be unclasped, felt his forehead for fever, and wondered whether to give him an aspirin. Finally, she returned to fixing his lunch. Without an audience Greg subsided.

When she placed him in his chair again, his shrill whines began anew. She placed his plate in front of him with cubes of food to spear with his fork. He tossed the implements overboard, and began to push his plate away, refusing the food. Mrs. Lang was nonplussed, decided he didn't fell well, and offered him his favorite ice cream. Again, he sat helpless, refusing to feed himself. When she offered him some of the mush, he submissively allowed himself to be fed a few spoonfuls. Then he knocked the spoon out of her hand and pushed the ice cream away. Mrs. Lang was sure he was ill.

His negativism may be invading the food area all of a sudden. I have seen it hit like an unexpected tornado, leaving the participants helpless. Many children begin to be negative about food much earlier, and it is not such a surprise to their par-

ents. But it does seem to be almost an inevitable development. Refusing certain kinds of foods, refusing lumpy foods, regressing to baby foods or to a bottle or to being fed are all symptoms of this turmoil. A parent will do well to give with the blows, to retain a sense of humor, and to try to ignore the full force of the tornado. If one tries to meet it head-on, by pressure to eat, by cajoling or ingenious attempts to get around the negativism, the chances are good that the feeding area will become a battleground. Many unnecessary feeding problems are laid down in this year. Underneath the more obvious motive of parents, to be sure their child gets properly fed, lies the less conscious struggle over allowing him to be the master of what he eats. As soon as this is pointed out as the real struggle, most parents can admit to themselves and to him that his need is important to explore, to establish his own "infant power" and its limits, to be able to say "yes" and "no" to certain foods and various kinds of foods. Although this may last for most of a year, he will learn a kind of autonomy in the feeding area which is as important to his ultimate development as is a rounded diet. Very few feeding problems can exist in an accepting environment.

Mrs. Lang extracted Greg from his embattled position, and placed him on the floor to play while she ate her own lunch. This, of course, wasn't what he wanted either. He continued to tease her, asking for food off her plate, which he devoured greedily. His eagerness disproved her theory of illness. When she ignored him and continued to eat, his efforts redoubled. He climbed under the sink to find the bleach bottle which he brought to her on command. He fell forward onto the floor and cried loudly as if he'd hurt himself. He began to grunt as if he were having a bowel movement and to pull on his pants. This was almost a sure way of drawing his mother away from her own activity, for she'd started trying to "catch" him and put him on the toilet. This was one of his signals for her attention, and she rushed him to the toilet. He smiled smugly at her, but refused to perform. Mrs. Lang felt as if she were suddenly embattled on all fronts—none of which she could win.

This is certainly a time to give up on an area as complex as toilet training. Although Greg may have been cooperative and compliant before, he is now going to make this developmental step into a battleground. Since the child's own motivation and autonomy are of primary importance to any real success in this area (see Chapter VII), I would urge even a mother who had been "catching" her child successfully up to this point, to pull out of the fray when he so obviously begins to use the training provocatively. Otherwise, it can become a battle, and his determined strength will always win (see Chapter VI). It may come out as constipation or holding back stools, or as wetting pants after he has been taken off the pot, or hiding in the corner to produce his bowel movements. All of these can be interpreted the same way—as signals of too much parental control, at a time when he needs to be searching for his own controls. Of course, the simplest and most foolproof method for successful toileting at this age is none at all. If parents can wait out this initial surge of negativism, there are more cooperative, imitative times ahead when success can be tolerated by a strong-minded baby like Greg.

When she turned to her own chores, Greg produced the bowel movement he'd been predicting. Immediately, he began to cry to be changed. Mrs. Lang was furious with him and refused to change him. When she finally did, her heart sank, for he had produced another of his mucousy, loose stools. For several months he had been having as many as four or five loose bowel movements a day. Some of them had mucus mixed into the stool, were very foul-smelling, and contained bits of undigested food. Mrs. Lang had consulted Greg's doctor about it, and they had constructed diets to counteract his "diarrhea." Skimmed milk and clear liquids for a day reduced the number of stools quickly. When she slowly added low-fat food, he seemed to stay all right for a while. Earlier, they had taken him off sugar and breads in order to rule out a condition known as "celiac disease."

This is a moderately serious response to sensitivity of the intestinal tract—its symptoms consisting of frequent mucousy

*stools which are not easily controlled. The condition depletes
the baby since it interferes with his absorption of nutrients.
He does not grow and gain normally, his body becomes
wasted-looking, his belly swollen and uncomfortable. The
weight loss and poor progress demand a solution. Often
restricting carbohydrates and grains (as in cereal and bread)
helps him recover, as he is likely to have an intolerance to
these foods which contain gluten. Allergies to milk or other
common foods may also mimic this condition. A pediatrician
should certainly be called in to help find out what is responsible for this condition.*

For weeks after his restricted diet, Greg remained in good
shape, having one or two solid stools a day. But almost any
change in diet brought on the old problem, and Mrs. Lang's
heart sank when she smelled him, for she knew what to expect: not only a terribly smelly diaper, but a painful-looking
diaper rash which would appear almost immediately on Greg's
buttocks. He whimpered to be changed and cried when she
did change him. She felt like saying, "Darn you, if you'd learn
to use the toilet like I've been trying to teach you, you'd save
yourself all of this." But she was too worried about the condition, and felt as if she were somehow responsible. Even
though she had watched all the things in his diet which she
thought brought it on, the diarrhea would return. It made her
feel desperate that she couldn't control it, and that she had
to resort to a restricted diet all over again.

*This is a common condition in the second year. I hear about it
all the time, and, as in Greg's case, it seems to recur off and
on throughout this year. Almost any condition which alters
the child's general balance seems to bring on the frequent
loose movements. Teething, a cold, a change in water or milk
when traveling, new foods—all of these can bring on a condition which seems ready to come to the surface. My own way
of dealing with it is that of reassurance—as long as the child
is thriving, that is, growing and gaining. I feel that it is so
common that it must represent an immaturity of the intestinal tract which is present in most children in the second year.*

As they begin to eat more lumpy, solid food, their intestines do not adjust quickly enough, and are ready to overreact whenever another condition lowers the threshold. When there are no more than four or five such movements a day, there is no real reason to worry. Mucus does certainly represent irritation of the intestine, and blood streaks in the mucus mean enough irritation to worry about.

But short of this, I am tempted to allow the child a normal diet—excluding as much fat from his diet as possible by using fat-free milk, lean meats, and little butter. When he does seem to be bothered by it, or more than five stools do occur, I urge a restricted diet to give his intestinal tract a rest. In Greg's case, I would advise a day or two of clear liquids and skimmed milk; then lean meat, bananas, cottage cheese, and flavored gelatin for another day. Bread and crackers may increase the symptoms, and this may be a clue to the fact that he has an intolerance to wheat and other grains which contain gluten. Gluten-free breads can be obtained in health food stores and won't add to his problem. I do feel that this condition, if taken too seriously, can become a real problem for parents who feel it is a sign of neglect on their part—and for children who get too involved in this part of their bodily function. It needn't be a problem. As they reach the age of two, their intestines simply aren't as reactive and they outgrow this tendency.

After Mrs. Lang changed him, Greg immediately ran to the toilet and began to stuff his truck, a towel, and a slipper into it. He flushed it to watch the water swirl. Mrs. Lang heard him and rushed in to retrieve the objects from the rapidly filling toilet bowl.

Greg's interest in the toilet seems provocative after he's just refused to perform on it, but it is also exploratory, and represents his attempt to understand for himself all aspects of the toilet on which those around him place such emphasis. Again, it is an attempt on his part to master the important things in his environment for himself.

Mrs. Lang had planned an excursion for them in the afternoon, a play group with a couple of other children of Greg's age and their mothers. She found it a tremendous relief to get out of the apartment. By lunchtime, she had developed real claustrophobia. She had waves of feeling that she might either crush Greg or be crushed by him in this struggle. She had found, as most mothers of small children do, that any kind of excursion broke the feeling of being locked up together. One of the most salutary outings was one in which there were other mothers with children of Greg's age. Not only did the other children provide an outlet for Greg, but the other mothers had the same problems with their eighteen-month-olders, and their anguished cries somehow comforted Mrs. Lang. Even the old competitive comparisons of one child with another, which had been so painful in the first year, took on a new aspect in the second. It was fun to compare the horrors that they had had to endure. The ingenious tortures which each child had dreamed up for his mother were a new base for comparison. And, of course, it was a relief to realize that every other mother spent at least half her day loathing this newly emancipated child she was stuck with. Occasionally, one of them came up with a new solution which had not occurred to the others. But, primarily, it was fun for Mrs. Lang to see other adults, and to feel that she wasn't losing any adult mentality she might have attained before Greg came.

These are such universal feelings that I hardly need to elaborate upon them, except to comment on the obvious fact that in our lonely, nuclear-family society they can become real sources of anxiety for young mothers. When they don't have another adult with whom to share their negative, ambivalent feelings about their child, it must be an isolated, frightening kind of anxiety which builds up. The incidence of child abuse in our society is increasing as a correlate to this kind of pressure, and the age group which is most abused is this one. This is no surprise, I'm sure, to any mother who has a strong, provocative two-year-old at home. The feeling of losing one's mentality and one's own identity represents the depth of involvement to which a caring mother (such as Mrs. Lang) descends in her mothering. She feels so identified with Greg's struggle, as it calls up memories of her own, that she begins to question her own integrity. Certainly, communication with other mothers who are going through a similar struggle takes on a therapeutic aspect—reinforcing the positive and ventilating the negative side of their ambivalence so that they can continue to provide a caring atmosphere for their babies.

When Mrs. Lang and Greg arrived at the play group, there were two other pairs of mothers and children who were a year and a half of age. Greg began to cling to his mother, holding her dress so tightly that she couldn't extract it from his grip. She pushed him to enter into the play, but the harder she pushed, the more he clung. She tried to turn her back on him, scornfully reprimanding him for being so clinging. This brought loud wails from him, and, embarrassed, she was forced to pick him up.

Probably the other mothers in the room went through this mixture of clinging anxiety and teasing that Greg is forcing on his mother. But Mrs. Lang felt exposed by it, felt angry at Greg for being "inadequate," particularly in front of her friends.

No one comforted her, so she and Greg sat in the chair, somewhat ostracized and angry—not only with each other but with the cool reception they had received. As Greg screeched, the other mothers stiffened, and the children stopped playing to watch him, with anguished faces, as if they were about to start crying, too. The mothers tried to divert their children back to the play situation, aware of how close the children were to breaking down.

Greg finally sat beside his mother, tears on his bright red cheeks, watching the two other toddlers longingly. When a door opened, he jumped and clung to his mother again. When she rose from her chair, he stiffened. She went out to get a glass of water, shutting the door firmly behind her. He started to wail again. This time the other mothers came to comfort him, and one of the toddlers came over to offer him a toy.

The identification with his anguish is real in all the others. At this age, the other children's defenses against it are too fragile. Both the babies and the mothers are intimidated by their own anxiety when they realize how close they are to the same reactions. When they can do something active to help, however, their own ability to cope strengthens their defenses against breaking down.

The kind of tension which comes naturally to the surface for a child in a new, strange situation can be dealt with in better ways than Mrs. Lang has done. She may have been surprised that Greg broke down, since they are in a familiar group. But new situations and strangers all press the child's coping mechanisms, and if he has had a bad day already, this kind of reaction may be predicted. Had Mrs. Lang talked about what they might expect, how she hoped Greg would try to live up to it, had she warned him that she wasn't planning to leave him —all of these preparations might have aborted this overreaction. When she became up-tight along with him, it increased his tension and his protest. And then her walking out on him, closing the door as she did, surely could have been the climax. A closed door at this age is symbolic of real separation, and most toddlers hate to see doors closed, even when their parents are in the room with them.

Mrs. Lang had revived by the time she came back, and she sat down on the floor with Greg and the other two toddlers, entering into their play. Quickly Greg lost interest in her, began to play alongside the other children. She was able to pull back and began to talk to her own friends.

The three children were in exciting parallel play. As one banged the floor with a toy, the other two banged the floor. All three giggled delightedly. They built up in tempo, babbling at each other. The babbling was imitative and each child repeated the form of the sentences of another child. When a word came out of the babbling, all three children tried the word. When they hit on it together, they all laughed. So much fun was it that all three mothers stopped to watch it. As soon as the mothers stopped their chatting with each other, the children's play became self-conscious. The spontaneous giggling and all of the verbal imitation came to a halt. Instead, each child became silly—squinting his face into a social smile. One banged a toy on top of another's head, and Greg pulled one's hair. This brought the mothers into the play situation and the delightful childish quality of the play vanished. Each child began to cry as his mother entered into the conflict.

Mothers find it hard to stay out of children's play situations, but when they can, the duration and quality are certainly enhanced. Each child is ready to separate off into his own mother-child cocoon. But if the mothers ignore this, and leave them to it, they will handle each other's attacks. These attacks are playful anyway, until they acquire a new value, that of provoking maternal reaction.

One of the mothers started the record player. The children got up to dance. They bounced in rhythmic movements, in perfect time to the music. They twirled, fell down, got up and danced again, all in synchrony with each other. As they danced, they laughed, babbled, held onto each other's hands. It was a thoroughly delightful picture. This gay enterprise lasted for nearly an hour. It was with some surprise that the father of the household opened the door, coming home from his work. Everyone—parents and children—had been so engrossed in the pleasure of this play and communication that no one had realized how late it had become.

Every toddler rushed to him, screaming "Daddy! Daddy!" He was surrounded by eighteen-month-olders, all demanding to be picked up, in chorus. When it was Greg's time to be picked up, he was carried along by the excitement for a moment. Then as if he were suddenly hit by the realization of the father's strangeness, his face became horrified, he turned away and began to cry loudly, struggling to get away.

This is a time for heightened stranger anxiety. Along with increasing independence goes increasing dependence. With it goes an increasing awareness of small differences. Big differences often aren't as overreacted to as are slighter ones. For example, the fact that Greg wanted the father also made it harder for him to accept him. This is a time when grand-parents, pediatricians, and strangers are hard to accept.

When Mrs. Lang and Greg arrived at home, Mr. Lang was already there. Greg rushed up to him, laughing, hugging, clinging to him. Mrs. Lang was just as glad to see him. They vied with each other to recount the day's experiences. Greg sat in his father's lap, talking as loudly as his parents, putting his hand over his father's mouth to shut him up. When his mother started talking, he screamed out one word over and over as if he were trying to drown her out. Each member of the triangle was competing for time on the air. It was an exciting and gay time for them, and it was difficult to come down from the excitement to get ready to eat and to go to bed.

While Mrs. Lang prepared his supper, Mr. Lang took Greg in to bathe him. Greg had recently come through the fear of tubs and of baths that is so common at this age (see Chapter I). He was still wary of the routine, saying "no bath, no bath" as he was undressed. When his father began to draw the water for his tub, Greg watched in anguish, saying "no, no, no." Mr. Lang then ran through the rituals they had developed together to overcome his anxiety. They tried a toy, a truck, a finger, a toe, a leg, an arm, and finally his bottom—getting each one a "little wet," then "more wet," and finally "most wet." Only with this playful routine could Greg make it into the tub. Of course, having his daddy do it all with him made it much more exciting. It was still touch-and-go when Mrs. Lang tried the same routine.

Having special routines with fathers relieves the load on mothers. It also gives the father a role into which he can step at the end of a long day. And it is certainly more exciting for the child to have a new, fresh look at the day's routines. It is a real help to have two parents in all of the mundane aspects of child-rearing.

Bedtime at the end of this exciting day was another hurdle which could better be handled by a father who was available and willing. When Mr. Lang was at home to put Greg to bed, the slide was greased. After supper together, Greg was so delighted to be allowed to draw off his father to himself that he barely seemed to mind the games which they played to remove his clothes and to put on his pajamas. Had his mother tried the same games, they would have been a transparent cover for the real intent. But Greg chortled as his father yanked off his shoes and pants in one pull. He giggled when his father put the pajama top on his own head first, then slid it over Greg's head. Soon the two males were comfortably settled in a rocking chair, reading together. Greg pointed to the objects as his father asked him the words.

I am aware of the apparently chauvinistic comparison of mother and father roles which comes through in this chapter. I can hear a critic say, "But why would anyone ever want to be a mother, or to go through this horrible day with an eighteen-month-older? After reading your chapter, I certainly don't want to be stuck with one at home." It is a difficult job for mothers with a child of this age. The contrast between the tired, familiar mother and the new, exciting father makes for this reaction from the child. But the reward must be in the form of other than superficial satisfactions for a mother. The job of being an all-important anchor, of being a source of strength which can allow the child his negativism, his swings in ambivalence, his testing of the environment and of his own ego resources, is a vital one in the child's life.

If the child cannot be tolerated and supported in this struggle at home, he must either suppress it or try to work it out in less supportive circumstances. We are all familiar with children who are still caught in this struggle in later childhood, who have not been able to work it out. And we are all saddened and repelled by adults who must have public tantrums, who have never worked out these struggles in childhood, who regress to a two-year-old status with any frustration or in response to any demand for an adult reaction.

CHAPTER VI

Withdrawn Child

Two Years

One of the most dangerous threats to growing up happily hangs over the child who is just older than the new baby. It arises from the situation of weaning, weaning not only from the breast or bottle but from what has been for a long time, a lifetime, in fact, the very close attention of the mother.

Joan, two years old, was the fourth child in her family. She had two other brothers, Larry who was six and John who was four, a sister Marcia who was three, and a six-month-old baby brother Paul. Mrs. Gary was overwhelmed by all of these children. She was in her late twenties. She had lost two teeth and had not had them replaced. She was letting herself get fat; in fact, she seemed to care very little about her appearance. Her husband was a year older than she, a quiet man who seemed to be submerged in responsibility. He had finished high school, had gone to a trade school for a year, but had given that up when Larry was born, in order to earn a living for the three of them. Mrs. Gary had been a lawyer's secretary when they married, and had been able to support her husband in school for the first year. The children came along so fast that his resolve to continue educating himself in night school had given way to a second job at night to cover the rapidly escalating expenses of the household.

Having children before a couple is really ready is hard to make up for later. A child does change the whole life style for young parents. And by the time a second child comes along, the family's flexibility is pretty much at an end. Now that we as a society have more choice about whether to have children at all, it becomes an opportunity for parents to make clear, responsible decisions about when to start their families. Implicit in this decision is an awareness of the kind of responsibility a child will mean. As adults accept this responsibility, and base their initial decision on it, they will be readier to be real parents. Each baby adds more stress to the family. Spacing of children is an important decision. I am convinced that the time between children is not very important to the children in a family, but it certainly is to the parents. Indirectly it becomes important to the children. Mothers worry about whether their children will "get along" or "like each other" as a major goal for such spacing. I feel that this is misplaced concern. Siblings rarely like each other in childhood, no matter what their relative ages. But if parents can tolerate the pressures of each new child, the children will certainly be more likely to thrive. So the planning must be done first and foremost on the basis of the parents' tolerances and the capacity of the family to include new responsibility.

The Garys lived in a three-family house with Mr. Gary's sister's family on one floor and his parents on another. The younger Garys lived on the second floor, which provided only two bedrooms, but they counted themselves fortunate. For the sister lived in the "attic apartment," with only one bedroom for herself and her three small children. The apartments were part of the elder Garys' attempts to help out. They owned the house, and felt that their contribution to their struggling married children could be in the form of a partially subsidized place to live. The grandmother was something of an anchor for the two young mothers, taking a role in helping with the children when she could. But she preferred to help with the babies in the family, and was less interested in each child as he reached his first birthday.

This pattern is common to all cultures. All of the women in an extended family play with a baby, but turn their backs on the two-year-olds. In parts of Africa, there has been a traditional practice of pressing mothers to wean their babies in the second year, in order to get on with life. The grandmother, authority of child-rearing tradition, will indicate the proper time for weaning and in many instances will take the child into her care, compounding the problem of nutritional deprivation with that of separation. Whether the child is sent away from the mother or not, the abrupt and definite weaning gives rise to protein and calcium deficiencies, as well as psychological depression with reduced desire for food resulting in a pathological condition known as kwashiorkor. Everyone remembers the swollen bellies and emaciated faces and limbs, symptoms of kwashiorkor, of the Biafran children so much publicized in the early 1960s. Milder forms of this physical and psychological depression persist in less stressed circumstances.

One can see pathetic, depressed two-year-olds leaning against doorways, trying to hang onto the skirts of their mothers or grandmothers, attempting to climb into an empty lap. But they give up easily and withdraw, beaten, when the lap is filled with a smiling younger baby. In polygamous groups, the husband has been sleeping with his other wives, and will not return to the new mother until she has weaned her own baby. Other women shame her for being too close to her baby, and for keeping him from growing up. When the baby enters a negative phase of development in the second year and begins to add his negativism to the cultural situation, the stage seems to be set for their separation. I interpret the mother's need to wean abruptly as evidence of how difficult it is for her to desert an infant she has cared for so much. But it is certainly hard on the infant.

I mention these cross-cultural observations because I think they throw light on mechanisms which are present in our culture. For example, there is an increasing number of young women who breast-feed their babies into the second year. This seems to become offensive to everyone around them, and the young mother is bombarded with critical disapproval—consciously expressed as well as suppressed, but coming to the surface in guarded ways. For example, she will hear, "I've always heard that mother's milk loses its value after nine months." The mother herself begins to feel guilty and questions her own motives, feeling she should push the baby away. As she does, the baby may abruptly begin to display normal second-year negative behavior. She takes this as a rejection of her at a time when she is still sensitive and not quite ready herself to be weaned. Then, in reaction to this "rejection," she swings farther than she might have—turning her back in essence, as she weans the child. The child's developing two-year-old negative behavior is a real trigger in all of this, and certainly does play an important role in isolating him from those whom he needs.

Joan had been a gay, laughing baby. Everyone carried her around—her mother, her older brothers, her grandmother, and even her aunt. Her father played with her constantly when he was at home. She responded with delight and vigor.

She was round, chubby-faced, and dimpled. She had developed quickly, saying many words at a year, walking and even running at a year. When she wanted anything, all she had to do was to point at it, and one of her large retinue produced it for her. Her brothers were delighted by her when she was learning to walk and to say words and they played with her as if she were a doll. Her mother had been worn out with four small children and was reliant on the rest of her family to cope with Joan. Joan was a year old when Mrs. Gary found out she was pregnant with the fifth child. She became depressed and spent much of her time in bed. When she was up

and around, she was angry and quick with the children. By the time Joan was fourteen months old, Mrs. Gary was beginning to feel awkward and uncomfortable. She resented the amount of care Joan required. She couldn't hide her feelings, and when Joan made an advance or a request, she either wept openly or refused Joan with an abrupt, angry answer. Since Joan had not met with anything like this before, she was stunned but not daunted at first. She turned to her grandmother or her father or her brothers, who tried to make up for the mother's withdrawal. As the months went on, everyone in the household began to reflect the tension, and Joan's world began to crumble. Her father and brothers became quieter around the house, and didn't play as much with Joan. Her grandmother was so concerned with her daughter-in-law's state of mind that she, too, left Joan more and more to herself.

Joan reacted to this change with a combination of quiet sadness and a kind of showing off when others were around. She didn't dare express herself in the loud, gay voice she had used when she was smaller, for everyone called out "ssh." When she wanted something and made a demand for it, her father or grandmother tried to quiet her. On one occasion, when she was tired at night, she began to cry and lay down on the floor to kick her feet. Her mother's eyes flashed, and she picked Joan up by one arm so angrily that she dislocated her elbow, and threw her still crying into her bed.

No one came to see about her. Her arm was painful when she moved it, but if she let it hang limply at her side, the pain lessened. Not until the next day did anyone notice that she didn't use her left arm. When they finally took her to the clinic, X-rays confirmed that she had a dislocation of her elbow.

This is not an uncommon injury at this age. Mothers or fathers give a child a sudden yank of the arm. This most often happens when the child needs to be pulled away from danger. The sudden pull dislocates the head of the radial bone of the forearm at the elbow joint. The child complains of pain in the shoulder, and the arm hangs limp, so that it is hard to diagnose it as an elbow problem. It is easy to snap back into place again with a simple twisting maneuver, and the pain goes away almost immediately. The only problem is that if one waits many hours before the bone is replaced, swelling of the tissues around the joint increases and it gets harder and harder to snap it back into place. If a child won't use an arm, it's possible to attempt a diagnosis: I always hold the good hand, then offer a lollipop at shoulder height to the arm in question. A child with a dislocation will refuse the lollipop rather than raise the painful arm. Immediately after the bone is replaced, he will use his arm normally. Parents feel very guilty after they have produced such an injury, but it is com-

mon and easy to cause at this age. As the joint ligaments become firmer with age, it is not likely to happen.

Mrs. Gary was terribly upset when she realized that she had really hurt Joan. She pulled herself together for a few days, making an effort to comfort and love Joan more. This fueled the two-year-old for more courageous behavior, and she began to show off for her mother—dancing, saying words out of her repertory, falling down to her own loud laughter. Her noisy antics were too much for Mrs. Gary and she turned away from Joan again. As the child's anxiety built up, she began to whine or to suck her fingers and to retire to a corner. These habits irritated her mother, who reprimanded her for them continuously. Joan was forced to try to give them up.

Mrs. Gary is conscious of her changed attitude and neglect of this child. Hence the behavior which is Joan's response to this changed attitude is guilt-producing for her mother. Mrs. Gary is already too unhappy to tolerate any guilty feelings, so she tries to suppress the behavior. This is a vicious circle, and Joan's only choice is to withdraw eventually.

Joan began to withdraw more and more. She became quieter, more sullen, sat for long periods with heavy-lidded eyes. She began to pick at her clothing, to pick at her nose and mouth, and to pull at her hair. There was none of the gay laughter or words that had been typical of her before, and by the time the new baby came, everyone spoke of Joan as a "quiet, sad child." She was slower moving, less interested in people, and much more difficult to get involved in play. She was left alone more and more.

This is a child who has gone into a real depression, based on a separation from her mother which she cannot understand. The three stages which John Bowlby speaks of as occurring in children who are separated from their parents have been demonstrated to some degree by Joan: (1) protest, as evidenced by her showing off, her loudness, and her inept attempts to reach her sick mother; (2) despair; and (3) with-

drawal, which followed when she met with nothing but disapproval. These stages are seen in children in hospitals all the time, and can lead to defects in their future development unless they are taken seriously and the child brought back out of his regression.

After the new baby came, the household focused on him and his depressed mother. When the other children made demands, they were shut up and pushed outside. Six-year-old Larry was given charge of Joan most of the time. Since he was at school during the morning, his homecoming became the time for Joan to be mobilized, dressed, and put outside "to play with Larry." Larry was dismayed by the recent turn of events with their mother. He and his brother tried to take an interest in Joan, and played with her the way they used to, as if she were a doll. She was a floppy, quiet doll at first, but as their attention began to feed her, she began to be a bit more lively. She sat smiling quietly while they pulled her in a wagon or played around her. Her attempts at speech began to return slowly. She called out for Larry and John quietly during the day. As she became interested in their play, she began to imitate some of their activities. Her imitation was confined to sitting-down activities with her hands, as she was too subdued now to want to follow them on foot. She played with beads, putting them on a long string. She placed blocks in a form-board puzzle.

She began to pick up things around the house and to put them in their proper places. This pleased her mother, so it became a repeated effort. When there were shoes on the floor, she carried them to the closet. Clothes left on the floor were picked up and put on a chair. Diapers from the baby were handed to mother for the disposal can. On one occasion Joan picked up a dirty diaper which left her hand smeared with the baby's bowel movement. Her mother lashed out at her and rushed her into the bathroom to wash her hand, saying, "Joan, why do you have to try to help, when all you do is to make things worse!" Joan's face darkened, and she cringed as if she had been struck. She crept to her bedroom and climbed up into her crib to suck her finger and pull on her hair.

Mrs. Gary is too overwhelmed to see what she is doing to Joan. The child's attempt to come out of her shell is evidence of how desperate and hungry she is. She can still be refueled by her brothers, and can begin to try to pull herself together in ways which approach normal two-year-old behavior, such as the organized activity of putting things where they belong. All of this is a testimony to the strength of a child's repeated attempts to cope with an overwhelming situation. As long as she can come out of herself like this, she shows that she is reachable and has not passed the critical period when she could no longer be brought out of it. She might have passed such an irreversible barrier, if her brothers had not stepped in to help.

After this episode, she lost interest in trying to please her mother or in trying to help her. As if she had given up, she sat alone and quiet all morning. Loud talking or sudden noises frightened her. When the boys came home, she revived a bit, and at night, when her father arrived, she looked hungrily to him for attention. When he played with her, she began to brighten, her color improved, and she looked happier. When no one was around, she again looked fragile and sad. Her hair was wispy now and all of her body reflected her depressed attitude. Her appearance had changed enough so that the relatives commented upon it and urged Mrs. Gary to take her to a doctor to see what was wrong. Instead, her mother was immobilized and put off by her attitude. She said, "Joan is just quiet because she's angry with me for having a new baby." She admitted that she liked Paul so much better that she didn't have energy for anyone else. And, she pointed out, Joan had her brothers, and her sister Marcia had her cousins. (Marcia was being cared for by her aunt much of the time.)

Mrs. Gary's way of turning to Paul and away from Joan might still be remedied if someone was ready to explain the child to Mrs. Gary. She sees Joan's withdrawal as a reaction to her own desertion, and she feels too guilty about Joan's passive behavior to be able to see how serious it can be for the child's future. Instead, because Mrs. Gary is overwhelmed and depressed herself, she tries to ignore Joan's side of it, by blaming it on the child. We can understand why she resents having so many children, but it is too bad that they must suffer so much.

If she were more aware of what was going on with Joan, it would not be hard for Mrs. Gary to give Joan more of a role in caring for Paul, to let her imitate her mother in household chores, to encourage her own mother or her husband to help Joan out of her depression. In an overwhelming situation like this, a mother simply may not have the energy or the capacity to think about each child's special problems. I always urge the parent of a large family to have a special time for each child —once a week will do it, as long as it is special for that child. This can make up for a lot, for it is a symbol to the child that his mother does care. In that weekly period, mother and child do keep alive the relationship and the understanding which is of vital importance to each of them. Mrs. Gary allows her guilty feelings to push her farther away rather than to mobilize her to do something positive for Joan. Her idea of turning her over to the older brothers is a good substitute, but the boys are too young to be able to do all that needs to be done. If Mrs. Gary gave the boys more encouragement and suggestions, she could do a great deal for Joan indirectly.

Joan had not been willing to cooperate on the toilet. She continued to use diapers. When her mother had sporadically tried to push her to go on the big toilet earlier in the second year, Joan stubbornly refused. At two, Mrs. Gary began to feel that Joan was being bad, and punished her for not being willing to use the toilet. She cajoled her, spanked her, put her in her bed. All of this Joan accepted passively, showing little reaction. During a spanking she cried out softly or looked back sadly at her mother, whose guilt and frustration were thereby increased. But when she softened her approach, Joan stiffened, turning away in stubborn refusal to be handled. Thus a new behavior pattern was developing, with the energy source being Joan's two-year-old negativism. Gradually, Mrs. Gary began to see that Joan's problems were increasing and were more than a simple reaction to the new baby.

Mrs. Gary turned at once to her own mother for advice and help. Mrs. Gary's mother worked all day and had little time to help out with her daughter's family. But she had been worried about her daughter with this pregnancy and had seen how hard it was for everyone in the family. When she was asked about Joan, she told Mrs. Gary honestly that she thought Joan had changed from a gay one-year-old to a sad, depressed two-year-old. She wondered if it wasn't in response to the overloaded household. She offered to take Joan out on the weekend if Mrs. Gary made an effort to help Joan more during the week. She suggested that Mrs. Gary urge her husband to pay more attention to Joan, too. She talked to her daughter about how desperate she must feel at having so many children, but she pointed out that little Joan needed her. As she listened, Mrs. Gary began to see things more clearly, and she and her mother talked about Joan's change over the past year. She resolved to try to bring her out more.

Mrs. Gary went back to her apartment full of good intentions. She rushed over to Joan to pick her up. Joan stiffened, arched away, and slid out of her mother's arms to the floor. She gave her mother a look which was a mixture of reproach and withdrawal. Joan lay at her mother's feet limply. Mrs. Gary was surprised, then angry, then turned off. Almost as if in retaliation, she went over to baby Paul, who chortled as she leaned over him, talking to him. Joan looked out from under heavy lids to watch her mother. Her face was set and pale, her eyes sad, her body limp and motionless.

Mrs. Gary took a deep breath, turned away from Paul to return to Joan. She tried to pick her up, but was met with the same passive resistance, then she sat down beside the child to talk to her and stroke her. She said, "Joan, why won't you let me pick you up? I'm not going to hurt you, I just wanted to say hello from grandma." Joan looked carefully at her mother as if she thought she was fooling her, but she allowed her mother to continue to stroke her.

The depth of hurt which Joan has suffered over this year is seen in how hard it is for her to accept any approaches from her mother. It would be easy to think that she was also retaliating a bit by pulling away so forcefully when her mother does try to reach her. In hospitals, we see this kind of reaction all the time—a small child, who has been longing for and crying for her mother, suddenly quiets to look stonily at her mother, then turns her back on her as she comes up to her crib. This must be a retaliative effort, and is actually a sign of strength on the part of the child. That she can submerge her longing in order to punish her mother for having deserted her shows that she has retained an awareness of what she can expect from her mother—both the loving side which she misses so much, and the reaction that her retaliation will elicit from her mother. Certainly if she didn't have an awareness that her mother cared for her and that their relationship could stand it, she never could have dared to use these tactics. A child who has never experienced a really meaningful relationship doesn't dare *test out an offer of affection. Such a child has not experienced an intense relationship and its many facets—the good and the bad. So Joan is thinking back to a time when she and her mother were closer and their communication was better.*

Mrs. Gary continued to talk to and to pat Joan as she lay on the floor. She felt an urgency about reaching out to her. She said, "Come on now, Joan, let me pick you up." As her voice took on an urgent, demanding quality, Joan pulled away again.

Joan will have to be reached out for consistently and patiently. She is too fragile and too wounded—more like a frightened animal. But this oversensitivity surely reflects the need she has for being reached.

Finally, Paul cried out for her, and Mrs. Gary gave up on Joan. As she went to him, Joan turned away, hardly watching her go.

Unfortunately, a child's behavior may represent her defense against longing rather than a more direct expression of her needs. Joan must be seen as a child who has protected herself for some time now, not allowing herself to wish for the things she had experienced at Paul's age. The "trust" which is necessary to bring her back would need to be built up over a long time.

Joan's sad, quiet behavior began to be accepted as a part of her personality. After a few more months, no one remembered any of her former characteristics. Adults and children alike felt her sadness, and her brothers played with her less and less. She became more isolated in this large family than she might have been in a small one. Paul was boisterous, and pleased his brothers as a playmate. Marcia was really being raised by her aunt and escaped thereby. It was easier for everyone to leave Joan to herself than to encounter her sad, reproachful looks.

Her only protest now came in her refusal to use the toilet. Her mother's desperation increased, and she sat her on it for several hours at a time, trying to "catch" her and to force her to use it. Joan was able to hold on to her bowel movements, but not her urine. She became more and more constipated as time went on, and as her mother's efforts to train her increased. Over the next few months, her stools became increasingly large and hard, and her bowel pattern changed to a weekly one. Her mother gave her laxatives which worked for a time, then used suppositories, and finally resorted to weekly enemas to "control" the pattern which was developing. Joan submitted dutifully and impassively to these manipulations.

One can see how this pattern of constipation develops as one small part of the struggle in a sad child. Her withholding and her unwillingness to comply with the demands of those around her are remnants of strength in her. Her mother's efforts to control the situation are adding to the child's unconscious need to hold back even more forcefully. As her mother senses this and presses harder, the struggle becomes a more deep-seated one which at some point will no longer be reversible. Although Mrs. Gary would protest that she must be sure that Joan doesn't hurt herself by staying constipated (and there are many old wives' tales about being "poisoned" by retained feces, about being "blocked up" for life), her efforts are misdirected, and one can see that this child's need to control a small part of her life is centered in this area. This area even becomes a source for the attention from her mother which she has been unable to stimulate in any other way. Even negative attention is better than none at all. Perhaps this gives the reader an insight into the genesis of an incipient psychosomatic disorder. In Joan's case, the manipulations might be seen as punishment, and the discomfort and pain which follow her successful holding back might be seen as self-punishing. As we see Joan from a distance, this pattern can also be seen for its strength. She is a sad, lonely, deserted child in her own eyes, and she accomplishes several tasks by this symptom: (1) She maintains a kind of integrity against outside pressure to give up a part of herself. (2) She resists urging from the environment to grow up, at a time when there is little reward for her in that. (3) She protests her mother's desertion in a more effective way than any other so far, and draws her mother back into an effective interaction with her. Her sad, passive pattern of turning inward is now being reflected in her body's physiology as well as her outward behavior.

In Joan's case, one might foresee a poor outcome for her future, if her behavior is not met by those around her as a cry for help, before the pattern is irrevocably entrenched. If she is allowed to continue with this locked-up resistance to those around her, she may well become a frightened, neurotic adult with many physical symptoms which mirror her earlier appeals for help. She is not likely to change when she is first pushed out into the world to go to school. Few in our present, overcrowded school system have the energy or sophistication to reach out for a quiet, withdrawn child. And by the time she is forced out of the family as an adult, she will have years of these patterns to overcome. Unless her symptoms are recognized and treated in early childhood, each year makes it less likely that the gay, attractive personality Joan demonstrated as a baby will be recaptured. If, on the other hand, someone like her grandmother or a teacher could be touched by her, could reach out for her and continue to reach out until Joan

*could learn to trust someone, she might be saved. If her
mother could see Joan's needs as independent of her own, she
too might still be helped to reach her. But it will take patient
and persistent effort to overcome the defenses which Joan has
already set up around her, as a result of the early disappointment and desertion she experienced.*

*Even if someone reaches out to Joan, the period of return
will be a painful one at times. At first it will be slow, and
those around her would have to watch carefully for faint signs
of responsiveness to encourage. As she begins to come out of
her shell, she will be obnoxious at times, as well as violently
demanding. These will be signs of healthy recovery. Although
she will need limits on these swings, she will need understanding, too. Her parent or care-giver will need to interpret them
to her, letting her learn to control them herself. This period of
recovery is fragile and constitutes a kind of tender feeling out*

of the environment. If she is treated harshly at this stage, she may retreat again. She is like a frightened, wounded animal and her recovery will be slow. A parent cannot always prevent such an experience for a child, and Mrs. Gary's case demonstrates how easily it can happen when a mother is overwhelmed and depressed by too much responsibility. But if these symptoms in the child are recognized at a time when they are still reversible (and in Joan's case, they may well be, for she had a good start, and people who cared about her along the way), her whole future may be salvaged. Instead of a sparse, lonely, neurotic future life, a caring adult could still offer Joan a brighter pattern. But it would demand devotion and understanding.

CHAPTER VII

Demanding Child

Two Years

The Weiners felt they had lived through a long second year with Jess. Although he was their second child, he seemed like their first. Four-year-old Mark had been taken care of by Mrs. Weiner's mother while Mrs. Weiner taught school, so they had been removed from much of his second-year turmoil. In addition, Mark had been an easy, compliant child and had made little trouble for those around him. Living with Jess was something different! Mrs. Weiner had stopped teaching before he was born, and had never returned to it—partly because Jess was so demanding and partly because she wanted to be at home with her two small children. Jess had been a strong, loud baby and had established himself as a definite person from the very first months of his life. He fought at every stage of development, protesting loudly when he couldn't walk alone and needed help, having loud, long, violent tantrums when he entered the second year. As if open protest wasn't enough, he began to have breath-holding spells when he hurt himself. Mrs. Weiner thought she'd never forget the first of these episodes.

He was just learning to toddle alone and had navigated successfully for about a month. In his typical headlong fashion, he began to hurtle forward, half running instead of walking. He fell a great deal and often hit his head. On one occasion, as he crashed on the back of his head, his mother heard him scream once, then she heard no more. She came in from the next room to see him turning blue. He had stopped breathing after the injury, and his color changed from ashen to dusky blue. As he became cyanotic, he passed out, his eyes rolling up in his head, his body becoming completely limp. She screamed for help and began to try to give him mouth-to-mouth respiration. At this point, he began to breathe again—at first in short gasps, then in deeper, longer, and more regular respirations. His color returned, and he began to return to consciousness. After he revived, he was limp and exhausted. So was his mother. She felt as if she'd just been brought back from the dead. She was too frightened to move from Jess's side at first, then she called her pediatrician. He tried to reassure her, telling her that breath-holding spells were common at this age, and, other than the horrifying effect they had on everyone around, they did not hurt Jess. Mrs. Weiner needed repeated reassurance that this was not an epileptic seizure, that he hadn't damaged his brain by lack of oxygen when he turned blue. She and her husband begged for a solution or a medication to prevent a recurrence of this ghastly episode.

Breath-holding spells occur commonly in the second year, and are one more evidence of the violent struggles which are going on in small children. They are very much like the kind of internal struggles which tantrums represent. Usually, they occur after an injury, just as the child starts to cry. Instead of letting out the cry and wailing with deep breaths, he holds on to the first deep inspiration. His immature breathing controls don't respond properly; he holds his breath until he loses consciousness, and then his breathing begins again. As the active holding of his breath gives way to the normal chemical responses of the body, he begins to take deep breaths to counteract the low oxygen content of his blood. The most amazing thing is that a baby this age has the strength and determination to overcome a body mechanism as powerful as is the regulation of breathing. But the struggle is this fierce.

Parents are fearful of the consequences of these periods

when a child does not breathe. Fortunately a brief period of low oxygen will not damage his brain, and there are no sequelae from such episodes. Other parents wonder whether these are precursors of seizures, or of epilepsy. There seems to be little relationship, and certainly these spells are not likely to increase a child's chances of developing epileptic seizures. There are a small number of children who do have seizures when the cyanosis, or low oxygen, occurs. Those children already have a lowered brain threshold for seizure activity, and this is an indication that they may need medication to raise their threshold. But they are very few compared to the large number of breath-holders who have no later problems. The biggest danger of these spells is the effect they have on the people in the child's environment. So terrifying are they that a parent's resolve to teach the negative toddler any controls or limit becomes shaken. So frightened of setting off a spell by crossing the child that the parent avoids any confrontation. Normal frustrations become something to be avoided. The parent hovers protectively over the baby in order to keep him from becoming upset. Advice to require normal limits or to punish the child when necessary falls on deaf ears.

I have seen parents at the mercy of a child as a result of these spells. The child becomes jazzed up as a result. He begins to be more and more demanding, manipulating his anxious parents. To control them, he seems to learn to produce spells at will. This cycle represents the evolution of a "spoiled" child—an anxious child who knows he needs limits, desperately wanting them but unable to place them on himself, and not receiving them from the adults around him. Unless the parents can break this cycle, the danger to the child's personality development is far greater than any danger to him from the breath-holding spells.

The pediatrician explained all of this to Mr. and Mrs. Weiner at their next visit. And he urged them to continue to treat Jess as normally as they could. Although it was an ordeal, they became a little less worried each time they lived through these spells brought on by mild punishment or frustration, or by episodes in which Jess had been hurt unexpectedly. After the Weiners realized that he would recover spontaneously, they began to be calmer in the face of them. The spells began to disappear, as his physician had predicted.

Jess's struggles to become independent were so violent and demanding throughout the second year that Mrs. Weiner was both repelled and fascinated. If she had any doubt about returning to work, Jess's personality resolved it. His need for her was too obvious. She felt that she couldn't leave him with her mother or her mother-in-law with the possibility of having such spells. She looked around halfheartedly for a sitter whom she felt she could trust, but gave up after two turned him down, because of his "problem."

If she had to work to earn a living, it might have been a more serious complication. Finding care for a difficult, demanding child with a tendency to such spells could be an insurmountable task. I have seen an entire day-care center become involved in such a child, and make this a worse problem for him. They made the mother feel so hopelessly inadequate that she became more and more so. There is a real danger in caretakers, other than parents, overreacting and perpetrating problems which might otherwise be normal deviations in development. A parent who must use help with a child has a double job—to protect both the child and his self-image as a parent from such an overreaction.

After this hurdle had been passed, the end of the second year seemed like a reward to them. Jess himself seemed grateful that he wasn't constantly in turmoil. His mother had a feeling of reward and accomplishment when she saw Jess becoming more organized and less negative. Mr. Weiner began to look forward again to the end of the day with his family. Mark had been quiet and overwhelmed by all of Jess's violence. Now he began to be a more definite person himself, and to make demands of his own, as Jess settled down.

I often warn parents that it's liable to be a "good bear, bad bear" situation. When one child gets better, the other gets worse. It's as if children sense that the parental system can tolerate just so much. So one child waits until the pressure is off in the other quarter, storing up his aggressive feelings to throw at them later. Mark could have worked out some of his aggressive needs by identifying with his tough little brother, but he needed to be brought out of his shell. And with that came his negative, aggressive feelings.

The first signs of Jess's becoming better organized began to surface around twenty months of age. He began to follow commands, and seemed to gain pleasure from his parents' pleasure when he completed them. When his mother asked Mark to find her pocketbook and bring it to her, Jess returned with it, proudly holding it out in front of him. In other ways, he showed more awareness of things around him. He began to see the appropriateness of situations. For example, he played baby and talked baby talk with an adult or an older child but never with his own age group. With his peers, his speech was lower-pitched and more definite, words being well formed. He was aware of the differences in the situations. He was playing a game as he regressed into baby talk and baby behavior with his parents. But as soon as Mark came into the room, all of this vanished.

Jess liked to imitate adult tasks. When his mother cleaned the house, he followed her with a cloth, trying to dust the tables. When Mark fed the dog, Jess helped him by getting the dog's dish. When his father shaved in the morning, Jess

took a toothbrush to imitate his father with lathering and shaving motions. He was learning to brush his teeth, even though his span of attention was short at this job and the cleansing ineffective.

Parents worry about when toothbrushing should start. They may try to do it for the child early in the second year. His resistance to having things done to him quickly becomes such a problem that two or three imposed brushings are the extent of success. But later, the child's desire to imitate becomes a powerful force and he wants to learn such tasks. So it's wise to wait until two years of age to introduce the toothbrush. Fortunately, the combination of nonpermanent teeth and the natural cleansing by foods (such as juices) provided by nature is protective despite the lack of any attention. Fluoride in the water and in toothpaste certainly seems to be an adjunct to nature's protection. In addition, restriction of sweets such as candy and chewing gum can be important in preventing dental caries.

Jess was intrigued by washing his hands. He slathered soap all over his arms, clothes, the sink, and the wall. He tried to

dress himself. Undressing had been a favorite occupation for some time. He loved to be naked. Now, he wanted to put things back on—he wanted to try shoes as well as socks. His mother showed him how to undo the shoelaces, how to slap his foot to push the shoe on. He himself added the idea of stomping his foot on the floor to push the shoe onto his foot. He learned to pull the laces tight. Mark was learning how to tie his own shoes at this point. Jess watched him for long periods, as if he were trying to digest this more complicated task. He got so tangled as he tried to copy Mark that he soon gave up.

Awareness of his own limitations is another sign of Jess's organization. Instead of plowing into a hopeless task, then dissolving in frustration, which he might have done earlier this year, he seems to have learned a more comfortable understanding of his capacity.

All of these tasks went better if the incentive to try them came from Jess. When his parents asked him to wash his hands or to brush his teeth or to help with a chore, there was an immediate blow-up. He seemed to listen, become a bit interested in the idea, then quickly shut down with the old negativism. He could still fall down on the floor to scream and howl as a result of a simple request. The tantrums now seemed to be conscious defenses against complying or giving in to something he might have wanted to do, but couldn't allow himself since the idea hadn't come from him.

Negative reactions could be circumvented by more sophisticated approaches. Although he hated to be dressed, his mother could elicit his interest and cooperation by saying, "You look so nice in your new shirt, let's put it on." If she wanted him to give up a toy, he still dissolved in tears when it was taken from him, but he would hand it over willingly if she had the patience to ask him for it, adding a "please" at the end.

The success of eliciting his cooperation points to his increasing awareness of the expectations of those around him, as well as an interest in learning about his role in them. His interest overcomes his resistance to being pressed into action.

He was learning manners such as "please" and "thank you." At the table, he could comply with "pass me that." He used his napkin to wipe his face after he saw his parents do it. He used his fork and spoon regularly, and made a few abortive swipes with his knife, imitating Mark.

At the end of a meal, Jess was helpful in cleaning up the pieces of food off the floor, in wiping the table with a wet rag. In fact, he was becoming almost painful in his concern about crumbs on the table, about bugs or flies around him, about putting things where they belonged. He would take a towel out of Mark's hand before he was finished to put it back on the towel rack. He began to pick up his toys at night, to his parents' surprise.

Mothers have been so surprised at this new, sudden cleanliness that they have reexamined themselves, wondering whether they have been too rigid in their expectations of the child. A two-year-old may reprimand a parent for not putting his shoes away, or scold him for spilling on the floor. This compulsiveness seems to come from within the child and is part of his attempt to organize himself. The mastery of ambivalence is apparent in this symptom. That he can now reproduce organization which he has absorbed in small bits along the way may represent his attempt to identify with the demands of those around him. The fact that he can allow himself to do it is a sign of having achieved a better balance of the "yes" and "no" responses which stymied him earlier in the year.

Jess spilled his milk, became concerned when his mother reprimanded him for spilling it, and then looked down at the puddle and said "bad milk." His awareness of responsibility was emphasized by his transferring the guilt onto the milk. It seemed to Mrs. Weiner that this was an optimal time to begin to toilet-train Jess. Mark had been slow in getting trained, and he still wet the bed at night. She felt that she had made mistakes with Mark. She had started to train him at nine months to please her mother. When he allowed her and her mother to catch him on the pot, they felt successful. But it was short-lived. The success lasted until he was fifteen months old, when he began to hide in a corner when he was about to have a bowel movement. He smeared his movements over his crib when he had them in bed. After his mother punished him, he held his bowel movements back for several days at a time, becoming quite constipated. She had used suppositories and laxatives for weeks before she finally realized that the solution was to put him back in diapers and abandon the training venture. He was still constipated at four years, but he had finally trained himself to use the toilet during the day. She was determined not to ruin Jess's training with all of this turmoil. She had heard that two years is an optimal time to introduce a child to the toilet and to expect him to train himself. His new orderliness made this seem an opportune time to start.

It is certainly possible to "catch" a baby and to train his sphincter reflexes—to hold onto urine and feces until he is placed on a potty seat. But this is all that is accomplished—a training of reflexes. It is not a voluntary act on the part of the child, and depends on a caretaker to lead to any success. In previous generations when there were no diaper services or washing aids to keep clothes clean, there must have been pressure on mothers to push this kind of training. In some "primitive" cultures mothers begin to train their babies in the latter part of the first year and achieve some kind of cooperation before the middle of the second year. Their reasons for wanting babies trained are urgent, too. Since the babies are carried by the mother most of the time, she doesn't want to be wet or dirtied by the infant. As soon as he can toddle to the outside of their living quarters, he is expected to do so to keep the hut clean.

In our culture, there is no longer any urgency to impose a method upon the child. This developmental step can be treated like others, like those of feeding himself or of making choices about clothing. We can wait for him to learn at his own pace. Our culture places emphasis on developing strong individuals who make their own choices in childhood, as preparation for an adulthood fraught with choices. To treat toilet training differently from all of the child's other tasks places undue emphasis on it. It becomes a focus for attention. He uses it for rebellion, for negativism, to tease those around him. If there is too much concern in this area, parents get hung up when the child fails to perform. Pressure to comply is not necessary when early timing is not at stake. The child can see it as an exciting new step to make on his own, and he will want to make it. The saddest part of pressing him to conform is that he loses the pleasure and excitement of achievement from mastering each step for himself. One of our children refused to get very far away from her pot when she understood the game—that of urinating on her potty seat. She wanted to be there when she needed to go for her own reasons, not ours. And we were asked to admire and participate in her achievement each time!

Mrs. Weiner took Jess to sit on his potty seat once a day at a routine time. At first, she let him sit on it with his clothes on, reading to him or giving him a cookie to reward him for sitting down. After he understood this step, he began to look forward to it. At this point, she took his pants off so he sat on it bare. The first time he sat on it with bare buttocks, he winced and said "cold." She felt the seat and realized that it wasn't cold, but it was unfamiliar, and he'd classified it. Each time she asked him to sit on it, she explained that it was Jess's toilet seat, while the big one was mother's and father's to use. She asked Mark to show Jess how he sat on it. This endowed it with immediate sanction, and Jess's interest increased. Mark was proud to be a "teacher," and he took his new job very seriously, sitting on it every day to "show" Jess.

Don't use the guards which are commonly provided on seats for training little boys, to divert their urine. Sooner or later the child gets hurt by them as he climbs on or off the pot, and it may slow up the training process. They serve no necessary purpose anyway, for he will be intrigued with the process of holding down and aiming his penis into the pot, as soon as he realizes he can make noise that way.

After a few days of sitting him unclothed on the potty seat at a regular time, Mrs. Weiner began to take Jess to it a second time each day when he had a bowel movement in his diaper. She sat him on it while she removed the dirty diaper to drop it below him. This helped him see why she wanted him to sit there and what was to go in the pot. Accompanied by Mark's producing a bowel movement on Jess's pot, the association was made easier for Jess. He began to understand what the fuss was all about. He tried to push and grunt as he sat on the seat. He produced a movement on two occasions, and began to urinate into the pot.

The amazing thing to me is that first children can and do make the association without someone like Mark to imitate. It certainly helps to have a peer to show the child, but it isn't necessary. A first child may be several months slower in catching on, but they do—all of a sudden. In a series of 1170 normal children in Cambridge, Massachusetts, whose mothers followed this routine, I found that 80% of them first began to perform on their own at an average age of 27 months. Not only did they achieve bowel training, but they were able to train themselves for both bladder and bowel simultaneously by 27.7 months. This represented to me their urgent desire to achieve complete control when they were old enough to understand what was expected of them—particularly as it was their achievement, not their parents'!

Mrs. Weiner's mother had constantly undermined her daughter's resolve to leave it up to Jess. She had hinted for months that Mrs. Weiner was much too lax in her timing, and she constantly predicted failure for Jess. Her criticism unsettled her daughter more than she cared to admit. But she had been fortified by her ineffectiveness with Mark. She had found for herself that early training was no solution, and she wanted to try a better method with Jess.

Any young mother who needs to be reassured that it is better to wait for the child's readiness needs only to poll her friends who are training second and third children. In nearly every

*case, she will find the experienced mother relaxed about tim-
ing, in no hurry, and ready to leave it to the child. I think that
mothers with first children feel early success is a sign of being
a "good mother," and they feel like failures unless their children achieve this step at an early age. Grandmothers play on
this and hint that waiting too long indicates lack of responsibility in an important area of mothering.*

Jess had been successful in urinating into his pot each
morning after his mother sat him on it. As he heard the
sound of his urine hitting the plastic surface and associated
it with his performance, his face began to light up, and he
gaily cried, "Jess do it!" "Do it" became his name for the
need to urinate. He began to rush to his toilet seat when he
felt a full bladder, crying "do it, do it." He proudly demonstrated his new prowess to Mark and to his father, when Mr.
Weiner returned at night. After a successful week, Mrs.
Weiner put him in training pants, showing him how to pull
them down so he could perform without any help. This became
fun for Jess, and he trained himself to urinate in his pot every
time in the next few days. He was still worried about using
toilets other than his own, and the Weiners respected this.
They took his pot along with them when they went anywhere.
He placed it out in the yard when he played outside, so it
would be near him when he needed it, and kept it in his room
during the day. He almost seemed to carry it with him every-
where.

*This is the advantage to having a movable potty chair. The
child's sense of independence, of doing it himself, is a pleasure
and can be added to by having his pot available at all times.
Putting him in training pants which he can remove by himself, if done at the right time, opens up a whole new feeling
of independence. I have found that introducing "big boy
pants" too early, before he has reached a stage of readiness,
may be too much indirect pressure. When he fails, he is embarrassed, for the pants feel like a diaper, and he may wet
through them before he's aware of it. This embarrasses him,
but he doesn't know how to keep from repeating his mistake.*

So, it is better to save the training pants for an appropriate time, when they can become reinforcement for his success rather than pressure on him if he fails.

Quickly Jess learned to stand up to urinate, after watching Mark. He chortled as he learned to spray the back of the toilet, and as he made water noise by pointing his urine into the toilet bowl. Mrs. Weiner had to watch the two boys to see that they didn't compete in spraying the walls and floor with their urine. Mark and Jess began to hold back their urine so they could urinate together.

The pleasure a little boy takes in standing up to urinate is a real incentive for his learning to perform like his father, or brother, or any male. His play with his newly found skill will naturally lead to more interest in his penis and to masturbatory activity—all of which is eminently understandable and normal! I urge parents not to prohibit, divert, or otherwise try to interfere with the burgeoning interest in this part of the body. It is fun for a little boy to find out about his penis, and it deserves exploration. Having been hidden under diapers heretofore, it's like a new toy. Masturbation is rarely a problem for new parents these days—largely because adults no longer see it as a problem, and don't reinforce it as one for their children. This period of exploration and investigation will pass, unless someone makes the child feel guilty for his normal interest. Then it may well become a problem.

As Jess became excited about his new achievements, he wanted to use the big toilet like everyone else. He couldn't get up to it easily, so Mr. Weiner fixed him a step up to it. He showed Jess how to sit on the seat, facing toward the back of the toilet. In this position, he could watch his penis and its performance, feeling secure about not falling through the seat.

All of this developed so rapidly that Mrs. Weiner hadn't realized that Jess was urinating but not defecating. He was becoming constipated. He had no bowel movement for several days at a time. When he finally did, he strained uncomfortably for several hours before he produced a rocky hard bowel movement. Jess seemed very uncomfortable with it. Mrs. Weiner urged him to go to the toilet for his bowel movements. The more she urged, the more he seemed to hold back and to try to prevent a movement from coming. After many more days, he produced a large hard movement, streaked with bright red blood. He cried after this one, and she found a fissure in his anal ring. His doctor advised laxatives and stool softeners. Despite medicines, he continued to strain and to hold each movement back. This rapidly built up into a real problem for Jess—of constipation, of anxiety about being hurt, and of holding his stool back.

This is not an unusual development at this stage in an otherwise successful training venture. Boys hold back their bowel movements much more frequently than do girls, even as they achieve urine training. For one thing, they give up the seated posture which is important in stool training, but it is more than that. They seem to value the bowel movement as part of themselves, and worry about letting it go down the drain. This doesn't seem to be as common with little girls who are training themselves.

The vicious cycle which has been created by allowing Jess to become constipated enough to hurt himself must be counteracted on two fronts now, both psychologically and physically. A stool softener must be used which will allow Mrs. Weiner to promise Jess that his bowel movements won't continue to hurt him. After a fissure, the anal sphincter automatically clamps down to hold back a stool which might hurt. His conscious holding back is reinforced by this. The psychological side should be approached with reassurance that the situation isn't a problem, that he needn't worry about performing on the toilet and that he has permission to wear diapers so he can have his bowel movement in them in the familiar manner. With reiteration and reassurance from his parents, he can begin to relax about it. Children do want to comply and they do want to master this step, so much so that it may be working the wrong way. I have seen a child groaning and crying in discomfort, saying "I want to go the the toilet!" He may not allow himself to defecate when he gets there. This is a kind of ambivalence, not unrelated to the earlier forms of it we have seen, and demanding time and patient understanding to work it out. Forcing him to give up his movement, or using manipulations such as suppositories or enemas, can be very destructive and parents should avoid them, although they may become necessary if the cycle becomes too deeply entrenched. An early understanding approach is infinitely preferable.

After Mr. and Mrs. Weiner consulted Jess's doctor, and were successful in finding a medical solution to his constipated stools, they began to reassure Jess and to relax about it themselves. In a matter of a few weeks he had proudly begun to go to his pot for his bowel movements, and he was completely day-trained. All of this over a total of six weeks!

Night training should not be attempted yet unless the child asks to be helped. (When he does, refer to Chapter X.) At this point it is preferable to give him time to solidify the gains he has made before introducing another complicated step. As we see with Jess, much of the pressure to succeed comes from within him—an internal pressure to master—and is not easily controlled by the environment. So don't open up another area until this one is settled. Since many second babies arrive at the end of the first child's second year, parents are faced with the question of whether to toilet-train the older child before or after the new one comes. As a rule, it never hurts to wait before starting a step as complex as training. The older a child is, the more resources and desire he has to achieve such a task. Imitative mechanisms become even stronger in the third year, and are easier to use as an adjunct to training. If this task is pressed at a time when he's making another big adjustment, it is more likely to fail. Adjusting to a new sibling is always a big task. If a parent feels the child should start to be trained before the new baby comes, or before a move, or along with any big adjustment, the training should be set up with as little emphasis on success as possible. The child should be expected to regress with the demands of the new adjustment. The parent should make it easier for him when he does regress in this area, by pointing out to him that it is all right, and that the parent understands why. Helping him understand himself will prevent his becoming clutched up inside about failure in an area where he had become successful before.

After Jess was trained in the daytime, he began to get worse diaper rashes from being wet at night. This surprised Mrs. Weiner, and she had to reevaluate her care of the diapers which he used.

It is surprising that diaper rashes are so common in partially trained children. Perhaps the skin loses its protective toughness when it is no longer continually wet and under stress. The urine is more concentrated and more scalding when his bladder retains it for longer periods. Powder in the diapers or antiammoniacal solutions as a last rinse for the diapers seem to help most in preventing this. In order to provide rubber pants necessary at night for large children as they outgrow normal-size rubber pants, several mothers in my practice have hit on the solution of cutting leg holes in appropriate-size plastic bags.

The bathroom became a focus for Jess's play. He brought his toy animals to sit on the pot. He flushed the toilet endlessly, dropping in various bits of dust, food, and toys to watch them swirl and disappear. He put in his clothing and his beloved blanket. He asked repeatedly where his bowel movement went when it disappeared.

This question crops up in older children who have presumably conquered their anxiety about the toilet. One of the most popular displays in a local children's museum was a sectioned toilet which graphically demonstrated where the contents of the toilet went when it swirled away. Obviously in the child's mind, the bowel movement is a part of his body even after he has learned to give it up to the toilet. Repetitive play and questioning help him conquer the anxiety he has about giving up this part of himself. Playing out something which has been frightening is a very important way of dealing with anxiety. As another example, mothers tell me that their children talk endlessly about coming to see their doctor, and try to push themselves into liking to come, in not being afraid to come. This talking and play about going to the doctor serves as an important force in the conquest of their fears about it.

Jess had made strides in motor achievements. He could walk up and down the stairs holding on to the stair rail by himself. He hopped on each foot and could imitate Mark in the game of hopscotch, landing on the lines as he did. He hopped like a frog, and played at being a bird, flapping his arms when he ran. He turned doorknobs and opened doors for himself. He was interested in everything, in how it worked, and in trying to fit things together. But it could be cause for concern. For example, he was "hooked" on electric cords and plugs. He begged to be allowed to pull a plug out, to fit one into an electrical outlet. Mrs. Weiner lived in fear of his playing with electrical outlets when she wasn't there to protect him. Mr. Weiner showed him how to handle a plug safely, allowed him to practice over and over while he was with him, and provided a dummy plug and socket for him to play with when he wasn't around.

This combination is excellent—of allowing the child to learn how to handle it, of letting him practice over and over until he wears out his curiosity, and of providing him with an appropriate toy substitute. Since there are an unpredictable number of dangerous tasks which children find and want to get involved with, this is a valuable lesson for avoiding trouble. If they are prohibited from exploring, children try to sneak off to find out for themselves. One two-year-old finally succeeded in pushing a chair up to unlatch the door to a prohibited room, entered it, and proceeded to destroy everything in it.

New kinds of play opened up for him. He could sort out objects by their size and color. He knew what was "his" and

what belonged to someone else. He called his toys "mine" and Mark's "his." He was learning the meaning of pronouns at the same time that he learned how things belong to certain persons. Along with this he developed a hoarding protectiveness of his toys in the presence of visiting children. When another child wanted to play with them, he gathered all his toys into a pile to hover over them protectively. To help him give up "his" toys, Mrs. Weiner explained the idea of giving, and of getting back. She pointed out that he liked to play with other children's toys at their houses, so it was only fair that he allow them to play with his toys at his house. He seemed to begin to understand fair and unfair, of giving and receiving, and the process of sharing.

These are all demanding of a kind of self-awareness. If he is not sure of his own limits and of his own strengths, he cannot afford to allow his toys, equivalent to parts of himself, to be passed out to someone else, trusting that they will come back. This is evidence of an awareness of behavior in others comparable to his own, and denotes the beginning of an awareness of non-self.

Along with sharing, he began to play more directly with other children. He put his hat and coat on another child, and laughed out loud, as if he were aware of a comparison. He could cooperate in a game in which the other children gave him commands. But he also had begun to be competitive, and tried to be the "first" in line or the one to give orders.

Again, these are ways of learning, in play, about the differences between one's own self and the other. Competition is fostered earlier in children with older siblings, but it also begins to appear at this age in only children. It is like a trial balloon sent up to test one's strength. A child incorporates another child's resistances, by learning how to overcome them.

Make-believe and role playing became a common kind of play. Jess fed, scolded, patted, and loved his teddy bear, assuming all of the tones and many of the words of his parents as he did so. He placed teddy on the toilet many times a day, saying "do it!" and then making a S-S-S-S sound and swirling the toilet water with his fingers. He sat teddy in his feeding chair to urge him to eat or to take his medicine, alternately cajoling or fussing at him in unmistakable voice inflections.

He explored his penis, his testicles, his navel, as well as his eyes, ears, and nose. He tried to insert the tip of a pencil into his urethra. He stuffed peas and other objects into his nose on several occasions, coughing them out as they slipped into his throat. On one occasion, a bean lodged in his left nostril and was there for several days before Mrs. Weiner became aware of it. By that time there was a greenish, foul-smelling drainage from the left side of his nose. It became necessary to take him to a specialist to have the bean extracted.

One-sided drainage from the nose or outer ear can be caused by a foreign body which is lodged in the canal, irritating it and producing a foul-smelling secretion. It is amazing that a child doesn't aspirate and choke on such foreign objects, but they almost never do. A child this age can swallow objects the size of a nickel without problems, as long as they don't lodge in the esophagus. If an object does stick, the child will complain of chest pain. Nature provides us with amazingly resilient bodies—and it is fortunate at this age!

In a play group, Jess was often a quiet observer for the beginning of the session. This was so unlike him at home that it alarmed Mrs. Weiner at first. Then she realized that he was sizing up the group situation before he entered into it. On the way home, he could tell her in detail everything he'd observed by acting out and interspersing a few words.

Participation in a group can occur in many ways, and visual participation is as important as more active participation. An observation period is often the way a sensitive child learns before he acts. Watching quietly is a new development in Jess, and may represent a new interest in learning different ways to do things. It is certainly to be respected.

One of the most exciting areas in Jess's development was that of speech. His mother and father counted the number of words he used in one week, and found about three hundred different ones. He was putting three and four words together regularly now. "I take my hat." Sentences had subjects and verbs. The objects of action were used after the action. Quite often he was using adjectives and adverbs in a sentence such as "I wanna go *bad*." The structure of sentences was indeed beginning to assume adult forms, instead of simple verbs or

nouns. Both Mark and his parents were conscious of helping Jess with his speech. For example, when he said "Wanna go," they added "I want to go." Or if he said "Gimme some candy," they corrected to "Give Jess some candy, please." This was an automatic response from all of those around him, and served to shape him toward more complex speech forms.

Older children in a family push the learning toddler pretty hard. They have just learned many of these forms themselves and are conscious of the younger child's immature form, so their pressure on the small child can be constant. This is one reason why younger siblings may not speak early. In such a

*case, it behooves parents to be aware of what is happening
and to let up on their own pressure. Symptoms of too much
pressure in a toddler might be stuttering, hesitating speech,
or regression to baby talk. The urge to learn to speak from
within a child is great. When it is overloaded with pressure
from the outside as well, he slows down or comes to a stop in
learning.*

Jess knew everything that was said to him, and could point
to pictures of things he'd seen only once. He could name many
things in the household and knew the names of all of his
mother's friends, as well as those of his own.

"What's that?" or "What's this?" were asked constantly to
keep his mother's attention. When they were in the car, he
pointed to one thing after another. At home, he never lost
contact with her, bombarding her with questions. She could
hear him calling "Mommy, what's this?" from another room.
When she tried to talk to anyone, he manufactured reasons
to interrupt her with "What's this?" This question rang in
her ears at night long after he was in bed.

*Of course, he is using it to control her and to hold onto her
attention. Its power to divert her from another interest is
great—she is accustomed to fostering his interest in things
around him, to supplementing his information—so this question strikes an unconscious chord in her which almost forces
her to respond.*

By now, he had learned to name such things as snow, wind,
rain, day, and night, and he could be asked to do so. The whole
family took pleasure in showing him off to anyone who would
listen. Even Mark greeted grandparents with "See what Jess
can do. Tell them which is your nose, Jess!"

*The delight in his achievements is a tremendous reinforce-
ment for learning in Jess. Mark's interest is partly an attempt
to get in on all of the adults' interest in Jess but also represents his feeling of having been responsible for Jess's learn-*

ing. It is a good way for Mark to handle some of his competi-tive feelings.

So many new things were happening, all showing real progress in Jess's development, that they softened the strain of the bad days. There were entire days when he couldn't be reached. He seemed to fall apart, screaming, early in the morning, and the horror of the day could be predicted from that time on. Mrs. Weiner had learned to ignore him for the most part on such days, but she was not able to withdraw from him completely. She would try various ways of cheering him up or of diverting him, by reading to him, playing with him, taking him out. On such days, everything seemed to turn sour—he spent most of the day in tantrums, or in screaming "no" or "I can't." After he had been through a tiring day, she could always expect this kind of falling apart. If she took him to visit, and hadn't prepared him for it, or if he became too jealous of her having a nice time, he seemed to fall back into his old tantrum behavior as if to dominate the scene.

This can be pretty discouraging to parents who hope they are over this hump by the time their child is two. But it needn't be, for this period lasts a year and a half in our culture. There begin to be more "ups" than "downs" as the child gets to two years of age, and this is as much encouragement as parents can expect. I see development in children as a constant homeo-static curve—the "ups" must be balanced by "downs." These regressions seem to be serving some sort of refueling purpose for the spurts in progress. It is difficult for parents to see the necessity for them, but if they can look on such regressions as necessary to ultimate progress, perhaps this will help them live through the bad days. In a Mayan Indian culture in southern Mexico where this behavior was not found, the chil-dren were quieter, more passive, more imitative, and less individualized, less able to cope with complexity as adults. We should realize that we are raising children for a compli-cated, individualized, demanding society. This turbulent be-havior seems to be a necessary counterpart to developing qualities which children need to meet our culture's demands.

CHAPTER VIII

Hyperactive Child

Two Years

Barney was a bombshell. He had entered the world kicking and screaming. He had never stopped. As an infant, he had seemed to cry constantly. Mrs. Stein had taken him to several doctors, who had treated him for colic, but nothing had worked. Medication, changes in feedings, swaddling, letting him cry it out, playing with him constantly, had all been tried at various times to no avail. Barney seemed unable to quiet down. As time went on, his crying diminished, but he became an intense, demanding, clumsily active one-year-old. He was a fifth child, with one brother and two sisters who were in their teens. Another brother, Hal, who was eight, had been forcibly enlisted to help out with Barney. The teenagers were grabbed as sitters when they could be found, but Barney had become a reason for their absence. He afforded little pleasure to any of them as he cried and thrashed his way through the first year.

Even at first, he had seemed to startle when there was anything unusual. A new sound, a new light, a new person—all of these set him off into crying and furious activity. Over the first two years, he had gradually learned to control himself, but he was still a baby who could not be taken into a new situation without having an initial period of protest. When a friend came to visit his brothers or sisters, the cry was, "Get

Barney out of the way." Upon the advent of a stranger, Barney would begin by crying, then he would reduce his crying to constant whining to be picked up by the brother or sister, then fuss to be put down, and end with constant, clumsy activity. This last consisted of rushing from one part of the room to another, picking up one toy or object after another, throwing it, kicking it, climbing up on a chair or table, falling off onto the floor, opening a door, slamming it, finally falling in the middle of the floor to kick and scream.

These stages of activity as responses to a new person or new situation can be seen as defenses on Barney's part. They are defenses against new stimuli and information which is too sudden. Barney has a very sensitive and overreactive set of stimulus receptors, like many children who are labeled "hyperactive." These children respond with activity in an attempt to assimilate novel information and to discharge the nervous energy it stirs up in them. Barney's initial crying is one way of shutting out these responses. When this does not work, his effort to be cuddled and shielded becomes a second attempt to reduce and control his responses. When even this doesn't work, he is "stuck" with his built-in pattern of responding to excitement—that of apparently undirected activity and a kind of pointless discharge of motor energy. Of course, the goal is just that—of discharging the nervous excitement which his sensitivity generates. In infancy, crying and thrashing probably served the same purposes. Now he has "learned," or has been trying to learn, more effective and acceptable ways to cope with his raw nervous system. Many of these hyperactive children can learn coping patterns which work for them. If those around them can understand this, and can help them find techniques for coping, these children may be saved from the misery of an intolerant set of peers and an unyielding, hostile school system which they must face later on. For example, when he was upset and hysterical, Barney could be taken gently into a rocking chair, held securely in someone's arms, and rocked until he subsided. Then, his caretaker could begin slowly to croon to him, gradually to talk, and when he was able to listen, to tell him what he had been

*through and how he had learned something from it. In the
strange situation, Barney could be told about what had bothered him, how he could gradually learn to calm himself first,
then begin to take in and even enjoy the stranger or the new
place. It would work eventually.*

In the face of Barney's behavior, the aim of the Stein family was to keep away from Barney and to keep him out of the
way. Many of the worst fights in the family were over Barney.
When Mrs. Stein wanted help with him, she had to demand it
of the older children. Hal was a more placid, compliant boy
than the three older ones, and she usually resorted to putting
Barney in his charge after he came home from school. By way
of bribing Hal, Mrs. Stein provided cookies and candy for him
in the afternoons when she wanted him to "sit." Hal was
rapidly gaining weight, as he sat in front of the television set
on these afternoons, munching his sweets, "sitting" for Barney.
Meanwhile, Barney alternated between attempts to distract
and interest Hal in playing with him and, giving up on that,
charged around the house picking up objects, putting them
down, climbing on chairs to rock, on tables to explore. Hal
gave a lazy call now and then which kept Barney's attention
focused on the television room. When anything crashed, as it
often did, Hal wearily picked himself up, came in to set it
upright, swatted Barney across the head or cheek, and returned
to his television watching. Barney took these reprimands in his
stride and continued his frenetic activity. Rarely did he join
Hal in the sedentary activity of watching cartoons and soap
operas. When he did, there was nothing of Hal's passive intake
in his response. He sat close to the screen, his body in rhythmic
motion, occasionally mimicking snatches of repetitive commercials. He had memorized a few and could sing them with appropriate intonations and even some distinguishable words.
Although his vocabulary was still limited to a few dozen words,
most of them were taken from his television experiences with
Hal.

*This is not an uncommon source for learning these days.
Many of the three-year-olds who come to my office and on*

whom I try the vision-testing chart can sing out the letters with tunes culled from "Sesame Street." They seem to have learned to read the letters, and have associated the letter with its appropriate background music. I have not seen two-year-olds do this yet, but mothers report that they can. At two, they do put words and tunes together in television commercials, and one can see this as evidence of television's powerful capacity to teach. As in Barney's case, I also see it can be a way of filling up an environment for a child who may not be getting appropriate interpersonal stimulation. I think personal stimulation is much more rewarding and important to a small child than any form of television, and I am sure that learning is richer and more individualized if it takes place in an interpersonal setting. The power of a medium which uses both visual and auditory senses to transmit information should not be underestimated. As in Barney's case, it may be sopping up learning energy which could ideally be put to better use.

In this child's case, integrating speech is likely to be a difficult task—in the same way as learning to read or learning to write will be later on—for it is a task which demands integration of his oversensitive sensory apparatus and his overreactive motor system. The mastery of cues which he must receive, integrate, and learn from, are more difficult for a child like Barney. And we know that he already has problems controlling his motor responses. There is little reason to think that the muscles and nerves needed for speech aren't affected by the same kind of rawness that we see in his gross motor patterns. In fact, many hyperkinetic children of six and seven still speak with jerky, overshooting muscular patterns of tongue and other vocal muscles which have not been mastered over the first few years. Barney is not as uncoordinated as more severely affected children, and his speech is not as delayed or distorted as the speech of many children with so-called "hyperactive syndrome." Barney's problems lie more in a "normal" range, and he would be classified neurologically as a normal, active child.

But, because he is in an environment in which there are many people, none of them really in tune with him and his difficult rhythms, he is less likely to find ways of mastering his uncoordinated patterns. Activity remains a successful outlet for stored-up energy. Had his parents or his siblings the patience to teach him bits of control and to interact with him in his own rhythms, he could learn. The fact that he can learn from a medium as relentless and unsympathetic as television is testimony to that. The one real advantage to the television set as a teacher for Barney is that it has no built-in expectation for him to perform, and it will not force this type of pressure on his already overworked system. The only pressure it adds is that of a constant bombardment to the senses. But, Barney has been learning ways of coping with that, by rocking, sucking, banging, and even running away when he is overloaded. These are certainly effective ways of reducing his own tension and of controlling his overreactions. To have learned them without help from his environment is testimony to Barney's strengths.

His parents could teach him other, more mature ways of keeping himself in check. They could help him to stay in the room by concentrating his attention on the events around him; they could gradually prolong his attention span by evoking his interest. Whenever he shows even a little more staying power, they should reward him with encouraging words. As he gets better, they should continue to support him. Gradually, he could be introduced to more new situations while under the "protection" of one or both parents, encouraging him to handle the confusion and excitement that the novel situation generates little by little. In other words, with a hyperactive child these efforts at mastery may have to be thought of as a slow learning process.

I cannot resist entering a plea for parents of young children to be more aware of the tremendous implications of television as a powerful influence on early learning. The energy which it takes to control the input from such an attractive source is demonstrated by a child who sits mesmerized in front of a set, unable to be reached unless a parent shouts in his ear, or physically draws him away. The cost to him is easily seen as he disintegrates at the end of a program—screaming, whimpering, and "raw" after a period of such intense involvement.

If a child is to benefit from such involvement, we must see to it that we provide him with programs that are appropriate to his stage of development. Programs which contain the kind of information he can use will certainly add to his experience. By the same token, programs which do not may do double damage by demanding energy of him which could be put to use in more appropriate interpersonal learning situations. So

it cannot be thought of as a neutral medium, to fill up time while mother gets her chores done, or to be left to the discretion of an uninvolved baby sitter. A small child's capacity for experience and learning is limited and it is precious. If we don't protect and treasure it, we may well raise a generation of selfish, insensitive, sensorially overwhelmed, and basically exhausted adults. Television is only one of many environmen-

tal pressures toward this, but it may be a potent one for small children. I would urge strict monitoring of the amount and the quality of programs to which two- and three-year-olds are exposed. And we as responsible adults must press for more and better programs geared to the capacities of small children.

Mrs. Stein realized that she was abdicating important responsibility to Hal. She had been so worn down by Barney's infancy that she often felt a desperate fear either of running completely away or of hurting Barney. She often felt as though she might smother him when he was crying so relentlessly, or strap him into a straitjacket when he was thrashing about, unable to stop moving. When she found herself ready to throw him down soon after she picked him up, she stopped holding him. When she rocked him to quiet him, he often became more upset, startling and crying louder. So, she stopped rocking him. Contact with him became less and less frequent. She knew he was sensitive and was responding to her anger and desperation, but this knowledge did not make it easier to live with him. She found she could stand about an hour at a time of his "protest" activity before she wanted to crack. So she had developed patterns for herself, of being with him, then of getting away from him.

The difficulty with such an infant is that he provides a negative feedback system for his mother. Everything she might do naturally to mother a baby meets with a negative response from him, and she cannot help but take it personally. She soon begins to feel his behavior is her fault, due to her inadequacy as a mother. And no mother can tolerate that feeling indefinitely. In fact, the more she may care about being a good mother, the more difficult this kind of behavior may be for her. Her response will inevitably be to turn away from this continuous negative assault—to avoid responding in kind by battering the baby. It is no wonder that a distant, insensitive, even hostile relationship gets built up around such a baby.

By now, Mrs. Stein has developed a habit of withdrawing from Barney, as a way of coping with the feelings she has about him. She can still care a lot about him, but for this very reason may need to get away from the helpless feelings her caring and his responses engender. This cycle, based on a raw, overreactive nervous system in a baby, can be self-perpetuating. Barney needs a low-keyed, patient caretaker who can be tolerant of his jagged rhythms and who can teach him smoother ways of coping. This need is not likely to be met by a mother afraid of her own overreactions, and longing for a baby who is appropriately responsive to her. By this age, there are almost irrevocable patterns of interaction set up between mother and child.

To an outsider who was inclined to be critical of Mrs. Stein, these patterns could appear to be those of rejection, and yet that would describe only half of her story. What a mother in Mrs. Stein's position needs, what anyone needs, is reward for effort put in. She is obviously not going to get it from the baby. One would hope that she would look for encouragement and guidance from an outside source, be it parent, friend, or professional. She needs a source of support who could first understand her side of the difficulties she has had with Barney—the demands, the fatigue, the sparse rewards. But then she also needs someone who would press her to have the patience and the gentle determination to keep on reaching Barney through his difficult patterns, to teach him how to handle himself in spite of them. This is a demanding, continuous process.

But, from Barney's standpoint, this is a very important time for him to learn how to handle himself. If he continues to grow up with the patterns of overreacting and hyperactivity, he will have a harder and harder time. His peers will not be able to tolerate him. In school, he will be a menace to the teachers, and they will reject him. He will rapidly acquire a feeling of hopelessness and helplessness which will add to his problems. If his parents can muster the patience and determination to teach him patterns of controlling his overreactions at this age, he will have a better chance of learning how to cope in more complex situations later on. Most of these children either outgrow or learn to compensate for their problems by adolescence. But by then their personality problems are great, and their images of themselves as failures are set. This

*is the time for the Steins to develop coping patterns for them-
selves and for Barney.*

Mrs. Stein spent every morning alone with Barney. She
tried to make beds, wash dishes, cook with him at her feet. He
would dash ahead of her into a room, empty the bureau
drawers or force the articles back into the drawers, pull the
pillows and sheets off the bed, pull towels off the racks into
the toilet bowl, upend the wastebaskets and then refill them
with all available objects. He could now turn a doorknob and
open the door, so her efforts to contain him in one room were
at an end. Her best maneuvers to control him were in the
form of showing him how to do things with her and waiting
for him to help her. At these times, she could patiently repeat
one action over and over until he could imitate her and learn
to master it. But these efforts took time. She could enlist him
in bedmaking, but most of his attempts to stuff in a sheet
resulted in the sheet's returning with his hand. When she
washed the bathroom, he managed to spill powdered soap or
clean linen on the wet floor. When she was cooking, he emptied the cupboards of all the pots and pans, managed to hide
the lids, and to pour liquid detergent into the empty pots
before she realized how hard he was working to imitate her
cooking maneuvers. His efforts to clean up after himself were
just as earnest as were hers. He put the pots in one cupboard,
the lids under the sink, the detergent upside down under the
stove. He foresaw her rising tension, and could leave the room
in a hurry when he realized that he had done one too many
misdirected things. He could hide then in a very effective way
—to be found only after a thorough search of the house.

*Some of these behaviors show resourcefulness and almost
precocity in a two-year-old. Although two-year-olds are characteristically imitative and are organized in their attempts to
put things in appropriate places, when Barney successfully
puts all the pots in one place, all the lids in another, it shows
an advanced capacity to relate shape to function. His sensitivity to his mother's reactions reflects how much affect he has
available to use in a social situation. He is investing a great*

deal of energy in his attempt to keep in touch with her. Most two-year-olds would be more distractible than this. It is another example of how hard Barney is working to learn how to master himself and his reactions.

When she scolded him for spilling the detergent, he looked very serious, wincing as she came near him, but taking her scolding approach without crying. Within a minute, he had returned to the spot where he had spilled the liquid, and was scolding the spot with gestures and voice inflections very much like his mother's.

One of his best-used phrases was "poor Barney," which he sang happily to himself most of the day. Mrs. Stein winced when he first began to sing this, but she began to see the humor in it. She was never able to find out who had taught him this rather appropriate phrase.

Many of a baby's early utterances seem to occur as if by chance. My own feeling is that there is much more verbal exploration than we adults are aware of, and when a particular word or phrase in this wide scanning hits a responsive note in the environment, the child knows it. Then he tries it again and then again, and his repertory is thereby fixed. In this case, everyone indeed felt that Barney was "poor," and this phrase called out a positive response to him more effectively than any other he could find.

When Mrs. Stein sat down to read or to sew, Barney would immediately collect toys or objects to bring to her. He started a constant chant of "What's that?"—more to keep contact with her than for any answer. When she answered his question, he stopped, grinned slightly, and repeated it again. She found she could answer the same question as many as ten times in a row, before he went on to another "What's this?" The best way to stop his continuous flow was to turn it around to him, asking "Barney, what's this?" as she held the object. His favorite game was that of being asked to name the pictures in a book. Although he could name only a few, he loved to be asked. Then, he would smile, look up at his mother, reply with "What *is* this?" to elicit her name for it.

After a very few minutes of these quiet, interactive games, Barney seemed to build up more excitement than he could handle, and he fell apart. Either he would begin to cry out louder and louder "What's this?" or he would take the object

from his mother to throw it. Then he would lie down on the floor to kick and scream in a temper tantrum. Mrs. Stein had too often tried to stop him or divert him at such a point. The more effort she put into her attempt to control him, the more upset he became. He was able to scream for as much as twenty minutes without stopping. She found that the most effective maneuver was for her to leave the room. In between long bursts of screaming, he seemed to sense that she was gone, his cries became less intense as he looked around for her, and soon he was up again looking for her.

As in Chapters I and VII, these tantrums must serve many purposes—to discharge built-up tension and conflicting feelings, to test the child's own control. In Barney's case, controls are difficult and he demonstrates this by the duration and depth of anguish he shows at such a time. I'm not sure that Mrs. Stein can do any more in the midst of the crisis, but I am sure that these tantrums are an index of the struggle that is going on underneath. When they are occurring frequently and are increasing in number and duration, a parent should look at the rest of the child's day to see whether there might be other ways of helping him learn to handle tension and achieve the necessary controls over himself. In Barney's case, we are aware of his need for, and even desire for, ways of handling his overreactions. It is interesting that for this child, as for many others, pleasantly exciting situations can lead to tension buildup and tantrums just as easily as unpleasant situations can.

For Mr. Stein, playing with Barney was a dreaded chore, and he openly admitted it. When he came home at night, weary after his long day, Barney's screams and constant activity made Mr. Stein wish he had stopped at the corner bar. At the end of the day, Barney inevitably built up to a peak of excitement and activity which tested everyone's patience. So the sound of his father's key in the door set off a train of increased, provocative activity in the child. He raced up and down in front of his father, pulled at his pants for a word, screaming "What's that?" or "What's this?" He pulled cloths off the tops of tables, pulled magazines down, knocked over chairs as he rushed around violently responding to the increased excitement in the air. Mr. Stein responded by closing himself off in the television room, falling into his chair in front of the television set with a can of beer. Outside, the torrent of activity continued. Mrs. Stein felt herself seething with anger when this happened, and didn't dare express the feelings she had about being left with all of the caretaking of Barney.

A major part of fathering may be that of taking off some of the drudgery of child care at the end of the day. If Mr. Stein could pull himself together first, then return to offer Barney a new look at life, it could mean a great deal to both the child and his mother. Fathers can offer an active outlet for energy at the end of a long day—a change of pace, an opportunity to learn about another side of the world, even another kind of discipline and control over one's frustrations. All of these are novel and offer a richness of experience to any child. For Barney, a father's more active way of dealing with energy might be especially therapeutic. For his mother, the symbolic value of his father's participation would be sanity-saving. No wonder that the women's movements in our society are crying out for equal time for men and women in and out of the home. We know how hard it is for Mrs. Stein to feel responsible for Barney, and it would mean a great deal if Mr. Stein could support her in this by sharing some of the responsibility at the end of the day. The amount of time he gave to playing with Barney would not be as important to Mrs. Stein as the fact that he was willing to participate with him, to acknowledge Barney's problematic behavior, and to credit his wife for what she did for the child. For Barney, a short time is much better than none. A great deal of imitating and identification can take place in a short time for a child whose need for new patterns of behavior is as great as Barney's.

Mr. Stein's observations of Barney were usually made from a distance, and took the form of criticism. Mrs. Stein took this criticism personally. At the table, he watched Barney try to manipulate his fork or spoon with clumsy attempts to spear his food. These often resulted in overshooting the mark with a ringing clash in the plate, or in knocking the food off the plate onto the table. Mr. Stein would try to correct the boy, adding more tension to the table scene. "Can't he ever learn? I'm sure he's hopelessly defective. What a bad boy you are,

Barney!" Since these were ideas which hit both Mrs. Stein and Barney in vulnerable spots, they made him behave more clumsily, and most meals ended in total chaos when Barney was present.

Mrs. Stein, of course, does fear that something is wrong or defective in Barney. And she already feels it's her fault— partly irrationally, as any mother does who has a child who is

ill or damaged. Her concern is reinforced by her own ambivalent feelings about Barney's difficult behavior. Barney has now heard how "bad" he is for some time. At this age, a child is beginning to know the difference between "good" and "bad," and is just beginning to care which he is. Mr. Stein's destructive remarks may force Barney to defend himself against caring, an attitude which can lead to antisocial, self-defeating behavior later on.

When Barney attempted to control his clumsiness with one hand by shifting his utensil to the other, Mr. Stein criticized him for that, too. "Can't you push him to be right-handed?

If he grows up to be a lefty, he'll never be anything but clumsy!"

Parents often ask whether a child should be pressed to a decision about which hand to use. I can clearly answer with an unequivocal "no." We already push children to be right-handed in our society. From the time we start handing them toys, most parents (especially if they are right-handed themselves) hand a toy or a utensil across from their right hand to the child's right hand. A left-handed infant may accept it with his right hand and then transfer it to his left. Or he may try it with his right hand for a period before he finds it easier to imitate with his left hand. So from the first half year he must sort out his own best way of performing in the face of our automatic pressure to perform right-handedly. In the second year, and as he learns to imitate, he may perform in a mirror-like way, using the left hand to mirror his right-handed parent's actions. This may enter into his choice. But, as far as we know, preferences in "handedness" and "footedness" and "eyedness" for skilled behavior are already set in the child's brain at birth. When dominance is all on the same side, the likelihood of confusion is less. But, even a mixture of dominance can be effectively sorted out by most children over a period of time. If, however, the environment adds pressure before the child can sort out for himself, I see this as adding to his confusion, not lessening it. If you've ever watched a left-handed person who has been "taught" to be right-handed falter as he suppresses an automatic left-handed response, you can appreciate the expensive delay that results from such interference.

Parents also ask at what age preference becomes clear. In answer, I refer to A. Gesell's statements about handedness. He says that a child may not demonstrate fixed handedness before the age of three. In many cases, this may be true because of the confusion of a mixed dominance cited above, or a potentially equal dominance in the brain. By the age of three, he will be able to learn how to make the decision which accompanies each act more smoothly and automatically. But in most children, I think dominance can be detected in the first year, and it is pretty clear by the second year. A two-year-old may still perform certain acts with his less-dominant hand or foot, but most automatic behavior will demonstrate his preference. A parent should not try to influence him to change. Fifteen percent of adults are reportedly left-handed, and as the pressure to change is lifted even more effectively for future generations, perhaps many more will be allowed to perform with their built-in left-handed preference.

Barney's two-year-old exuberance and negative behavior seemed to survive all of this criticism. But he spent more and more time teasing everyone around him. He began to have two patterns which were characteristic of him. One pattern could be called his social pattern, and in that was lumped all of the attempts to reach those around him which seemed to parallel his desperation. The second pattern was one of withdrawal and quiet frustration. When he could no longer reach his caretaker, or when he was punished or forced out of the room, Barney seemed to collapse in a heap—sucking his fingers, rocking as he sat and banging his head loudly against the chair or wall. At night, when he was put to bed, he repeated this rapid-rocking, noisy banging behavior. For as much as forty-five minutes after he was put to bed, he could be heard banging his head on his crib, the crib moving across the room until it banged on the wall. Again at intervals through the

night, Barney would rouse to semisleep, and rock and bang
for fifteen to thirty minutes before he quieted again.

*Barney's need for a pattern which both uses his excess energy
and comforts him as he moves from waking to sleep is apparent and understandable. Many children have such rocking and
banging patterns, and they do not necessarily have the problems which we have outlined with Barney. But I would urge
parents to use these symptoms as a reason to evaluate the
environments, both inner and outer, for the child. If he is
under too much pressure from those around him, this pattern
may reflect it. If he is frustrated because of his inability to
work out inner conflicts, perhaps a parent's awareness of his
conflicts may lead the parent to play a more effective role in
helping him with new solutions. Certainly, I feel that the
Steins could have been doing a great deal more for Barney.
For instance, they could see to it that his day contained
periods of very active play, periods for low-keyed teaching of
how to use his body, periods of rest and quiet reading—all
geared to his rhythms when possible.*

*Barney is not a seriously disturbed or impaired child at
present, although he could develop personality problems if he
continues to have to cope with his world ineffectively. Many
hyperkinetic children have a more serious underlying pathol-
ogy of the central nervous system, and they cannot learn
patterns of coping with their clumsy overreactions. These
children need to be evaluated by a competent expert in hyper-
kinesis or minimal brain damage, for many of them will improve dramatically with medication. Since medicating a child
is a serious step, it should not be done without expert evaluation and guidance. But the earlier it can be decided upon, the
better become the child's chances of fitting into his peer group
and into school, when that becomes necessary. Barney's parents could use professional guidance to help them organize a
program for him. He is still a little boy with resiliency and an
eagerness to please those around him. He will lose these assets
if he continues to be buffeted.*

*The very nature of a two-year-old's struggle means at least
two things: (1) It is a period when inner conflicts are being*

brought to the surface for a kind of open resolution, in a way that may never happen as easily again. (2) After the resolution of these conflicts is set in a pattern at this age, the child's personality and his potential for coping with conflict will either be limited by a fixed, inflexible pattern, or be enriched by a more flexible pattern over which he has gained control. In Barney's case, it is apparent that he is becoming fixed in an either/or pattern: either hunger for attention and approval, or withdrawal and resignation to having to cope by himself. This will further limit his capacity to overcome his original problems of hypersensitivity and hyperactivity.

CHAPTER IX

Working Parents [2]

Thirty Months

Adding a baby to their tightly knit family had come as more of a shock than the Camerons had expected. They had been married for three years, had known each other for two years before that, and they'd planned each step of their lives together very carefully. They had been in love with each other for a long time before they could decide to endanger their relationship and their careers by marriage. Both felt strongly about their work—she was a lawyer, and he an architect. They had worked hard to complete their schooling on scholarships, and were enjoying the success they were achieving in their professional lives. When they met in the late stages of the struggle to finish school, they had a great deal in common. Ambition to achieve the excitement of a responsible position, and satisfaction found in hard work were mirrored in each of them. They were both from traditional family settings where the female was "at home" and the male was "out in the world." They felt that their marriage must be on different lines. They planned and successfully achieved a sharing of household and career responsibilities in their relationship. Marriage did not shake their menage or the excitement they found in their lives together. After a few years of rewarding, deepening ties to each other, they began to plan for a baby.

Both Camerons had experience with younger children, and

had taken care of their own brothers and sisters when they were growing up at home. They felt they could anticipate some of the problems of being responsible for another dependent human being. And they wanted a third person to share the lovely glow which their lives together created. They planned each step of the pregnancy, of the new baby's coming, very carefully. Even before she allowed herself to get pregnant, she had determined where she could find a sitter, which day-care center was nearby, and how much it would cost. He had figured out the insurance coverage and the hospital costs of a delivery. For they were still repaying loans they had made to complete their schooling, and they sailed close to the wind on finances. But they had been able to save enough to cover each of the big expenses, and she checked out the possibility of maternity leave at her office. She had to tread lightly to find this out, for her boss was not sympathetic with women's career problems. He had hired her because she looked like a better bet for the long run than the thirty or forty male applicants for the job. But he'd expressed misgivings and had even asked her jokingly to sign a contract not to get pregnant. As she began to want a baby, she began to work even harder, to make herself more indispensable to the firm. By the time she finally announced her pregnancy, she had succeeded so well that her request for the allowable two-month leave of absence was accorded with stony consent. She, in turn, felt so guilty about leaving her niche and the responsibilities that had been multiplying for her that she offered to cut down her stay at home to six weeks.

This is her first mistake. As I said in Chapter II, leaving a baby before the worst hurdle of adjustment is over and before enjoying the rewards of having made it together (not until at least three months) is unfair to both mother and baby. They will never again have such an opportunity for cementing their bonds and learning about each other. Sharing this early period with substitutes means diluting it.

Her guilt about being a woman, and being at the mercy of a woman's classic responsibility, reinforces a chauvinistic attitude in her employer which is anachronistic as well as unjust. My concern is that it is unjust to the baby's future, as well as to Mrs. Cameron's potential as a mother. She will never be as fulfilled a mother under this kind of pressure. It is time that our society began to value the well-being of its future citizens. Women's roles need more responsible thought. In communal societies which have been established long enough to realize the significance of this early critical period for mothers and their babies, most have established laws which protect and foster a mother's being at home for the first six months. We don't know the exact length of the critical period, and it may be very individualized, but an option must be there for all women. By making herself more necessary at the office in guilty preparation for something she wants dearly, Mrs. Cameron has boxed herself into a situation which may work to deprive her of the more leisurely rewards of motherhood. She is already setting her homelife up as a secondary job, not as a pleasure. The resulting tension will reflect in the future family relationships.

In preparation for the baby, the Camerons had attended childbirth education classes, and had read all they could about pregnancy and childbirth. They made plans to share the delivery and the care for the baby afterward. The classes were made up of young, interested couples with similar problems. The Camerons discussed many of these before and after classes with the others. Each couple drew support from the others. Pregnancy was a rewarding, busy time for both Camerons. Mrs. Cameron had her work organized and ready for her absence by the time she delivered.

The delivery was smooth and exciting for both parents, and Mrs. Cameron was able to go through it all without anesthesia. Her husband had learned his lessons well; he had coached and supported her, and it was a thoroughly shared experience which was to them indescribably rewarding. The baby was a perfect little girl, whom they named Lucy.

Mrs. Cameron's heart surged with aching tenderness and glowing complacency when she held Lucy. She had never felt so thoroughly in love—and so helpless. She had been able to control excessive feelings in her life before by careful plan-

ning. But this new intensity was not one she'd been prepared
for. When Lucy came in to be fed, she forgot all of her preparation, and felt as if she might break this beautiful creature
if she even moved in the wrong way. All of her self-confidence, built up over the years, had fled. She felt all over again
like the little girl who once had been left with a screaming
baby brother, bleeding after a fall, albeit only from a loose
tooth. Each day she became more involved with Lucy, and
each day her feelings of helplessness increased. She was
aware that she'd almost shoved her husband out of their tight
little cocoon, and although she felt guilty about it, she did
resent it a bit when he wanted to hold Lucy. When he held
the baby awkwardly and she began to cry, the mother
snatched Lucy away almost contemptuously. He felt pushed
away by them both and struggled to regain the old closeness.
He tried to help at home and he offered to practice taking
care of Lucy in the hospital, as they'd planned. Tensions built
up between them which they'd not anticipated, and each saw
the other's hovering over Lucy as an attempt to possess her.
They were trying desperately to overcome their feelings of
helplessness and to shield themselves from this overwhelming
new responsibility.

*In other, less rifted cultures, this is a time when social cus-
toms serve a stabilizing purpose. The knowledge is secure in
the older generation, who quietly hands it onto the new young
parents when they need it. Most of the young parents in our
lonely small families are indeed adrift in a crisis period such
as this. As a result, unnecessary tensions mount that force
families apart at a time when more cement is needed, rather
than less.*

*When a new baby is born to Indians in southern Mexico, or
to Greeks in the islands, the women band together to take
care of the young mother and to indoctrinate her in her new
role. The men provide a more jocular fraternity to help the
father face his new responsibilities. The support of his own
sex frees him to fall back and gather courage as well as moral
support for his new role. In our society, we have lost the
strength that comes with mixing generations at a time like*

this. Even a peer group, such as the childbirth education classes, can offer support and shared experience which fills the otherwise deep void.

As time went on, the Camerons developed a shared system of caring for Lucy as well as the household. Purposely, neither enforced a female-type role on her. They bought trucks as well as dolls, dressed her in overalls as well as dresses, and avoided type-casting pinks and blues.

By the third year, Mrs. Cameron had found a day-care center for Lucy, and had taken her away from the family where she'd been cared for during the day for the first two years. The day-care center was a cooperative one in which young parents played a major role—in setting policy, participating in the care of the center, and teaching in the classrooms. The staff was made up of full-time professionals who were trained in early child care. Parents were expected to contribute four hours a week. There were meetings twice a month for discussion and sharing of mutual problems and for child development discussions with the staff. Although the Camerons had felt wearied at first by the thought of more meetings, they found that the center began to be more and more a focus for them as a family. The sharing of problems which went on in the meetings began to supplant their need for other groups.

One of the most valuable aspects of a day-care center for small children is what it can mean to the families. It can become a focus in the community for many families who share similar concerns. Unless a center demands mutual participation from all its member families, it loses this value to them. As parents are forced to give to such a center, they begin to feel more responsibility and more involvement. I am not of course overlooking the fact that parent involvement is vital to the economic picture of most day-care centers. But the advantages of involved parents go way beyond this. The parents gain through warmth of commitment, and the young children benefit when their parents are right there making decisions that directly affect their daily lives. If parents allow themselves to be drawn away, they begin to feel guilty and angry with themselves, at the same time longing for a closer touch with their children. Their unconscious response to such feelings will create a feeling of competition and hostility toward the caretakers in the center. This may come out in various ways, either as undermining the work of the center or as a kind of abdication of responsibility for this side of their children's care. It doesn't need to happen—if a day-care center presses the parent-child relationship as its major focus, rather than just care for the child.

Another important reason for having parents intimately involved is to preserve strong ethnic or individual beliefs. If parents can reinforce these beliefs in the center, the child will experience less of a gulf between home and center. When the values of the parents are devalued in the center, either consciously or unconsciously, the end result will be a conflict for the child, and an implicit undermining of parental values. Since these ethnic values are a major source of strength in our society, we should be doing all we can to reinforce and preserve them. Parents need sympathetic centers as much as their children do!

Mrs. Cameron was responsible for Lucy in the early morning. She could gather herself together in the morning, whereas Mr. Cameron was uncivil until ten o'clock. She treasured her times with Lucy as they got dressed together. She had taught Lucy to begin dressing herself, and they chatted with each other. Mrs. Cameron put on a garment, Lucy watched her and followed suit. Her mother waited until Lucy was ready, then she put on another bit of clothing. In this way, they played a game of follow-the-leader. On occasion, Mrs. Cameron asked Lucy to be the leader. At such a time, the child was like a whirlwind, putting on her underwear, socks, pants, and shirt with amazing speed. Her mother was only half dressed on the days of Lucy's leadership.

Mrs. Cameron went away to start the water boiling for coffee and returned to find Lucy talking to herself. She used two very different voices in a dialogue with herself. She said, "Put on your clothes, you bad girl!" in one low voice. In a higher-pitched voice: "They're tore; I hate 'em." "What's

wrong with them?" "They're boy clothes. I want a dress!"
"You *be* a boy today—hear me?" Mrs. Cameron realized that
Lucy was playing a mother-daughter game with her imaginary friends, "Mary the mother" and "Betty the daughter."
Betty was usually a bad girl and came in for a good deal of
scolding from her make-believe mother. She was blamed for
misdeeds, imagined or real, which Lucy might have done. On

one occasion, Mrs. Cameron had missed a favorite pair of
shoes from her closet. She couldn't remember misplacing them
and searched the house for them. Lucy had professed no
knowledge of their whereabouts. Her mother finally found
them half hidden beneath Lucy's toy chest. When she realized
that Lucy had been lying, and had taken the shoes herself, she
was very upset. As she explained to Lucy, it wasn't hiding the
shoes that worried her, it was having Lucy lie to her that
really disturbed her. Lucy said, "Betty made me do it."

This is the beginning of a period for heights of imagination. Imaginary friends begin to be especially important to a first or only child. The friends take many forms—a bad friend who perpetrates all of the misdeeds, a good friend who takes the role of the ideal self. Two and a half is early for a child to be able to talk about them; they are usually kept very private. For when they are shared, they become open to ridicule, punishment, or any of the terrible things that happen to children in real life, and they lose their magic. This magic is precious, and the value of the imaginary friends in enriching a child's private world and in working out his real problems is obvious. S. H. Fraiberg's beautiful book The Magic Years *carries adults back into this delightful world of fantasies.*

It is of some importance that Lucy talks about boy-girl clothes. She shows her need to work out some of her struggle with sexual identification even more since her environment has not established it either way. In fact, I would suspect that, in an environment where it is consciously underplayed, the developmental process will still go on, but relegated to the realm of fantasy where it is dealt with in a private, protected sphere.

Mrs. Cameron caught the gist of this and she said, "Wouldn't you like to wear a dress to the center today? You've been wearing those brown pants for almost a week now. Maybe you'd like to dress up for a change." Lucy fairly shouted, "No! I promised I'd wear my pants!" "Whom did you promise?" "My friends."

The outward denial of any uncertainty about this does not deny the possibility that she may still be in the midst of a sorting process. I agree with the Camerons' feeling that we have overstressed sex-typing in our society and, in the process have undermined many adults who do not feel comfortable with polarized female or male prototypic roles. Today, when we are pushing toward a mixture of roles for each person, we are aware of the contradiction of pressing a child into a rigid sexual prototype. But the child will need to explore the limits of each sex role before finding his or her own identity and own blend. If we try to deny him or her experience with either end of the spectrum, we may find the child locked into a new kind of identity conflict. I remember the families of pacifists whom I observed. They tried to banish toy guns from their children's early experience. The boys still found twigs to use for guns. When a rare child accepted this banishment of aggressive play, he seemed to have a tougher time handling aggressive feelings as he grew older. This is the time of life to find out about and play out all of the possibilities in the spectrum—in sexual identification as well as in any other area. Mrs. Cameron is handling this well for Lucy, by leaving it to her.

Lucy was sent in to awaken her "lazy daddy." She climbed up on him, bounced up and down, roaring at him, "Wake up, wake up, lazy bones!" Mr. Cameron grunted, turned over to hide his face, and was assaulted as she pounced on his back. Lucy said, "Wake up, you big b.m.!" With this, her father came wide awake. "Where in the world did you get that kind of talk, Lucy?" Lucy giggled and repeated the phrase over and over. Her father turned red and hastened to get dressed in order to consult with his wife about the latest in Lucy's vocabulary. As he thought about it, the thing that bothered him was that she was not being "ladylike." He also had vague feelings about having let her get out of control, and thought that perhaps he should have stopped her or reprimanded her for her new kind of speech.

This experiment with exploration of "bad" language is just beginning and it will get much worse. Children find the things that bother adults around them in just this way. They pick up words from each other, usually from slightly older, more experienced playmates who have already found what words are taboo. Lucy is more adventurous and precociously free than many little girls who are being raised to be feminine, but so what? Is this really a necessary part of the Camerons' mores? For, as the father sensed, she is already trying things out on them. If they are actually bothered by such linguistic provocation, they'd better figure out how to let her know it. If they are not, they'd better not overreact. Her provocations are bound to become even more painful in the next few years. If her parents want her to leave them out of this kind of teasing, they'd better either pay less attention or tell her firmly that she can talk that way with her friends but not with them. I would recommend the first.

After breakfast, Mrs. Cameron took Lucy to the center. On the way, Lucy began to talk to her mother in a loud, insistent way. She repeatedly asked her questions as they walked. Many of the questions were nonsensical, and their repetitious demanding quality put Mrs. Cameron on edge. As they drew closer to the center, Lucy began to cling, and asked to be picked up. Mrs. Cameron carried her up the long stairs into the main waiting room. As they came through the door, Lucy whimpered, "No, no, mommy! No school!" Mrs. Cameron had one moment of hesitation, then realized that she needn't feel so bad about leaving Lucy. She hugged her, assured her that her daddy would be back that afternoon, and offered to stay with her for a little while until Lucy felt at home. The offer quieted Lucy, and she began to help with the job of taking off her outer clothing. As they walked into Lucy's room, Lucy began to moan a bit, and clung again to her mother, asking to be picked up. As Mrs. Cameron turned to lift her, the teacher called from across the room, "Come over here, Lucy, we need you. We're just about to paint. Bring your mommy over to show her the work we do after she goes to her work." Lucy rushed over to the group, crying gaily, "Mommy, come!" As Mrs. Cameron stood watching, the teacher first involved Lucy in the game, then stepped up to Mrs. Cameron for a "report." Mrs. Danforth asked her each morning how Lucy had been, what sort of things had happened overnight, and generally tried to bridge the separation for Mrs. Cameron as well as for Lucy.

This separation is the hardest part of the day for both mother and child. A teacher who can help both the child and the parent with this in such a sensitive way is giving strength to the mother-child relationship. She does it by acknowledging the importance of their tie to each other, rather than setting herself in a competitive role. She does it by softening the actual separation—first, by drawing the child into the group's activity in a gentle welcoming way, and second, by creating a continuity between Lucy's homelife and the activities of the center. By pointing out the parallel between Lucy's and her mother's day, Mrs. Danforth gives Lucy an image of her mother to internalize and carry with her. The lovely maneuver of asking Mrs. Cameron about the night before helps her bridge the gap between home and the center and gives them a comradeship in Lucy's care. One of the worst pitfalls—competing for, instead of sharing, responsibility for a small child's care—is thus avoided.

As Mrs. Cameron left, Lucy stopped playing, walked with her to the door, and watched her go down the hall. Her mother didn't look back, but if she had, she could have seen that Lucy had already returned to the activities of her group.

Separation is often more of a problem for the parent than it is for the child, at the time. I'm sure there is some deeper cost for the child which cannot be measured in observable behavior. But if the center provides a warm, nurturing environment and cares about the child, he or she can gain a great deal to compensate for it. Learning about other children and adults, learning how to handle feelings in the many situations which a center provides, can be a real opportunity. Most families in our society must depend on alternatives today. Lucy's center is an ideal one. Unfortunately there are many grossly inadequate centers, poorly staffed, or lodged in homes which are patently dangerous for the children. We must move to correct this by providing more safe and enriching centers for young families.

This center had a carefully regulated curriculum for the children. Each group was composed of five or six small children per adult caretaker. They were about the same age and stage of development, and activities were geared to their cycles of activity and recovery. For instance, climbing, running, active games were provided as the tension built up in the group. After a period of vigorous play, there was a quiet time in which reading or sitting games took over. The rhythms of each group were different, and each teacher took this into account. They had found that the most important aspect of gearing a day to a group of children was to be aware of the underlying rhythms of individual children. They had several groups going, and this allowed for a switch-off between groups and a choice for the children. For instance, if Lucy was having a "quiet" day she could join the quieter, slower group. If she was vigorously active, as was more usual, she could be a part of the active group.

Lucy liked boys and particularly the tough ones. She swaggered like her friend Mac, whom she most admired. He fairly rolled across the floor with a sailor's gait. He scorned the house corner and the doll table, using trucks to wham into walls, tables, and the other children. Lucy usually gravitated to truck play with him. As they banged their trucks into each other, she got giddier and giddier. Finally, she threw hers up in the air with a "whoop," landing it on top of Mac's head. He broke into a loud wail, and retreated to his teacher. Lucy sat, stunned, watching him collapse. After a moment, she got up, crept over to him, patted him gently on the head, and said "Poor Mac. Lucy sorry." Her tenderness was anything but boyish, and Mrs. Danforth patted her head, saying, "Lucy, that's nice. Now you're being a good mommy for Mac when he's hurt."

It is impossible to describe behavior without labeling it boyish or girlish, I find. It will take a long readjustment not to stereotype qualities as typically male and female. Such an unconscious label leads to a kind of reinforcement for what we tend to think of as "appropriate" behavior. I am certain that few adults would have reinforced Lucy's vigorous play, but when she shows tenderness, it is seen as "appropriate" for her. By the same token, the teacher might have had a slightly different attitude toward tender behavior in Mac, and a more accepting approach to his vigorous play. These almost imperceptible differences in what the environment accepts and reinforces, shape typed behavior in children in a subtle but powerful way. We must be careful as we try to change our conscious attitudes that we don't simultaneously undermine progress by our unconscious ones. If we do, we will set up a conflict in children like Lucy and Mac which will result in their feeling guilty about their behavior—which does not fit the stereotype, but which everyone says is O.K. They will sense all too easily that what we say and what we respond to are very different. (This is not a comment on the understanding solace which Mrs. Danforth offers Lucy, and which shows what a good teacher she is. She avoided blaming Lucy for the unintentional offense. See Chapter III.)

At their quiet time, Lucy wanted to read. She had been learning to read letters, and had already learned a few words. She had pushed her parents to show her words as they read to her and she had memorized them. When Mrs. Danforth began to read a book, Lucy climbed into her lap, and put her hand on the page until she was allowed to read the words she knew. Mrs. Danforth tried to explain to Lucy that she was holding up their reading, that all the children wanted to hear the book, and that she could read words later. But this mild reproval didn't deter Lucy. She began to be more insistent. As Mrs. Danforth tried to reason with her, getting firmer, Lucy became more upset. She screamed loudly, "I want to read!" and snatched the book, crumpling the pages as she clutched it to her. A teacher from another group came over to sit down beside Lucy to quiet her. All of the children watched, mouths agape, as Lucy raved. Mrs. Danforth retrieved the book and continued reading as if nothing were happening. No one could hear her low, calm words, as Lucy's vocal efforts increased. Finally, Mrs. Danforth was vanquished. She closed the book, picked up Lucy's body of squirming legs and arms, carried the fighting mass of extremities into the "quiet room," and dropped her on the couch, saying as she shut the door, "Lucy, I'm sorry. When you get control of yourself, come out." Lucy's piercing screams continued for a full five minutes before they subsided. A few minutes later, she crept sheepishly to the door, and peered out for a long time before she got up courage to rejoin the distracted group of children.

Lucy's vitality and strong will become difficult when they get out of hand. The tantrum which she prolonged so vigorously became a problem in a class setting. It makes any activity more difficult for everyone. The teacher must get angry. Lucy certainly does not gather any sympathy, and she feels guilty afterward. A tantrum in a public place, even at this age, is expensive. It is not the same as it is at home and in privacy— even at two and a half, when it must still be an expected form of behavior.

As Lucy crept back into the group, she tried to take a beloved doll, a dirty wreck which showed its importance, from Rita, one of her classmates. Rita let out a protective screech. Lucy was about to lose the struggle when she said to Rita, "Look at that!" and pointed to the light overhead. Rita looked up just long enough to lose the doll, which Lucy had snatched as she dashed off. Too late Rita realized her mistake and roared. Mrs. Danforth wearily extracted the doll from Lucy and returned it to poor sobbing Rita. Mrs. Danforth decided she had two choices in dealing with Lucy's mischievousness. One she couldn't do legally—to spank her. The other was to take her off by herself to read the words that had set off the initial power struggle. She hated to give in to Lucy's spoiled behavior, but she saw the day deteriorating and stretching on endlessly otherwise.

Is it important that Lucy learn the consequences of her maneuvers? They were rather an ingenious way of working off her frustration, but it's hard to put up with such demanding unfair behavior in a group. Probably the best Mrs. Danforth can do is to go ahead and give Lucy a little reading time while she tries to point out the unfairness of this kind of reading for the rest of the children.

The teacher put the others to play with another group and went off with Lucy. "Now," she sighed, "read, Lucy, and show off all the words you've learned." Lucy was elated, and she missed the edge in Mrs. Danforth's voice. Doggedly she started to pick out the words she recognized. Mrs. Danforth realized that there were ten or more that Lucy could recognize and name. Although she was impressed, she began to wonder how hard the Camerons were pushing Lucy to learn at this early age.

This brings up the whole question of early learning—is it good or is it bad? Should parents of a child as driven to learn as Lucy encourage her to learn to read? What, if any, are the deficits—particularly if the pressure comes from the child? I hear these questions often in my practice in Cambridge, Massachusetts, where many of the parents are young intellectuals. In such a setting, their children are exposed to reading as a way of life, and as a way of "being like daddy and mommy." Many of them show signs of readiness to read as early as two and a half and even press their parents to teach them to read

and to spell. They memorize familiar words in favorite books. They recognize how rewarded their parents are when they perform in this area. So it's no wonder that they are driven from within.

Parents reinforce the child's inner drive without realizing it. The cycle is set up for early performance. I have seen three-year-olds read familiar sentences, and four-year-olds read unfamiliar ones. It doesn't surprise me that children can learn to type and spell words at four, before they can write them, as O. K. Moore demonstrated. But before I would encourage it too universally, I would like to know how expensive such precocity might be. Is this task an appropriate one for these ages? Is the nervous system mature enough so that this becomes easy and natural? If not, what are more appropriate tasks? In earlier chapters we have seen some of the struggles which are going on in the child's developing personality at this age. If Lucy performs such a demanding cognitive task, will she use energy that might be devoted to other areas, such as personality development? Or will certain cognitive processes become fixed as she learns by rote memory? Then, when she enters later stages which demand more and more complex learning formulas, will she be able to apply this fixed formula?

I do not know the answers to these questions, but I feel that a parent should try to answer them for himself before he encourages and presses a child into a precocious learning pattern. Precocity is usually expensive. In Lucy's case, the only sign that this is anything but good for her is the head of steam she demonstrates to perform and to show it off. This could mean that her main motive is not to satisfy any need to learn but to create a performance for adults around her. She may be trying to fill up a hunger for approval which could be better served in other ways. I have seen several early readers who read well for their first-grade teachers but refused to read in the second or third grades. One could blame the unstimulating school system, but I also wondered whether the children hadn't just run out of steam in this area. The earlier excitement of reading in a one-to-one situation for a proud parent or an impressed first-grade teacher was a situation which was difficult to reproduce in a school setting. Motiva-

tion from within has ever increasing rewards, and gets con-
stant refueling from the sense of mastery in the child that
accompanies each step. Motivation injected by those around
him is more likely to need ever increasing amounts of fuel
(from outside) to fire the system. At a certain point, the need
outgrows the supply.

So, I would warn Lucy's parents that she's embarked on an
expensive experience. Is it worth it to her? She is certainly
not gaining friends or her teacher's approval with her driven
performance.

After lunch and an enforced rest period, the group was back
in full swing. The noise level was high, the activity was constant, fights were impossible to prevent, and Mrs. Danforth
began to watch the time, longing for the end of the day. The
teachers found that it helped to switch groups in the mid-
afternoon. A new adult changed the pace and had new, fresh
expectations to which the children responded.

Lucy found it hard to change authorities. She began to try
to attract the new teacher's attention. First she danced to
show off, then she tumbled on the ground, then she tackled
Mac. All of this seemed to be done in an effort to get Mrs.
Hearn's attention. The new teacher tried to draw them into
group play—to hopscotch around the room. Lucy broke this
up by clowning and tripping the other children. In exaspera-
tion, Mrs. Hearn sent Lucy off to sit down by herself.

Lucy watched Mrs. Hearn as she became involved with the
other children. Carefully she began to leave her assigned
chair. As if she were aware of the consequences, she crept
carefully around the group to a chair where "poor Rita's" doll
sat, alone, waiting for her mistress who was involved with the
group. Lucy picked up the doll, hid it behind her, and sidled
back to her chair. There, she hid the treasure well under the
table. Mrs. Hearn called her into the group. When Rita became tired, she looked for her doll, couldn't find her, and began to whine. Every child in the group became upset about
Rita's loss, and joined in the search. Lucy pretended not to
know about "poor Rita." She waited until the others had
been searching for some time and Rita had become encased in

Mrs. Hearn's lap for comfort. Lucy mumbled a few words which sounded like "Betty told me"—and produced the desired object from its hidden spot. The entire group gathered excitement as Rita revived. Lucy strutted as if she were indeed a heroine. Mrs. Hearn, alone, looked puzzled and sad.

This episode presents reasons for a kind of "stealing" which goes on at this age. Lucy's complicated trick had the simple motive of gaining attention. But her behavior has a meaning which carries her act beyond the tolerance of the group. She will certainly be branded soon as a "devious child." Her teachers have already become disturbed by her tricks. The other children will soon shun her. Each child identified with Rita in her distress, and Lucy's trick would be a personal blow at each of them. Although Lucy may have simply been trying to get back at the group, or command its attention, her trick was too far beyond the children's comprehension, and is infuriating. This attempt to satisfy her need for attention and control of a situation is indeed eerie. It should be called to the attention of her parents as signs of a kind of desperation which is already beyond her age. It represents a hunger which must be satisfied now—not after it is incorporated in an established pattern and it is too late. If they can see her behavior as driven by a need to gain attention, and can supply it for her themselves, they can help Lucy change this painful pattern for the future. It would take more genuine, and less ambivalent, attention from the Camerons at just such times. Then, when they had demonstrated their affection for her, they could interpret to Lucy how her behavior turned people off at a time when she needed their affection.

At four-thirty, Mr. Cameron came to pick up Lucy. He looked forward to this time of day and always arrived on time. He sat down at the edge of the room, greeted Lucy with a nod, and waited until the end of their play. Lucy, too, waited for the end of their game, accepting his coming rather coolly. As if she were reluctant to end her stay at the center, she waited until Mrs. Hearn or Mrs. Danforth went over to her father to speak to him. As at the beginning of the day, each parent had an opportunity to discuss the child's day with the teacher before leaving. Mrs. Hearn tried to pass along some of her concern about Lucy's self-centered behavior. Mr. Cameron seemed coolly interested and seemed to hear her remarks as negative rather than constructive. He asked whether Lucy had been "bad." Mrs. Hearn said "not really," but tried again to explain her concern. Mr. Cameron defended Lucy's generosity at home, and indicated that he thought they were seeing another Lucy at school. His defensive manner essentially cut off any chance for them to communicate, and with a sigh, Mrs. Hearn returned to her group of children. Lucy competently gathered up her outer clothes, kissed Mrs. Hearn on the cheek, and ran daintily to her father, holding his hand as they left.

One gets the feeling that there are ominous times ahead for Lucy. Her father's inability or unwillingness to listen to cues from her caretakers seems as if he were defensive about her. His attitude assumes that they don't care as much about her as he does, and hence they aren't willing to understand her. This may be true, but it is a dangerous bind for parents to get themselves into. An extraordinary degree of maturity, to avoid being oversensitive and overdefensive, is required of day-care parents if this necessary social experiment is going to work. They may miss important messages from people who can be more objective while still caring for the child. If the Camerons could hear the message, they might be able to reevaluate their relationship with Lucy. She is certainly showing a kind of desperate need for approval and for the center of the stage which presages a narcissistic character. She isn't as desperate as this behavior seems to indicate, but she is developing a counterproductive pattern which will isolate her even more from those who could offer her the affection she needs. I feel her patterns are not uncommon in children of this age, and most often reflect a lack of quite knowing where they stand with adults around them, or of how to cope with their own, more secure peers.

I would urge the Camerons to reconsider their rather ethereal treatment of Lucy. She needs an earthier, more thorough understanding of herself. She may need firmer limits, a tougher reality on one hand coupled with a more fulfilling acceptance of her as a little girl who is loved for herself, not her performance. As it is, she seems to be trying desperately to be an adult in an adult's world.

Mr. Cameron took Lucy home in the subway, buying her a candy bar. On the subway, he asked her about her school. She told him about "bad Rita," but he couldn't understand her story, so he smiled blandly, nodding approval for her role in it. She tried to show him how she'd danced and sung at her school. He watched her proudly as she twirled around in the subway car.

When they reached the apartment, he helped her take off her clothes, shooed her away, and began to make the supper for them all. He became engrossed in supper preparations and left Lucy alone in her room. She wandered about the apartment aimlessly, finally ending up in front of the television set. She turned it on and flopped in front of it to watch a cartoon in a glazed-looking attitude. When her mother arrived, Lucy was glued to the cartoons, and Mr. Cameron was concocting an elaborate dinner. Mrs. Cameron sighed with relief, and fell into a warm tub. After thirty minutes, she dragged herself out, feeling that something or someone must need her. She dressed leisurely since there were no demanding sounds from without, and went in to join Lucy.

After an hour's television Lucy was exhausted. She fell apart, crying with stored-up tension when her mother came to greet her. Mrs. Cameron was not prepared for this, and she felt rejected and tired after a long day. She stormed into the kitchen to remind her husband of his responsibility for Lucy. "After all, this is your end of the day, and Lucy needs you. Let me finish the supper, and you go to her." He had worked very hard to concoct a soufflé and was disappointed not to cook it himself. But he realized the wisdom in what she said, and he wanted a bit of time with Lucy. He realized that he'd not fed her, and that she probably needed a bath, so he went to find her. She was in her bed, curled up with her beloved "baby"—an old teddy bear that bore the ravages of time.

Lucy was huddled in a corner of her bed, half asleep, teddy clutched to her chest.

Mr. Cameron picked her up, cuddled her, and took her in to feed her. He realized that she'd passed her capacity to wait it out for a supper with them. He fed her a hamburger and a glass of milk, then carried her to the tub. Her head nodded heavily as he bathed her, and he hurried to get her into bed. He had planned to read to her, to have their time together at the end of the day, but before he could get out her book, she was fast asleep. He'd missed his chance, and somewhere he felt a gnawing sadness. He hurried back to the kitchen to his wife and to the unbaked soufflé. As he heard about her exciting day and told her of his, he forgot his feeling of having missed something. He and his wife were back together again.

Lucy is still something of an intrusion in their lives. They are doing their adult best to make a place for her. Each of them cares deeply about her, somewhere—but it doesn't seem as if she were a major part of their lives. And it isn't just because each of them has a busy life of his and her own—sadly, it is more than that. There are plenty of busy parents dedicated to their careers and to their own lives who still have enough left over to give a primary place to the children. Lucy hasn't got enough of a place in theirs—despite their excellent attempts to create one for her. After the major effort in the beginning adjustment, life became too much for them, and their early resolve wasn't enough to carry them on. For example, Lucy needed them when she came home at night. She needed to be fed and cuddled, even treated like a baby. She needed a real commitment of their time and attention to her as a child, not as another adult. She needed to be thought of first—her hunger, her fatigue, her rhythms needed their first attention. When she didn't get it, she was forced back onto her own inadequate resources. The day-care center was a fine one, but it was an impersonal experience compared to the needs she had for their deeper, more individualized understanding. This doesn't demand long periods of time, but it does require commitment in short periods. The crucial periods which the Camerons had available—at the beginning and at the end of the day—could do enough for Lucy, if she were their primary focus. They are too involved in their own lives and miss such opportunities with her. As outsiders, we can see what precious time in Lucy's life they are missing and what opportunities they are wasting.

CHAPTER X

Learning Inner Controls

Thirty Months

Mrs. Bond knew the end of a long era was in sight when she heard Joe respond "No! No!—I mean—Yes!" As if on the wind, this sudden change blew in one day in his third year. His automatic "no" was open to discussion or could be considered, and both he and she knew it. Even Mr. Bond noticed a change in Joe which he labeled "growing up." When Mr. Bond suggested that he and Joe pick up the toys in Joe's room, Joe looked at him with the usual "no" but smiled after it, as if he, too, saw the humor in the response. This came as a real change, for just one week before, he would have collapsed screaming on the floor after such a suggestion. It took Mr. Bond's firm command to push Joe to action. By the time he mobilized the boy, Mr. Bond was usually so angry that he had no desire to help him pick up the toys. What started to be a joint venture then ended as a command solo performance. Today the two "men" could laugh and play together as they started to put away the roomful of blocks and puzzles.

Not that they got very far. Mr. Bond began to build a block tower, which Joe knocked down. Mr. Bond felt that was pretty unnecessary and said so to Joe. Joe lay down in the corner to suck his thumb, and had to be reproved to get to work again. By the time this new command was executed, they were into their old pattern, of Mr. Bond getting angry and then guilty while Joe sullenly and slowly moved to the job. The scene ended with his father furiously picking up most of the room, while Joe moved in slow motion to put one or two blocks away. At this point, Mr. Bond retracted his earlier statement about Joe's maturity and stormed out of the room.

Although there is a point at which everyone, including the child, suddenly realizes that he has had it with negativism, it is not as dramatic a point in time as it seems. The whole year and a half between twelve and thirty months has been devoted to the task of learning about inner controls rather than having to set off outer controls from parents. This year and a half of testing, of flaunting negativism, has obviously been the child's way of testing and adjusting first to parental limits, then to his own. (It's obvious after it's over, but not at the time.) As in Joe's case, the ability to say "yes" seems to come all of a sudden, but is still fragile. When his father presses him or reminds him of the old relationship and its struggles, there are too many rewarding old habits to fall back upon. It is rewarding to get a father upset, to tie him up in angry knots, even if it means losing a rather pleasant play period together. Joe is becoming more aware of his own power —to manipulate and press his male parent into battle. This will serve him well as they enter the oedipal period, which starts soon and lasts for three long years. Mr. Bond had better stop letting his guilty feelings about disciplining Joe get the better of him.

But still, things had changed. Mrs. Bond could now offer a suggestion, ever so gingerly, with some hope of success. "Would you like to go outside and play, in a little while?" Joe would look up from his emptying of the cupboard under her feet, with a look that used to mean that he was about to start stiffening out in a tantrum. Instead, he caught the last phrase and seemed to allow it to penetrate his armor. He sighed a "no" rather softly. Then he returned to his work of dragging out the double boilers. When she suggested a bit more firmly that it was time to go outside and play and that she'd help him into his coat and mittens, Joe looked up and, with a bland expression on his face, said "O.K." Both of them laughed in relief as they buttoned him into his jacket. Joe literally skipped to the door to let himself out to play.

The relief that a child demonstrates when he has made it over a hump like this is very touching. A week or a month or even a day before, he could not have let himself do what he really wanted to do—for outside meant play and friends and fun. But inside, he was caught by his struggle—the struggle with compliance versus independence, and that's an important one at this age. In order to comply as Joe did here, he must have become aware of an inner independence of decision-making which just wasn't there a year and a half before. When his tantrums and negativism first started, they were indices that he was beginning to want to become independent but hadn't any idea how to get there. Now Joe can even say "yes" to his mother—which points to a real independence from her. For she and he both know he could have said "no" and gotten away with it. Now he can say "yes" and enjoy it. What a step toward maturity!

She barely had time to get back to the dishes when she heard the front doorbell ring. Joe was standing at the door with a bug he'd picked up to show her. She dutifully took it, placed it in a jar, and shoved him out the door again. Before she could wipe her hands, the bell pealed out a second time. By this time she was beginning to see the pattern. He would call her out as often as she'd come, partly to touch base in making the transition to the kids outside, and partly to tease her about whether he must leave her or not. She thought of two alternatives: to leave the door ajar so he could come in or out freely, or to go out with him to get him used to the children outside. They had a safe, open yard in the housing complex where they lived, and it was usually teeming with small children.

It is still early to expect a child to feel strong enough to separate easily or to enter a group of noisy, rushing children by himself. She is making it much easier for Joe to overcome his resistance to both big steps. His "bug" was a clear plea for touching base with her, and she accepted it as such. Leaving the door open says it's all right to want to not separate. A mother who had her own difficulty with separation might have acted quite differently at this point, and by either giving in or pushing him out forcibly, she would have undermined him in his struggle. Mrs. Bond was understanding, supportive, and helpful. Joe will be able to make this kind of separation much more easily because she is free enough to help him with his side of it.

Mrs. Bond stood by her front step, with Joe beside her watching the five other children as they tumbled around on the grass. As she stood silently, Joe reached up to touch her skirt, never taking his eyes off his friends. After a few minutes, he dropped his hand, stuck out his stomach, arched his back, and strutted a few steps toward the group. After another stop, he made a deep sigh and headed toward a pair of three-year-olds who had separated from the others. When he reached them, he pulled on the toy they were struggling over, pulled it deftly away from them, saying "mine!" The two children looked up in surprise, and one of them said "Joe!" and pulled him to the ground with them. He let out a giggle and began to roll over and over on the ground with them.

I never cease to be delighted with the greeting behavior of little children. Especially little boys in our culture seem to look at each other, approach, lock in each other's arms, and start rolling over and over on the ground. Girls are more characteristically gentle and wary, slower to "lock" in a greeting —when they finally do, it is more likely to be with a game or with dolls as a cementing bridge.

Mrs. Bond took this as dismissal and returned to her kitchen, leaving the door ajar. She began to hum a tune as she finished the dishes, realizing how much she really enjoyed this brief bit of independence. After a few more minutes, she heard a familiar loud wail. The piercing quality of the scream made her jump, and she ran to the front door expecting a maimed child. Joe came staggering in holding a finger aloft with both hands as if it were a precious treasure. Between loud wails, he sobbed, "My finger's hurt!" She looked at the intact finger, and tried to find the wound. She pressed on it, moved it, found a tiny laceration at last. He continued to cry relentlessly. The other children had followed him inside, impressed with his vigorous crying. Mrs. Bond had been through such episodes before and knew the solution. She said, "Let's wash it off to get the dirt out, then we'll put a Band-aid on it and you'll feel much better." At the magic reassuring word "Band-aid," Joe stopped crying.

As independence increases, so do unreasonable fears. Fear is obviously a way of expressing the anxiety which comes with responsibility. In this case, Joe's overreaction may be stemming from an increasing awareness of his body and his own responsibility for it. As the aggression which accompanies increasing mastery comes to the surface (for example, his aggressive play with the other children), the child's fears help keep it under control. Perhaps he'd become aware of how excited he was and also how exciting it was to play aggressively

—at just about the time he hurt himself. This awareness could be kept under control by giving in to such a minor hurt. His mother responded appropriately, by taking it just seriously enough and by offering a low-keyed kind of reassurance and a symbol of intactness—the Band-aid. Fears and aggressive feelings will increase in strength and frequency in the next few years. The next period of development becomes one of learning how to master aggressive feelings and feelings about protecting his self-image in the face of imaginary as well as real onslaughts. At this age, the child is just beginning to see his own role in this struggle. Before this, the anxiety related to fears and injuries could be transferred easily over to the parent-protectors. Mrs. Bond is accepting this now, but by her cool approach, not getting very involved, she lets him see how dramatic he is being over a minor injury.

After the Band-aid was applied and the tears were kissed away, Mrs. Bond offered the wide-eyed gang some cookies and sent them back out into the yard.

Each of the children suffered with Joe and were reassured vicariously by Mrs. Bond's serious but underplayed concern. Had she ridiculed him, she would have been devaluing all of them, for each had his individual concern about injury which surfaces around a playmate's wound. This hidden concern is the reason for the teasing about being a crybaby that surfaces at this age. She avoided teasing for Joe by taking him at face value. Hopefully, each time he will need to dramatize his fear less, as he gathers experience.

The group's play was fun to watch. In a short period, there were many different ingredients. They paced themselves in their contact play. Mrs. Bond could see the children change in a flash from hugging each other to bopping each other on the head or arms, or throwing each other down to wrestle on the ground. Such play was vigorous and rough, and she wondered why more injuries weren't "reported." But it seemed apparent that injuries were recognized only when they served a purpose, to space the play with relief periods, and were largely ignored otherwise.

Imitation was automatic. As a child began to hop on one foot, the one next to him picked it up out of the corner of his eye. He hardly seemed to watch, but soon he was hopping on one foot also. Within seconds, the entire group was hopping around, squealing with delight. When one fell, the whole troop followed suit. Up on hands and knees, they played at aggression. They began to act like bears, growling ferociously at each other. As they growled and made feinting bites, one child voiced her anxiety about being bitten. Quickly the game subsided, as if everyone identified with her and wanted to be free of the threat she had just vocalized.

Compare this to the uncontrolled biting of a sixteen-month-older who bites but doesn't realize what it means to the other person. By now the children have imbued the "game" of biting with all of its implications: aggression toward another, and fantasy of being bitten in return. They are learning and experimenting with such mechanisms in play. This provides very important opportunities for a child to learn about himself.

After this, the children sat around on the grass talking together. They shared the one doll and carriage in make-believe play. A little girl hugged it close and crooned to it. Joe took the doll away to force medicine into it, using a stick as a spoon and as a thermometer. Then he scolded it for not taking the medicine more easily, saying, "Bad girl—it's your med'cin!" One of the other boys took the doll away to look under its dress. With each of these maneuvers, all the other children participated eagerly, as if they were being the actors themselves.

This is the beginning of real identification processes. In the earlier bit of play we have seen the use of imitation as the children directly copied each other. Now we see how small children really "become" the child who is acting for the group.

With this process of identification comes an opportunity for cooperation, learning from and sharing experiences.

As the children explored the doll's body, they voiced their disapproval. "Where does she weewee?" "No hole." "Doesn't have a penis. How does he peepee?" The excitement over such communication built up, and soon the children were off and around, yelling "you b.m." at each other. This built up into sand-throwing, and reached an inevitable peak as one child was hurt by sand in his eyes. At this juncture, they all subsided, following him with serious faces as he ran crying for comfort to his mother.

This episode demonstrates the kind of rhythms which underlie all of children's play together. A quiet period can be expected to be followed by a buildup of activity ending in a peak of excited play, and then disintegration before another quiet period for recovery. This follows the pattern of a homeostatic curve which is characteristic of all the response curves of the body: attention–nonattention in the brain and activation–recovery in all other functioning organs of the body. In small children these periods of activity and recovery are shorter and more obvious than they are in adults, and they are important markers for planning a small child's day.

The giddy excitement which builds up around sex play even at this age reflects the heightened concern about sex differences that will soon ripen at four, five, and six. Already, these children are aware that there are differences, are curious about them, and even can name them. Yet they generate a certain kind of prohibition among themselves about going too far with their curiosity. The afterreaction of giddiness, scatological names, and building up to an injury are obvious results of their guilty excitement.

By the time Joe was brought in for lunch, he was exhausted. When Mrs. Bond went out to find him, he was hidden behind a pair of bushes with two other boys his age. They had pulled down their pants, and were investigating each other's penis. They were saying, "I'm the doctor, you lie down" and "What's that, doctor?" as they pointed out their belly buttons and genitalia. Most giggling came out when Joe pointed to another boy's anus and buttocks and said, "Here's your b.m.!" Mrs. Bond flushed as she realized what the boys were doing, and was tempted to rush in to break this up and punish them. She felt embarrassed to be spying on them, and angry at how horrified she felt. However, she mustered her self-control, walked around the bushes, saying, "What are you boys doing? Are you finding out about yourselves? Each of you is a boy like the others, and each of you has a penis for urine to come out, and testicles—that's what's in the little bag there. You have an anus where your bowel movements come out, and a belly button. Do you know what your belly button is for?" The boys were worried and silent at having been "caught" at first, but as Mrs. Bond entered into their play and brought it out into the light by talking about it, they recovered. They were eager for her to answer her own question: "The belly button is where each of you was fed by your mommy when you were inside her tummy." Each boy looked down at himself carefully. One boy said, "How were we fed through a hole?" She explained that there was a tube for food at that hole which wasn't there now. The tube used to connect the baby with the mother. It was no longer needed when the baby came out of the mother's stomach and was able to eat by himself. Joe looked at her with wide eyes, "Did you keep me in *your* tummy?" Mrs. Bond smiled a "yes," and wondered what the next question might be. At this, Joe looked down at his own stomach wonderingly, puffed it out, and said, "I'm hungry," as if he were changing the subject. All of the boys jumped up in relief at this change. Each ran off merrily to his own house. Joe looked up seriously at her as he took her hand to walk home. As they entered the front door, he said "*my mommy.*"

Mrs. Bond took advantage of a rare opportunity and set the stage for future communication by her response to their sex play. Had she burst in with recrimination and disapproval when she caught them, she would have reinforced their guilty feelings which were there ready to be mobilized. It isn't easy for adults not to respond with their own taboos about such investigatory play. Many mothers would quickly translate this to more dangerous sex play, to distorted sex information that children give each other, to their own fantasies about homosexuality and the dangers of boys becoming too intimate in such play. But these children are under three. They are in the first throes of investigating a part of their bodies which has been covered up with diapers heretofore. They are just finding out the fascination of these parts of their own bodies, and their similarity to other little boys. They are also beginning to be aware that, although they look somewhat alike, there are differences too. They are beginning to differentiate themselves as individuals in this area as well as others, and it's very exciting. The more obvious differences between boys and girls call forth an even greater excitement and wonder. To make this kind of curiosity and exploration into a "bad" thing would put all sexuality and sexual identification into a highly charged "bad" context. The excitement is natural and well founded. If told that it's wicked to be excited about such things, then even a very small boy begins to figure out ways of hiding his excitement. His guilty feelings would protect and nurture this excitement and lead it into less healthy ways of exploring and expressing itself. All children must find out about their bodies—all parts of their bodies.

How nice that Mrs. Bond could see this, participate in it with them, and offer them permission to explore, wonder, inquire, and bring their questions to her as someone who might be able to give them considerate, honest, uncharged answers. Joe is indeed a lucky boy, and he will be able to return to her from time to time with other, deeper questions as they arise. She's given him permission to do so by not closing him off.

For lunch, Mrs. Bond had made an egg dish and salad. Joe had never seen the dish before, and immediately refused it. Mrs. Bond bristled and said, "Joe, you try a bit of it and if you don't like it, you can have a scrambled egg." "No." "Please try a bit, just for mama." The "no" increased in intensity. Mrs. Bond began to cajole, press, offer him bribes, and finally to threaten him with no dessert. From the first, Joe had been adamant, and he continued to refuse to give in to her bargains. When she realized she'd lost her argument, she asked what he would eat. He replied, "Peanut butter and jelly sandwich," which was his inevitable reply at lunchtime. By this time, Mrs. Bond was so exasperated that she gave in to him, fixed him the usual sandwich, and fairly shoved it at him. The meal was soured, and she choked down her lunch cheerlessly.

This is certainly a different kind of approach to him than she has yet demonstrated. She must have hang-ups in the food area, for her approach was doomed to failure from her first

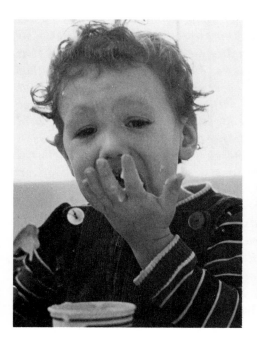

response to his refusal. To allow meals to become a battle-ground or a place where bargains are made is already putting the wrong emphasis on food. It is a precious area for the child, and if it is highly charged for the parent, he is bound to use it as an area for testing. Mrs. Bond undoubtedly would de-fend herself by saying that she didn't really care but that

Joe must eat something after a long active morning. If I told her that he could get along on one or two meals a day, and a minimum of calories and food requirements (see Chapter I), she probably wouldn't hear me. She might reply, "But he's got to grow up and take more responsibility by trying new things, and by learning to eat things that are good for him." It is not time to expect such responsibility in the feeding area. By four or five, there is a change in a child's interests. If the feeding area has not been charged with such tension as there is now at the Bonds, he is more likely to explore new foods, imitating adults around him, and he will begin to eat proteins, vegetables, and other things. At this age, it is not yet the case.

Parents ask me how they should handle important things like medicine and vitamin supplements, since the same kind of refusal invades the child's willingness to take these. I feel that they should be treated in an entirely different way—that there must be no ambivalence in the parents' minds about whether the medicines or vitamins are important and are necessary. If the parent isn't sure they are necessary, he'd better forget them. For if the child senses that there is a choice, he will surely respond as Joe does to the egg dish. On the other hand, if medications are treated with decision on the part of the parent, the child will know it, and will accept them more readily as a result. But it is impossible to push each meal with this kind of determination, and if one does push food at this age, it can certainly lead to future problems in the oral area for the child.

After lunch was over, Mrs. Bond took Joe in to use the toilet before his nap. He had been staying dry during the day for the past four months. He proudly stood on a stool at the big toilet, urinating in a noisy way into the toilet bowl. He had just learned from his friends the fun of standing up to urinate, and he giggled as he splashed into the toilet. All of a sudden his face darkened, he stiffened, stopped urinating, and called wildly for his mother. He seemed to be immobilized, and she realized what was happening. As he'd begun to urinate, he began to produce a bowel movement unexpectedly, and he was caught in a terrible predicament. He didn't want to miss the pot for either production and he couldn't figure out what to do. His mother turned him around, sat him on the big toilet, and he was able to finish with relief.

Learning to stand to urinate is no problem for a boy—it is usually a new pleasure. Once he achieves the degree of control that Joe has, he can enjoy the fun of watching his urine splash and spraying the "universe" with it. A child learns from his father, or from watching other little boys. In all likelihood, he and his friends have been showing off in this area to each other outside. In the past four months he had learned enough control to be aware of the signals of an oncoming bowel movement and could now control it until he was seated in the appropriate place. This is pretty great at two and a half years, and demands real mastery from the child. This mastery would not have been as likely if Mrs. Bond had taken over this area by pushing him into being trained before he himself was ready.

As she put him in for his nap, she asked him whether he wanted to wear his "big boy" training pants and to try to stay dry for his nap. He was still so excited by having controlled his bowel movement that he asked eagerly to be put in his training pants. She knew he would sleep hard during his nap for he'd had such a busy morning, and she worried that he might not be able to control himself.

Too deep a sleep can interfere with the child's still conscious control over his urine. Control is not yet delegated to unconscious mechanisms, as it will be later. There are children who just don't get the necessary signals in deep sleep, and continue to wet the bed long after they might have achieved control in lighter sleep. Deep sleepers do have more difficulty learning to control enuresis. I think that being dry at night comes about when a child's determination to be dry reaches deep into his unconscious, and not before. Until he is ready to be sensitized to appropriate cues even in deep sleep, he will not be sensitive enough at the bladder level to hold on and wake up to urinate

*in the appropriate place. Until he himself is ready at an un-
conscious level, pressure from the environment to stay dry is
likely to work the wrong way—adding pressure at a time
when it is a job for his unconscious, and essentially he can do
nothing consciously about controlling it. Pressure will increase the likelihood of failure, and add on guilty feelings
about the failure after it occurs. Night control is attained at
an unconscious level and must operate when the child's conscious mechanisms are out of the picture. Hence, the desire to
be dry at nap or at night must come from deep inside the
child. And it is based on wanting to be responsible himself, as
well as a desire to please those around him.*

*When he is really ready to assume such responsibility, par-
ents can help by maneuvers such as getting him up to a con-
venient pot near his bed before they go to sleep and before he
is already wet. They can provide him with a night light, a
luminous pot, or even an alarm clock to waken him for the
next urination, but none of these can or will work until he
wants to be dry at a deeper than conscious level. It is testimony to this that girls who should have less sphincter control
anatomically are usually several months quicker in achieving
day-time control, and three months quicker in mastering
enuresis (night wetting).*

*If Joe should wet the bed, Mrs. Bond would be wise to put
him back in diapers at nap time without a word of reproval.
He would feel the failure far too much without adding her disappointment to it. If he tried but failed too often, it could
undermine his other training achievements. At two and a
half years, it is too early to expect much success in night
training. The average age for success in this area in my series
of 1170 children was 33.3 months.*

Mrs. Bond was right about Joe's need for a nap. Although
he did not always sleep at nap time, he was exhausted today.
He slept two hours and could have slept on, but she awakened
him, so that he wouldn't be up all evening. She needed his
nap as a time to break from him and he from her during the
day, but she also looked ahead to time alone with her husband

in the evening. If he took a long nap, it usually meant that they'd have Joe up and with them in the evening.

As she awakened him, she thought once more of how very beautiful he was when he was asleep. He looked so easy and at peace in sleep that she dreaded breaking the spell. As he awakened, he was cuddly, and he snuggled up into her lap.

After she took him to the toilet, he asked her to read to him, and repeated all of the words and phrases after her as she read. She realized how far he'd come in developing language in the past six months. He used baby talk very little now, although he still had a tough time with "th," "sh," "ch," "l," and "r." But he had mastered pronouns and called things "my" or "your," or used possessive nouns such as "Johnny's." He knew some colors as she pointed to them—red, blue, and yellow. He lumped all variations of other colors under these. He could get as far as ABCDEFG–XYZ in his alphabet, rushing quickly from G to X because he knew there were letters he was omitting. He could count to ten. And he wanted to master these things himself, now and without help. When his mother filled in a sentence for him now, he looked up at her, repeating it his own way again as if in defiance. If she slipped into baby talk, he corrected her. And if ever she couldn't understand him when he spoke, he repeated his statement over and over, louder and louder, as if she were deaf. His urgency to learn to speak and to say everything seemed to be pushing him on to new heights of trying to understand. He'd ask her questions which were hard to answer—"Why does a tree grow?" "When was yesterday?" "Where is tomorrow?" "How far to grandma's house?" He seemed to be getting the ideas of time, of space, and of causality. No longer was his desire to understand led by her and his father—it was apparent that it was a burning desire in him.

In the afternoon, Mrs. Bond had an appointment for Joe with his pediatrician for a checkup. She dreaded it, for Joe had been frightened and had fought the examination on his last visit. He had had several illnesses in the past year, and had needed to be taken to the clinic at times when he was feeling bad. During one of these illnesses, after she had allowed him to refuse fluids with a sore throat, he had become dehydrated before she realized it. When she finally got him to the clinic, the doctor was so worried about his dehydration and unwillingness to take medicine by mouth that he felt he must give him an injection of penicillin to turn the tide—which it did. She had learned an important lesson from that illness.

When a small child is ill and feels nauseated or has a sore throat, he will refuse fluids. As he begins to become dehydrated, he will sleep more and more, and when he rouses, he is likely to vomit what fluid he has ingested. If he is allowed to make the choice, he will refuse and sleep himself into serious dehydration. A parent's job is to combat this, by virtually forcing small bits of clear sweetened fluids into him repeatedly at short intervals. This regime will counteract his nausea, and will keep him hydrated. Then, if medication becomes necessary, it can be given by mouth, rather than by more painful methods such as by injection. When a parent says to me that he just can't *get a sick child to drink or take medicine, I remind him or her that a hospital nurse will be successful at it, and that real dehydration would leave us no alternative but to turn him over to a hospital crew. This usually reinforces for the parents the importance of hydrating the child, and they usually succeed after my threat. For, as we have said earlier, a child knows very well when his parents mean business, and when they do he will usually comply—even if he feels terrible.*

Joe remembered the penicillin injection and hadn't forgiven Dr. Carter for it. He had screamed at the mention of his name thereafter. But Dr. Carter had urged Mrs. Bond to bring him in to his office just for a lollipop on two occasions after the painful episode, and she'd done it. Joe now was not afraid of the office, but still was very worried about being examined.

Being examined is an intrusive and frightening event for most people for most of their lives. To a small boy who has had a bad experience, and who is in the midst of normal con-

cerns about his body and its integrity, it is especially threatening to be exposed and undressed.

Mrs. Bond read him a book about going to the doctor, and tried to prepare him for each part of the routine. As she read, she could feel Joe's body become tenser and tenser. When it was time to go, he cried in protest and had to be dragged to the bus. As they rode, he huddled next to his mother. She tried to assure him that there would be no injections and no pain, but he didn't seem to hear her.

A child's fear is of the intrusive, searching aspect of being examined, not necessarily a fear of pain. Hence, saying "It won't hurt you" is missing the point and raising another. Half the time he hasn't been worried about being hurt, but about the exam itself. When a parent repeats that phrase over and over, she establishes a focus for his fears—that of pain. So that phrase is not necessarily a reassurance to the child, and its anxious repetition by a tense parent is certainly anything but reassuring. I really dread mothers who try too hard to control their frightened children by anxious patter or by such repetitious statements as "He won't hurt you," or, to me, "He's bound to cry." These statements keep alive the very fears which the child is trying valiantly to master.

When they arrived at the clinic, the nurse showed Joe the toys and tried to put him at ease. When it was their turn to go in, Mrs. Bond picked Joe up in her arms and tried to comfort his fears. He began to be more and more teary, until she said, "Now, Joe, I know this is tough for you, but I expect you to be grown up about it, and I'll do my best to help you. I know Dr. Carter will, too." With this firm expectation from his mother, Joe seemed to pull himself together, and with a quivering lip, allowed her to undress him.

When Dr. Carter came in, he spoke gently to Joe, saying that he knew he was worried but he needn't be. He asked questions of Mrs. Bond while Joe settled in his mother's arms. When he examined Joe, he allowed him to sit in his mother's lap, and showed him each new maneuver by performing it on Joe's mother first. After he saw the stethoscope on his mother's chest, Joe relaxed and allowed Dr. Carter to examine him with it. When he was shown how the otoscope and the light for his throat worked, he began to enjoy the rest of the exam. Soon he was smiling and talking to Dr. Carter, and at the end of the exam Joe was giddy with relief and the sense of achievement. He had made it through without crying!

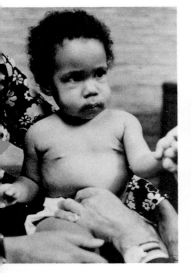

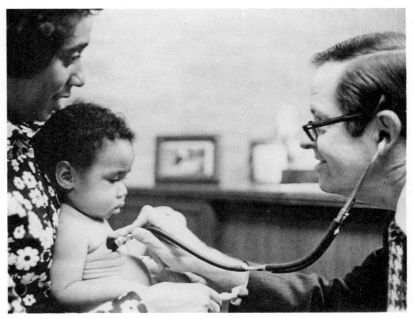

I use all of these maneuvers to quiet an anxious child. They give him the security of knowing what will happen and of seeing it acted out for him. I use his shoe, or his "lovey," or his mother to demonstrate each maneuver. It certainly breaks the ice in a marvelous way. What a boost it gives the child to be able to master such a worrisome experience! After one such success in being examined, he is your friend for life. Of course, a physician performs a much better exam when the child is cooperative and he can see what kind of person the

child really is, rather than seeing him in frantic reaction to a stress situation he can't handle. It's more than worth the extra effort on my part to consider a child's feelings about being examined.

Mrs. Bond had questions to ask about Joe's repeated sore throats. She wondered if he had "bad tonsils." After Dr. Carter had ascertained that Joe's colds lasted only a week,

 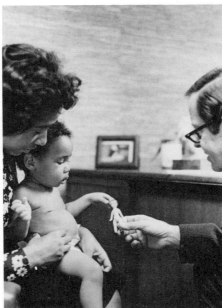 

that he didn't snore at night, that he did not have earaches or blocked ears with his infected throats, he assured her that his adenoids and tonsils were not acting in an obstructive way and were not "bad." He felt that the repeated sore throats were to be expected. As soon as a child begins to get out to play with other children, he must build up immunity to the infections which they carry. In order to do this, he must have a certain number of infectious illnesses which serve this purpose. After he has had a number of these, he could be expected to handle the following illnesses with healthy immune responses. Hence, some of these infections are a necessary part of growing up in a community of children, such as the Bonds' housing project. The physician's problem became that of assessing whether these infections were wearing Joe down, or whether he was suffering from any complication from them. If not, the infections could be seen as serving a long-term purpose, particularly if he could be allowed to handle a number of them without antibiotic therapy. The alternative to allowing him to build up immunity to infections that he would contact was to restrict Joe's association with his friends, and this seemed unreasonable and unnecessary.

Her other questions concerned Joe's back and his feet, for he was flat-footed like his father, and he toed out in a duck-like gait. Meanwhile, his back swayed forward with a lordotic posture, making him look very pot-bellied. Dr. Carter prescribed arch supports for his feet, to direct his feet toward the front and improve his gait. As his feet improved, so would his sway-back. Dr. Carter agreed with Mrs. Bond's concern about Joe's not getting too heavy, but he assured her that Joe was not overweight yet. He sensed that trying to manipulate his diet might add even more concern to the feeding area.

We now know that fat cells which are built up in infancy and early childhood remain with the child and are ready to be used later in life. They enhance the possibility of being fat as one gets older. So a plump baby is no longer the ideal, and a fat child is no longer equated with a healthy child.

When Mrs. Bond and the boy walked into the apartment, Joe's father had already arrived. Joe hurtled into his arms, yelling, "I saw him, I saw him." Mr. Bond needed to be reminded that their visit had been to Joe's doctor, but he proudly listened to Mrs. Bond's account of how brave Joe had been. The father said, "Joe, I knew you could be brave, for I've seen you lots of times. I am proud of you, and I know Dr. Carter is, too. You are really growing up. You're almost a man already." With this high praise, Joe began to fall apart—

to act silly, to show off, and to throw himself around on the floor like a much smaller child.

A child at this age can hold himself together through a crisis, but after it's over, he's bound to collapse. I have seen small children whose parents were under stress who could "be brave" for a week at a time, but then they had a regressive reaction after it was all over. This is marvelously economical and points to the capacity of the child to postpone the immediate reaction. The capacity to postpone is a sign of maturity.

After supper and a hearty play session with his father, Joe was ready for bed. He loved to have his father read to him and put him to bed. He proudly demonstrated all of his recent achievements for Mr. Bond. He took off most of his clothes by himself, even unlacing his shoes in a very efficient way. He brushed his teeth, washed his hands, and splashed his face very gingerly. He said his alphabet—ABCDEFG–XYZ—and counted to ten very proudly. He urinated in the toilet standing up, and asked to be put to bed with no diapers. Mr. Bond sensed that this might be more bravado than Joe would live up to, and he consulted with his wife. She assured him that it had been too big a day to expect Joe to make it through the night. His father took the responsibility for the diapers by saying, "Joe, I know you can do it now. You've shown me what a big boy you are in lots of other ways. But tonight I don't think you should try to be dry. Let's try it tomorrow night and then I'll come to get you up myself."

The night was a somewhat turbulent one. Joe couldn't get to sleep at first, and he called out for water, for a bottle (which he'd given up months before), for the potty. He ran the gamut of tests to bring his parents to him. When they didn't come, he began to cry. Mrs. Bond came in to comfort him briefly, and he followed her out into the living room. Mr. Bond returned him angrily to bed, saying, "If you can't stay in your big bed, we'll just have to put you back in your crib. Big beds are for big boys who can stay there." His definiteness convinced Joe that he meant business, and Joe subsided into sleep. During the night, he woke twice more, once to cry out and once to sing and talk to himself. By the time a parent reached his bedside, he was almost back to sleep, rocking on his belly on top of his balled-up blanket. In one of these waking episodes, they heard him talk as if he were on the phone, saying, "Hi Rocky, come over," "Doctor like Joe," and "Daddy play ball with Joe." He seemed to revive important events from the day as if he were dreaming and reliving them.

Children of this age do dream and can recall bits of experience from the daytime. These periods of light sleep seem to be important in many ways. They serve to discharge fears, anxiety, and even peaks of pleasure which are left over from the day. A child who can get himself back down into deep sleep from these peaks can master his own sleep pattern in a mature way that parallels his increased mastery during the day. Although there are certainly times when children at this age do need comfort or interference from their parents in their sleep, most of the time they are better off if they can be in control of this part of their lives, too. A sleep problem that involves parents is a sort of regression or abdication for a child of this age. Of course, getting used to being alone at night must be dealt with by parents long before this. If it isn't, all concerns, fears, and excitement can be expected to interfere with his night's sleep in a way that will increase his dependency—at a time when independence should be well on the rise.

CHAPTER XI

Toward an Awareness of Self

The struggles and the achievements depicted in these chapters are common ones for most children and their parents in our culture. In other cultures where children are expected to assume adult roles earlier, and where conformity is prized, this age may not appear so turbulent a period. But in a culture which values individuality and open self-expression, it is during this time that the child must establish individual patterns of behavior partially independent from those of the parents. The child is now equipped for independent exploration with his new skills: walking, the capacity to manipulate objects with a refined skilled grasp, the burgeoning capacity to speak and express himself, and the new-found power of imitating and acquiring the behavior and the characteristics of the people around him. That the power given him by these skills must dawn on him all at once and overwhelm him should come as no surprise to anyone who has watched him acquire the precursors of these skills so painstakingly through the first year of life. But the suddenness of the struggle to control and assimilate this power does come as a shock to most parents of toddlers.

The intensity of this struggle to sort out which results *he* wants to achieve with his new skills, and which results he does not want, is a testimony to the strong wills we build into our children in our culture today. We may wonder whether we want to continue to foster such turbulent children, who go through such upheavals whenever the environment reminds them that there is a choice to be made. Nevertheless, the strength to protest and to bring the struggle out in the open is very healthy. It is expensive to struggle alone, to suppress open expression of one's turmoil. It is cheaper in the long run to externalize one's conflicts and to involve those around one. Joan's pattern (in Chapter VI) of turning away from her environment, and suppressing the feelings with which she needed help, will endanger her future development much more than the open struggles which most of the other children demonstrate. Although children aim their struggles broadside at their parents' vulnerable spots, both the parents and the children manage to do much rapid learning during this period. The adult learns that he must allow the child to settle his own struggles; the child learns that he can!

That any parent can live through this tumultuous period without actually destroying his or her child (and many do abuse their children in this second year), or without walking out in order to protect the child from the parent's own angry feelings, is a testimony to the strength of parental ties to the child. One cannot like a child all the time through this period. One can admire the strength and depth of his conflicts, but watching him struggle calls up too many painful memories of just such unresolved struggles in most parents for them to remain constantly loving and uninvolved. As a result, most parents end each day with an angry reaction that is equivalent in force to the turmoil in the child. If they can, they turn this anger inward on themselves, or attempt to save it for their spouses.

What of the ones who can't, and who fight back on the child's own level? All of us are guilty of turning on the child at times, and the shame which we experience after we realize we've just thrown a two-year-old's tantrum ourselves virtually incapacitates us. Should we feel so guilty? I am convinced that a parent's angry outbursts serve a purpose, too. The child's inner struggles are contained, at least temporarily, by the limits set when a parent can't tolerate him any longer. Compare the prolonged struggle that exhausted Susan in Chapter I when her parents weren't aware of her need for firmness, with her relief when her parents acted decisively. If a child is surrounded by smiling acceptance through such a period, he is left to find the limits for himself. The role of honestly open reactions from parents in helping a child handle his struggle is a powerful, important one. Definite limits from the outside allow the child to explore himself more freely.

But what of children whose parents are not in tune with their struggle? A child like Lucy in Chapter IX demonstrates personality characteristics that worry all of us as observers. Are her problems built in by now, and irreversible? Will they ruin her future life? Not necessarily, for though she appears to be developing an unappealing pattern of showing off to gain attention from preoccupied adults, she has the advantage of a family and a day-care staff who are deeply concerned about her. The Camerons had made a big adjustment to her when she was an infant and seemed to have done it very well. At present, her needs are unrecognized, but the love and care they have given her in the past suggests that they will find ways to help her when they do recognize her call for help. This family has the strength of being able to care for and respond to one another. That is a basic requirement for a child's normal development. Without it, a child's identity does not develop. When real caring is not evident, the child's personality will not be strong, as it is in Lucy's case, but will become submerged in the struggle for survival, as in Joan's case in Chapter VI. Joan will indeed have a tougher time unless her difficulties are soon recognized and met. She will need a long period of patient caring to bring her back. Just as Mr. Gray approached Bobby with insight in Chapter IV, one of Joan's caretakers will have to see her withdrawal as a symptom of distress, and encourage her gently and patiently. But unless she is brought out of her present system of defensiveness and withdrawal, she will be a very restricted, maimed person for life. Her capacity to love and be loved could be permanently impaired.

There is no one way to help a child through this negative period. Each parent is faced with his own childhood solution to the turmoil he meets in his two-year-old. He is bound by this earlier solution as surely as he is by his other limitations.

Hence he must help the child in a way that will mesh with his own personality, or they are doomed to more devastating future struggles. He may not be comfortable with the mirror image of his own early struggles as he watches the child. He must remind himself that the child will find strength from his own honest feelings and reactions as a parent. Together they can and will work out a solution; if abandoned in the struggle, the child will turn to less than adequate ways of coping, such as Joan's withdrawal or Barney's hyperactivity in Chapter VIII.

But this adjustment of a child to his environment takes time. The year and a half outlined in this book is obviously a small segment in the lifetime adjustment of individuals to their own needs and to the demands of those around them.

What tasks are achieved in this period? And what is lost if they are not achieved?

Learning about Independence

With awareness of the capacity to move away, the child begins to measure what it means to him to leave the warm attention in which he has spent the first year. As he finds he can control the distance from home base, first crawling and then walking, he must decide how far and in what directions he can afford to go. Piaget points out that an awareness of the permanence of unseen objects surfaces in children at this age. If he loses sight of an object or a person, he now has the cognitive capacity to recognize that it is still there. Coupled with his ability to make a decision about coming or going, is the ability to hide objects and recover them. Now he can test out his own concepts of permanence in play with objects. He tests them by leaving and coming back to them. Most important of all, he can test these concepts with people. He sees his mother and father go but they come back. He leaves them, but when he returns they are still there. As he tests these new concepts, he becomes aware of a whole new kind of independence. *He* is in control of this! No longer is he at the mercy of "their" handing his food on his tray. He can find it for himself. No longer can he be simply put to bed and left. No longer must he wait till they come to him. He can climb out and go to them. He can also decide where he will be and when he will cooperate, for he has found that he has certain controls over *them*. The awareness comes as an avalanche.

As with any new achievement, the awareness of it comes far ahead of its mastery. And as in any other developmental step, real mastery follows prolonged exploration of all of the facets of the new achievement. Piaget calls these time-consuming experimental processes accommodation and assimilation. Mastery of the steps toward independence will take the rest of childhood and most of adulthood. But the most turbulent, churning period takes place in this year and a half. It is painful to the child, as witnessed by his negativism and his temper tantrums, and it comes as a painful new era for doting parents. That either can let the other go is the amazing thing, and testifies to the degree of a child's need to be independent as well as to the parent's awareness of this need. The drive for the child to become independent is a force that is built into his maturation process. It first appears when a baby stands up at about the age of five months. He brightens and giggles as if he were saying, "This is it! This is what I've been waiting for!"

The storms which the process of separation brings to the surface take many guises. Most of them are described in earlier chapters. When the separation is stormy, it testifies to the strength of the ties which are being loosened. When insecurity makes the child unable to let go, fear of separation may surface in different ways, such as the withdrawal of Joan (Chapter VI), the regression to an earlier stage of development of Bobby Gray (Chapter IV), or as the kind of adult-demanding "spoiled" behavior of Lucy (Chapter IX). Each of these are symptoms of inadequate readiness for this big step in maturation.

Open negativism toward his parents is a toddler's way of expressing his need for independence. With his "no" he establishes himself as separate from his parents. Every time he says "no" or acts out a negative response to a demand from those around him, he is learning about himself as a separate individual. He learns about his parents' expectations, and he learns about how he will act in response to them. Although his immediate reaction may be an automatic "no," he will gradually learn from the environment's reply to his "no" that this is not a satisfactory way to respond. He then has a second chance to decide whether he must conform or can afford a second but more tentative refusal. The negativism quickly becomes a first line of defense in order to stall for time— time for inner decision and evaluation. As the child nears two and a half, many decisions can be made more quickly. He is surer of his own limits, of his own independence from his parents' demands after a year and a half of sorting them out, and can settle into a new phase of equanimity. This new stage may unsettle parents by its very lack of turmoil!

Strangers and new situations present other opportunities for learning about oneself. They are bound to be more difficult for a child to assimilate in this period of stress. A stable environment brings with it a set of known values. In a novel situation, with a set of unknown demands and of unpredictable values, a two-year-old must cope in new ways. He must set up new antennae, and if he dares, he must try out all his new-found strengths—his negativism, his provocativeness, his exhibitionism. It is more than likely that he will *not* dare, but will regress to more infantile behavior until he learns ways to cope with the new situation. In either case, he learns about himself. If he must regress, he learns that this is a way to deal with an overwhelming situation. If he can muster the courage to meet it head-on, he gains self-confidence and learns how new people greet his new skills.

The anxiety which strangers produce becomes a stimulus for self-evaluation. In the second year, stranger anxiety is at a peak as a result of the toddler's increased awareness of himself in relation to his environment. His sense of integrity and of identity is threatened by an approach by an unknown person. The threat is engendered by his awareness that he may not know how to react in the novel situation. Novelty is a threat when one is trying to establish secure and independent boundaries of self because it may shake those new and unsteady boundaries. With each new conquest of novelty, the child's awareness of himself increases. After the novel situation is over and conquered, he experiences the exhilaration we saw in Joe in Chapter X.

Such "crutches" as thumb-sucking, head-rolling, head-banging, rocking, blankets or other "loveys" can be seen as necessary and healthy ways for a child to ease the struggle toward independence and separation. They are a way to preserve the image of what he must give up at a time when he is locked in the active struggle to give it up. Only when he ceases to use the crutch to further his struggle, and retires with it into a cocoon, must one see his crutch as a mark of failure and a cry for help (as did Mr. Gray in Chapter IV).

Learning the Importance of Limits

This second year is a period for establishing firm limits. Unless parents can accept the responsibility for limiting the child and for using appropriate punishment where it is necessary, they are deserting the child. His new-found freedom is fraught with danger, and a child this age recognizes it. He demonstrates his awareness of the danger every time he goes toward a prohibited place by turning to look back with a wicked gleam in his eye, fairly pleading for a parental "no."

More complicated provocative behavior in older children is of the same order. Their need for limits is conscious enough so that they seem to deliberately produce a violent reaction by their "spoiled" behavior. I see such testing behavior as representing a wish or thought that they feel must be prohibited. The child realizes that he might not be able to control it himself, and therefore behaves so provocatively that he demands an answer from his parents. Punishment should be immediate, it should be appropriate, and it should be limited in time so that the adult and child can make up the rift. Nothing is so harrowing for a child as a long, drawn-out withholding of affection. After discipline is meted out, and the episode is terminated, the adult can comfort the child and point out that someone else still has the controls which he must learn. Implicit in these controls is the promise that they can be incorporated by the child himself.

When a parent disciplines a child in a firm but understanding way, the child's sense of relief at having found limits motivates him to learn how to set limits for himself. I am convinced that children do not enjoy anxiety, and that they are aware in some way that getting out of control produces anxiety. Hence they will search for discipline from those around them as they begin to lose control. A "spoiled child" is one who is searching for an end to such anxiety. His provocative, "bratty" behavior pushes the onlooker to want to control the child himself, and he regards the child as "spoiled." An adult's understanding discipline brings relief, and with it the sense of "This is what I want! This feeling of being in control!"

Repeated episodes with controls from those around him finally bring about enough experience to make it possible for the toddler to know how and when to control himself. By the end of the third year, children whose parents have provided them with such experience have acquired a real sense of inner control, and no longer need to provoke or tease for discipline. The Camerons in Chapter IX will have a longer period of two-year-old provocative behavior unless they realize soon that Lucy is aching for honest firmness from them.

Learning from Play

Locomotion provides the child with new opportunities for learning about the world around him. He can find out about distance and space, and about the stability of objects in this space. With his newly acquired fine motor skills, he can manipulate objects and learn about size, form, and relationships of objects. Awareness of what is "mine" and what is not is an inevitable sequel to these motor explorations.

A child who is handicapped by motor deficits, or by sensory ones such as visual or auditory defects, must fight much harder to acquire the experience of space, shape, distance, and of what these mean to him. Unless the adults caring for such a child are aware of the terrible lack of experience which these handicaps bring about, the handicapped child is in danger of incurring an even more devastating lag in learning about the world and himself. His actual handicap will be compounded by a failure to develop the motivation to separate, to learn for himself, and to sort out the world around him. Dr. Kate Kogan describes a study of mildly retarded children whose mothers were asked to teach them a new task. She found that, as opposed to mothers with normal children, these mothers pushed the child to learn by pure imitation, giving them no time to digest each step before they were pressed on to the next in the learning sequence. When they began to fail or to experiment, the mothers of retardates pressed them even harder, stripping them of normal exploratory steps needed to feel mastery in learning a new task. Learning by pure imitation became a secondary handicap, and lack of motivation was added to their retardation as a compounding force.

In the same way, an emotionally handicapped child will not dare to explore, to try new skills. Like Joan, she or he will need to conserve, to protect the fragile ego against the insecurity which independence might bring. One of the most observable signs of such fragility is the child's inability to play. In play, a healthy child tests out reality and differentiates it from his inner world of fantasy. He tries out ways of approaching new tasks, of coping with separation; he assimilates the ways which work for him; he discards those that don't. And in play with others, he learns about himself. Variety in play and freedom to explore the facets of a learning situation become two more signs of healthy development in this age group. A child of this age who does not and cannot play will not develop fully. Parents must be aware of their responsibility to provide opportunities for play in this age group, both with toys and with other children.

At this age the child begins to show tremendous excitement at learning things for himself. In the first year, many of the child's learning experiences are provided by those around him. Reinforcement and encouragement are provided by caretakers or older siblings as each new step is mastered. The second year provides a new, more independent way of learning; much of the child's learning experience is sought out and provided by his own actions. Although the people around him offer contingent encouragement, it is already less necessary as he becomes more and more aware of the inner excitement he feels in mastering new steps for himself. R. A. White calls this a "sense of competence" and labels it a major motivating force in childhood. When the pressures to learn come from adults and outweigh any pleasure the child may be able to find for himself, learning becomes more automatic in nature. As in Chapter IX, Lucy's motivation to read is likely to be self-limited, because it is too dependent on those around her for approval.

Learning from Wishes and Fantasy

There are other ways that the child can learn about himself. He learns to play with fantasies. As he becomes independent by two or two and a half and learns how to enjoy independence, he is freer to enlarge on his own world. He can "play" with ideas, with wishes and with dreams. He can afford to divide up this newly found person—himself. He can let a part of him be like the grownups around him, and save another part to be like the two-year-old "him." Now he can afford to let one part of himself be a baby, sucking on a longed-for bottle and wetting again into warm diapers. At the same time, he can be a mommy or a daddy who doesn't approve. He can try out what it's like to be bad, or even very good, using only an imaginary part of himself for each of these. But at this tender stage he often finds he has acted upon some of these wishes, as well as dreamed about them— and then he's caught. For though *he* knows the difference between these magical wishes and what is real, those around him see only the results of his actions. It becomes a scary game—unless he finds a way out. Often he finds one: he can lie or blame the misdeed on a friend. Not on any real friend who could deny it, but on an imaginary friend who can get away under the pressure of disapproving parents.

These imaginary friends become important as ways of dealing with reality but not being too overwhelmed by it. Without them, he is stuck to the ground in leaden boots. With them he can explore parts of his personality, parts of himself which he could never learn about otherwise. And he learns about experience with the world this way. He finds out what his parents will or won't allow by letting his "friend" try things out for him.

Lying directly about situations becomes the next step in the testing of his imaginary world. He needs to explore his new fantasy world to learn about himself. When the imaginary friends cannot be held responsible for actual or wished misdeeds, he begins to assume responsibility himself by lying. He finds this a way of accepting responsibility but denying it at the same time. The magical world of which he is becoming aware makes such a split possible. In his magical world he can be absolved if he can create a convincing story. When his story does not convince the adults around him, he can even pull away into his new-found world to feel mistreated. The exploration of this imaginary side of himself is an important process in growing up, as the child learns the differences between the real world and a wished-for world of fantasies which he owns and controls. Lies protect this precious world, and it must be a real surprise to him when they are taken too seriously by adults around him.

But there are children who don't have such friends and such fantasies. What of them? Do they suffer? A child who is never allowed or can't afford to have fantasy friends or magical experiences is faced with two choices—being content with the reality around him and his own limitations, or acting upon his desires and feelings. Since the latter is liable to bring the world of adults down upon him, the first choice may be more bearable. So he must limit his world to a reality world. Perhaps Joan is a child like this.

Stealing may begin at this age. It is a common way for a child to try out some of his wishes. He can reach the sugar bowl now and he can find his mother's pocketbook. Lying and stealing are common in three- and four-year-olds, but most children begin to try these out by the age of two and a half. If a parent takes these mechanisms too seriously, and projects them into the child's future as problems, this over-reaction may act to set them up as patterns. The child may be intrigued by the concern he creates around him. He may feel pressed to try them out again. Or he may make more effort to hide his tracks—for instance, his lies may become more elaborate or more believable, and his thefts may be better covered. So, parents should be warned that lying and stealing are "normal" at this age. Instead of treating such acts as problems, they might see them as ways the child has of trying out a whole new fantasy world. At these ages, such behavior reflects a kind of flexibility and strength in the child. He need not be given freedom to use lying and stealing as a way of life for the future. But learning the difference between wishing and acting upon a wish is a slow process, and it can be worked out over the next several years. If the child is frightened too much by parental disapproval, he will not learn the difference, and living in fantasy, or lying and stealing can become fixed as problems for the future.

Learning by Identification

The process of learning by imitating others is a subtle one. Since birth, the infant has been shaped by everyone around him. He has learned to imitate their voice patterns, their style of walking, their ways of putting on and of taking off clothes, and even to sense the times of day when they will be more likely to say "no" to his requests. All kinds of subtleties he has learned become apparent if one watches a toddler as he orates in imitation of his mother on the telephone, or puts on his father's hat with a characteristic tug, or watches for his mother's mood out of the corner of his eye, at the end of a long day, to see whether he dares play with the forbidden television set.

He has also been making certain choices, as to which behavior to imitate. After walking is mastered, a boy's swagger may be a very subdued imitation of his father's walk. A girl's more graceful way of sitting down in a chair may have incorporated some of her mother's smoother, more flowing approach to sitting. Certainly in the second year there are observable differences in motor behavior between boys and girls. Whether the differences come from the child, or are built in by different sorts of reinforcement from the environment, cannot be easily determined. For, even in these days, when we are consciously trying not to reinforce stereotyped sex roles which may not be productive for the child's future, it is virtually impossible for parents not to treat boys and girls differently.

I believe that there are differences in behavior styles even in newborn infants, and that infant boys are likely to be more vigorous and motor, while girl babies are likely to be more sensitively observant and quieter about their motor achievements. However, these are likely to be minor differences. Parents single out these differences and enlarge upon them. I feel that a father's reaction to a boy may be only slightly different in early infancy, but as he finds a welcoming response from his baby son to vigorous play, he increases it. By the age of one year, their relationship is already grounded in physical interactions which are comfortable and rewarding to each of them, which are not consciously "masculine," but form a basis for the little boy's identifying with the more physical behavior of the father. If a father unconsciously plays more tenderly with a girl, he will form a very different kind of nurturing relationship with her, and by the time she is toddling to him, he may gather her up very differently to cuddle her in his arms. In each case, the nature of their physical behavior together may have come in part from inborn differences in the child, or they may have been engendered by preconceived notions on the father's part about what girls and boys "need from a father." Whatever the source, it is self-perpetuating, and I doubt that we can eradicate these subtle influences upon our handling of children in less than several generations of reconditioning. I am not sure we want to, either, for I feel that the "fit" that a parent feels when his behavior meshes with that of a child is so rewarding that we as parents shall continue to search for and respond to subtle differences in styles and rhythms. If indeed such differences are inborn, they will continue to be nurtured.

If one does assume that there are reasons already built in by the age of a year which lead a child to imitate certain behavior in a parent, it is easier to see how the child can absorb whole chunks of behavior from each parent. For example, a little girl may imitate the way her mother moves around the room, or fixes her hair, but she may want to imitate her father's gentle voice as he cuddles and reads to her. She may prefer to watch another two-year-old girl out of the corner of her eye, to imitate her technique for playing with a doll. Perhaps her preference was influenced by "feminine" treatment at home, or she might find the girl's movements more easily imitated than a boy's more vigorous movements as he pushes his trucks. But in all likelihood she will try both, and will imitate the behavior of each of these, her peers. Children will try out the movements, the voices, the subtleties of each parent. They may have to decide which behaviors will be theirs by long trial and error. All of the techniques—of negativism, of play, of fantasy—will be used in their attempts to sort out which pieces of each parent, of each sibling, of each peer, to adopt as part of themselves. These two years become a period in which the child imitates, digests or discards, and identifies with each important person around him. This is a complex process and it takes time, for it is a matter of sorting out the bits and pieces which will go into the jigsaw puzzle of a future complicated, individual personality. These years need the sensitive nurturing and the appreciation of strong, vital parents who are not too threatened in their own life styles, for it is painful to see one's own defects appear in full bloom in the next generation.

Learning by Acquiring Skill In Language

By the time the toddler is able to make clear words and less clear phrases, there is a pattern of communication between him and his parents which has long been in use. As he makes a vocal utterance, they reinforce it by repeating it to him, adding an approving gesture or inflection. In all likelihood, they will also add another word to it, to try to lead him on. When he begins to come close to an actual word in his "baby talk," they shape it into the word, attempting to push him to clearer speech. He may or may not make further attempts at the time, but he is aware of their pressure to learn to speak the way those around him speak. As he imitates long strings of unintelligible inflections, he first receives delighted, surprised approval from everyone around him. Then, quickly, they begin to push him toward intelligible utterances, and he finds himself pressed back into single words or phrases. From this he learns that he must conform rather strictly to an adult code for his speech.

There is less opportunity in this area than in any other for the exploration and the negativism the child shows in other areas. He must practice and try himself out when he is in bed, or when he is off by himself, in order to have any real freedom for experimentation. For when he is in the midst of his family, he is under constant and often severe pressure. Siblings are even more demanding of a two-year-old than are parents. They correct him, "teach" him, make him repeat words and phrases after them until he is perfect in his production. Even two-year-olds who are just learning themselves take the time to correct another two-year-old's mistake. As a result, he learns a kind of rigid conformity which places him under real inner pressure. It is small wonder that most toddlers stammer or stutter as they begin to put words together. What is wonderful to me is that, at a time when every other kind of learning moves through periods of negativism and regression, a two-year-old will master language in rapid spurts. Long sentences seem to come from nowhere. Phrases and words he can scarcely have ever heard come spouting forth. And complex memories of events in the past take shape in words, to the complete surprise of adults who give small children no credit for memory.

With the language and the putting of ideas into words comes a whole, rich new world for the child. He can communicate with adults on their own terms. He can call for, command, and direct their actions. He can express his wishes. He can negate them or change them. And most important of all, he can begin to put ideas into words. He can solidify his thoughts for himself as well as for others. With this capacity to make thoughts and ideas into concrete language comes a new capacity for playing with these ideas. He can manipulate his new inner world with words rather than with actions. And he is freer to try out the world around him, without the consequences of action.

The capacity to formulate sentences seems to parallel the capacity to think in more abstract ways. Linguists claim that the acquisition of language helps to structure and reinforce the developing behavior of the child and to concretize his burgeoning capacity for cognitive development. More complex types of thinking, of fantasy, and of awareness of himself seem to take shape around the child's new and uniquely human capacity to communicate with language.

Where Do We Go from Here?

By the middle of the third year, the small child has begun to master all of these processes in the service of learning about himself and his world. For parents, the six-month period from two and a half to three years of age seems like a lovely plateau after the turbulence which precedes it. The child is almost miraculously at peace. He conforms, he understands, he cooperates, and he even tries to please those around him. As if he had achieved some sort of longed-for goal, he suddenly settles down to enjoy it—for a few months. This six months is a plateau which seems devoted to digesting all of the enormous steps which have been taken. Most three-year-olds are surprisingly introspective, as if they also feel a need to understand these developmental achievements and what they might mean. They seem to be continually thinking, trying to understand themselves and the world around them. Speech and the ideas which come forth at this time are complex and convey the depth of thought with which the child is busy. This time seems to parents like a calm sea before another storm. And indeed it is—on the surface. All of a child's development seems to be made up of these spurts in achievement, followed by plateaus for digesting the last spurt and for gathering energy for the next one.

Parents who have struggled through the year and a half from one to two and a half deserve the respite. It is not easy. I find in my practice that the more parents care about their children, the more involved they become with the child in the turmoils which he encounters in the process of growing up. So parents need a plateau too—for time to appreciate the child's gains, to enjoy them, and gather energy for the next spurt. What fun it is to have made it with a three-year-old who can act for himself, who can think for himself, who can be gay and amusing, who can express his thoughts independently, who is beginning to realize his independence from you. How rewarding to find that at last he can afford to let himself care about you as another person—not just as an extension of himself!

BIBLIOGRAPHY
INDEX

Bibliography

AINSWORTH, M. D. S. *Infancy in Uganda*. Baltimore: Johns Hopkins Press, 1967.

BOWLBY, J. *Attachment and Loss*. Vol. I: *Attachment*. Vol. II: *Separation*. New York: Basic Books, 1969, 1972.

BRONFENBRENNER, U. *Two Worlds of Childhood: The US and USSR*. New York: Russell Sage Foundation, 1970.

DELAGUNA, G. *Speech: Its Function and Development*. Bloomington: Indiana University Press, 1963.

ERIKSON, E. *Childhood and Society*. New York: Norton, 1963.

ESCALONA, S. K. *Roots of Individuality*. Chicago: Aldine, 1968.

ESCALONA, S. K., and GORMAN, H. H. *Scales of Sensory-Motor Development*. Unpublished, Department of Psychiatry, Albert Einstein School of Medicine, New York, 1967.

FRAIBERG, S. H. *The Magic Years*. New York: Charles Scribner's Sons, 1959.

GESELL, A. *Embryology of Behavior*. New York: Harper and Row, 1915.

GESELL, A., and ILG, F. *Infant and Child in the Culture of Today*. New York: Harper and Row, 1945.

KOGAN, K., WIMBERGER, H. C., and BABBITT, R. A. "Communication between young mental retardates and their mothers," in *Child Development*, 1959.

MUSSEN, P. H., ed. *Carmichael's Manual of Child Psychology*. Vols. I and II. New York: Wiley and Sons, 1970.

NEWTON, N. *The Family Book of Child Care*. New York: Harper and Row, 1957.

PIAGET, J. *The Construction of Reality in the Child*. New York: Basic Books, 1954.

PIAGET, J. *The Origins of Intelligence in Children.* New York: International Universities Press, 1952.

STONE, J., and CHURCH, J. *Childhood and Adolescence.* New York: Random House, 1968.

THOMAS, A., CHESS, S., and BIRCH, H. *Temperament and Behavior Disorders in Children.* New York: New York University Press, 1968.

UZGIRIS, I., and HUNT, J. McV. *Toward Ordinal Scales of Psychological Development in Infancy.* Urbana: University of Illinois Press, 1973.

WHITE, R. A., *Competence and the Psychosexual Stages of Development.* Nebraska Symposium on Motivation, 1965.

Index

M

N

O

THE AUTHOR

T. BERRY BRAZELTON, M.D., a distinguished pediatrician in Cambridge, Massachusetts, is Associate Professor of Pediatrics at the Harvard Medical School. He is Chief of the Child Development Unit at the Boston Children's Hospital Medical Center, where he also conducts research in Mother-Infant Interaction. From 1970 to 1972, he was Chairman of the Child Development Section of the American Academy of Pediatrics. Dr. Brazelton's Neonatal Behavioral Assessment is now in use in twenty research centers in the United States and several foreign countries. A monograph and training films authored by him have recently been issued, and Dr. Brazelton travels extensively to consult and train people in the use of his assessment and scale. Dr. Brazelton's first book, INFANTS AND MOTHERS, was hailed as "the new Dr. Spock."